Guerrillas of Peace

On The Air

Guerrillas

⇛ *of* ⇚

Peace

On The Air

Blase Bonpane

Radio commentaries, reports and other works which examine and promote the ideology of peace

Red Hen Press 🐓 *Los Angeles 2000*

Guerrillas of Peace on the Air

Cover image "Bartoleme's Front Step"
by Mark E. Cull
Copyright © 2000

Book and cover design by Mark E. Cull

ISBN 1-888996-25-0

Library of Congress Catalog Card Number 00-109072

First Edition

First Printing, December 2000
Second Printing, June 2002
Printed in Canada

Published by

Red Hen Press
www.redhen.org

To my wife, Theresa Killeen Bonpane
and to my children, Colleen Maria and Blase Martin.

Contents

Introduction

Pacifica Radio Commentaries
KPFK 90.7 FM / Los Angeles, Calfiornia

The Peace Reports
and other works

Introduction

Guerrillas of Peace on the Air is a compilation of my 1996–1998 commentaries over national and international radio. It also includes "on the ground" reports of direct action from various parts of the world up to 2000

Back in 1949, the humanist, pacifist, Lew Hill began a listener-sponsored radio station, KPFA in Berkeley, California. This was the beginning of a unique network dedicated to creating a peaceful world. The Pacifica Network was established to give the *other side* of commercial media. Access to the *other side* of Pacifica is available by exposure to any commercial media outlet.

It seemed clear to us programmers that we should concentrate on the very issues ignored or censored out by commercial media. Often the form of our programming was rough but the content gave a view of the world from the base.

Pacifica became the voice of the voiceless. Rather than suffering exclusion by corporate media, poor people, ethnic minorities and highly qualified critics of government policy were given a platform. The uniqueness of the Pacifica Network can arguably be cited as the impetus for the formation of PBS and NPR.

Pacifica became the clearest and most powerful voice of dissent in the United States. It was advocacy and it was anti-war. There was no attempt to mimic the corporate media's claim of "unbiased" coverage. The de facto bias of corporate media is such that holocausts such as Vietnam, Central America and Iraq are justified as "honorable." Indeed, corporate censorship is more sophisticated than government censorship.

We determined that we could not fulfill the Pacifica Mission Statement by mimicking commercial media. Voices from death row and during the Iraq Massacre, voices from the Gulf Peace

Team camped on the Iraq/Saudi Arabia border were aired on Pacifica. As the network evolved professionally, world-class journalists like Amy Goodman far excelled the "news readers" of the commercial stations. Amy was frequently on-the-scene in critical and life threatening situations such as the Indonesian military's attacks on East Timor and military/corporate oppression in Nigeria.

I began as a Pacifica volunteer programmer in 1969 with "Latin American News."

I left the station and moved to La Paz, California to serve as editor for Cesar Chavez as he reestablished the United Farm Workers newspaper, *El Malcriado*, 1971–72. After returning to the Los Angeles area I continued with prime time world affairs programs and news commentaries originating from KPFK until 1997.

By 1995, however, it became obvious that the Pacifica National Board had an agenda at variance with the Pacifica Mission Statement. Dissolution of the Mission Statement by the Pacifica Board was protected by gag orders imposed by station managers. Station managers could comply with the mediocrity of the board or get out. It appeared to me that a monetarist policy in sync with the new economic order had been set in place by people who were well trained and badly educated. Some board members were actually trying to sell Pacifica on the open market.

KPFA in Berkeley, the birthplace of Pacifica, became a battleground as the much loved station manager was fired by the Pacifica Board. Working journalists were forcibly removed from their posts.

The legal battle for the integrity of Pacifica began when California Attorney General Bill Lockyer granted Pacifica's listeners standing to sue the Pacifica Foundation. A letter from the Attorney General's Office said in part, "The allegations set forth by the Relators raise substantial questions of law or fact regarding whether there is compliance with the purpose of the Pacifica Foundation charitable trust, whether its articles of incorporation are being adhered to, whether its assets are being properly protected, and whether it is being managed and directed in a manner consistent with the requirements of the California Corporations Code. The answers to these questions require judicial resolution."

The listeners won this case. It was an act of faith conducted nationally by the listeners together with programmers and dedicated legal counsel. Upon this victory I ended my four year strike against KPFK and renewed my radio commentaries.

We are in the process of establishing a new Pacifica National Board with members who will adhere to the Pacifica Mission Statement. Our intention is to carry on the vision of Lew Hill. He knew that we live in a war system and that we are socialized into accepting that system as a given. It is similar to the socialization of people during the days of slavery when good people would abhor involuntary servitude and express "TINA" (there is no alternative). The abolitionists both sought and obtained the alternative, no more slavery! The cult of militarism has all the characteristics of slavery; "Keep your mouth shut, do what you are told and follow orders." The relationship of soldier to officer is similar to that of slave and master. How many fine young people have gone off to die as the enemy in places where they were not wanted. In classic mind control fashion, soldiers learn to love the very commanders who send them to their death.

But what about the need for national defense? The nation state is as outdated as the city states of old. The Charter of the United Nations, however, is structured for international peace-keeping. But our nation acts as an enemy of the UN in a way that is reminiscent of the time it destroyed the League of Nations after World War I. Had the League been allowed to develop, there would have been no World War II. If the Security Council resolutions pertaining to the Middle East had been kept, there would have been no bloodshed between Palestine and Israel and the two states would exist peacefully side-by-side.

Our disregard for international law is creating an international disaster. A signed treaty such as the Charter of the United Nations becomes part of our constitutional law. We continue to ignore this reality to our own peril.

Now that the National Board has been restructured the network can realign itself with the international movement for peace and justice. Daily announcements of movement activities are once again a catalyst for community organization.

These commentaries are written with the belief that we can build a peace system to replace the dinosaur war system. May we always have a listener sponsored national network dedicated to that end.

Nineteen years ago we founded the Office of the Americas as a non-profit educational corporation dedicated to world justice and peace. Our work and the mission of Pacifica are once again in harmony. *La lucha misma es la victoria*! (The struggle itself is the victory!).

Blase Bonpane, Ph.D., Director
Office of the Americas
8124 West Third Street, Suite 202
Los Angeles, California 90048-4309

Phone: 323/852-9808
Email: ooa@igc.org
Website: www.officeoftheamericas.org

Guerrillas of Peace

On The Air

Pacifica

Radio Commentaries

KPFK 90.7 FM

Los Angeles, California

January 2, 1996 to April 7, 1998

Hello, this is Blase Bonpane with a comment . . .

The Second Anniversary of the Zapatista Uprising

January 2, 1996

On this second anniversary of the Zapatista uprising in southern Mexico, a new political opposition movement has been formed. The movement will be peaceful and non-military. It will not be a political party and will not seek power. The new movement will be known as the "Zapatista National Liberation Front." It will be open to people who do not seek elective office but who wish to push for a new constitution and democratic change in Mexico outside the political system.

This declaration from the collective farm, *La Realidad* on the periphery of the Lacandón jungle in Chiapas, is a follow up to proposals made at the August 1994 Zapatista National Democratic Convention and the International Consultation made by the EZLN or Zapatistas Army of National Liberation. The next series of peace talks in Mexico will begin on January 10, 1996.

In the midst of this Zapatista action for a nonviolent future there is cause for alarm. Some twenty kilometers from San Cristóbal de las Casas in Chiapas, Mexico at the collective farm of Oventic, a group of 120 indigenous people prevented a military convoy of 150 soldiers from establishing a camp 500 meters from their cultural center. These centers are designed for democratic dialogues with the population and are referred to as *aguascalientes* (a stage, wooden benches and a plastic tarp covering). Such construction can hardly be considered a military threat to Mexico.

These non-threatening community centers are being destroyed by the army. The one located at Guadalupe Tepeyac was destroyed and replaced by a military camp. The people of Oventic shouted, "Soldiers get out" and "The people united will never be defeated." At that point the Mexican army soldiers took up attack positions. There are four other aguascalientes in the area Altamirano, Ocosingo, Las Maragaritas and San Andrés Larraínzar.

Immigration authorities are now restricting passage of foreigners with tourist visas in these zones in spite of the fact that they have not been declared conflict zones. The situation in Mexico is clear—while the Zapatistas are preparing for peace, the Mexican military is preparing for war.

As United States citizens, we must understand the role of the so-called "War on Drugs" in this conflict. Our country is giving equipment to Mexico. Some of the latest helicopters can only be flown by United States pilots. While the stated agenda is "war on drugs," the reality is counter-insurgency.

It is incumbent on concerned citizens to write to the President of the United States and demand an end to military aid to the Mexican army and to the training of Mexican officers in the United States. Have we not seen enough of such United States-directed slaughter in the devastation of Central America? We should also write or fax the president of Mexico and urge him to support the new Zapatista program for political peace in Mexico. Even if its motives are opportunistic, the Mexican government would be wise to support this new and nonviolent opposition movement known as the Zapatista National Liberation Front. This program which comes to us from La Realidad is reality! It is the result of consultation with millions of people throughout Mexico and the rest of the world.

International peace making is not easy, it is often sloppy and frequently unfair. But 1995 was a year of clumsy, welcome peacemaking in Haiti, Balkins, South Africa, Middle East, and the Irish Sea. For the first time since its inception, Israel is at peace with the Palestine, Jordan and Egypt. There are talks are under way with Syria.

But Afghanistan has seen its capital, Kabul, destroyed. Kashmir wants out of India. Turkey continues a scorched earth drive against Kurdish rebels. Conflicts in Georgia and Chechnya are not settled. East Timor is still ravaged by the Indonesian government. Progress was made in 1995—let us all be a part of continuing that progress in 1996 by waging peace in Mexico and Guatemala.

The Republicratic
Corporate Capital Party

January 9, 1996

A corporation has been defined as "a person with nobody to kick and no soul to cast into hell." In over a century since the corporation has been so defined, the concept has turned into a monster.

We currently have government of the corporations for the corporations and by the corporations. Such a government will certainly perish from the earth. There are two large political parties of corporate capital. There is the Republican Corporate Capital Party and the Democratic Corporate Capital Party. The parties represent various differences within corporate capital. We have a Congress that is elected by corporations.

There is one small problem with the corporate model. There is no democracy in a corporation. We hear of corporate voting, but it is not democratic voting. Each share is a vote. If I have 1000 shares I have 1000 votes. If you have one share you have one vote. If you have no shares you have no vote. This is not a democratic structure of one person one vote. This is the antithesis of democracy.

What about the people who work for corporations? They give their lives to the monster but they have no vote. Indeed, we have seen some attempts at structural change through employee stock ownership plans.

United Airlines is employee owned, but not exclusively. Employee stock ownership programs are a promising change in corporate structure. But much more remains to be done. Our intention is not to simply say, "Isn't it awful?" Our intention is to say, "It is awful and this is what we can do about it."

Let us look at some specifics:

- In 1974 the ratio of corporate chief executive officer to the pay of the average worker was 34 to 1. Currently it is 159 to 1.

- Worker productivity is up but the current level of pay has decreased to 83 percent of what it was in 1973.

- 230 times more toxic waste is dumped into low income neighborhoods than into affluent neighborhoods.

- In the 1940s corporations paid one-third of the taxes of the United States. In the 1970s corporations paid one-fifth of the taxes of the United States. Currently corporations pay one-tenth of the taxes of the United States.

- The average return of profit for Fortune 500 corporations currently is over 20 percent per year.

Aside from what may be able to be done through the courts, we are developing a new political movement. This movement will undoubtedly lead to a new and effective political party which is something that the majority of the American people want. As it stands now, corporate power not only controls the economy, it controls the mind by controlling the media. NAFTA and GATT are two examples of corporate rule. There is no democracy and no consultation with the people in this new and destructive economic order.

There is a gauge which counts and which should be on the news every evening in place of stock market reports. It is the *Gross Social Product* (GSP). The GSP gives us an understanding of the quality of life. The *Gross National Product* (GNP) has nothing to do with quality of life. What is the rate of literacy in 1996 as compared with 1995? What is the quality of the air? What is the quality of our schools? What is the level of health care delivery? With corporate government, those who are healthy are insured. Those who are sick are denied coverage. Can you imagine, that they will not cover a pre-existing condition? The corporation is not designed to heal the sick, it is designed to make money for the few.

Once we recognize that giant corporations now govern, we can understand that such structures are the major causes of poverty, community destabilization, discrimination, ill health and environmental destruction. We will learn to end corporate rule by imitating community groups in India that forced two American giants, DuPont and Cargill, to close down their operations through well planned and persistent direct action.

We have had it with corporate welfare, reckless deregulation, corporate crime, corporate buying of politicians, multinational corporate erosion of our national sovereignty, corporate munitions trade, corporatist education, corporate dominated media and corporate environmental destruction.

We support the new movements to nurture cooperative, worker, community owned and controlled enterprises.

A Fire in the Kitchen

January 16, 1996

Prisoners of war are entitled to food, shelter and medical care. This is international law by way of the Geneva Accords. It is time to declare the homeless of the United States prisoners of war. Prisoners of war are not free, but they have rights. Similarly people who are homeless are not free to sleep under the freeways, but they must at least be given the same consideration as prisoners of war. Currently the homeless are being ignored. They have become invisible. Why do we have homeless people? We have homeless people because those who have been entrusted with our taxes are guilty of malfeasance of office.

When you make a contract with the Department of Water and Power, to deliver water and power, you intend to receive water and power, right? Suppose instead of water and power, you received a maudlin homily about wedlock from the entity that had pledged to deliver water and power? You would undoubtedly say, "Hey, I don't want your silly sermon, I want what I paid you to deliver, water and power . . . that is all I want from you, okay?"

This is the case with Pete Wilson. There is a fire in the kitchen and he wants to use the only available water to make cocktails for his cronies.

We gave him our money for the common good of the people of California. What has he given us? Methyl bromide for the children, leaking gas storage tanks for our subsoil, a freeze on the electric car industry, a license for more smog, disdain for youth, disregard for our schools and a sick xenophobia for the strangers in our midst. But we gave him our money for the common good.

Are all homeless nice? Of course not. Are all prisoners of war nice people? Of course not. Whether they are nice or not, both prisoners of war and the homeless must be dealt with humanely. Now if you want the Guatemalan model, you will simply shoot the prisoners of war and the homeless. Perhaps there are some in that category, but it seems to me that most people are not barbarians. The homeless simply need options. As it stands they do not have any options. Step number one is professional evaluation of each homeless person.

Annually there are 120,000 to 223,000 people homeless in Los Angeles alone. Among these, are 59,000 families including 42,000 children. The homeless population is increasing by 13 percent each year. On any one night there are 43,000 to 77,000 homeless on the streets of Los Angeles. 25 to 50 percent of the homeless population have severe mental disorders like schizophrenia and major depression.

Some 40 percent of the homeless population have alcohol and / or drug addictions. 12 percent of the homeless population is dual diagnosed with mental problems and addiction. One-third of the adult homeless are veterans of the Armed Services. In the course of a year there are some 12,000 homeless youth. 10 to 15 percent of the homeless are HIV infected. This data is from the Shelter Partnership, Inc.

What is the Governor doing while the needs of these Californians go unattended? It seems clear to me that he intends to break his social contract with the people of California to serve the common good. He is conspiring to give our tax money to the wealthiest people in the state and to profit glutted corporations. The wealthy will receive up to $30,000 each from what the Governor calls a surplus. Middle-class people might get as much as $200 to $300. The poor would receive nothing.

Rather than return $7 to $9 billion to wealthy Californians it is incumbent on Governor Wilson to address this state and national emergency.

I suggest a class action suit against the Governor to stop him from giving money back to the richest people in California. That money was not collected to fatten the rich. It was given for the common good of the people of California. Let us get on with the lawsuit and stop this illegality.

Beavis, Butthead
and a Love Based Society

January 23, 1996

What is the proper civic and social environment of a society? What is the proper social ecology? Does a society function best on terror? I do not think so. How about a mean spirited society? Does that work well?

"Let's take some money away from the poorest . . . Yeah. Let's do it. Let's close the county hospital. Yeah . . . let's charge tuition for schools that were free in the height of the great depression. Yeah . . . Let's do it. Let's give the state the right to murder people. Yeah."

If this sounds like Beavis and Butthead, well that's what it is. I think that a mean spirited society creates mean spirited people.

But let us get real. Can a society make a system out of love? Why not? A love based society would insist on a zero tolerance of violence. Citizens who could not abstain from violence would be lovingly incarcerated. They would remain locked up until professional judgement determined they were rehabilitated. If not rehabilitated and still prone to violence, they would be able to spend the rest of their lives in prison. But the prison would be a place where they could reflect, convert, study and pray. It would also be a loving place with a zero tolerance for violence.

We have seen love in our social and political systems. Have we forgotten our history?

Those with a great love in their hearts fought for an eight hour day. And they won while many lost their lives in the struggle.

Those who fought for the forty hour week understood love of their families and love of the people.

Those who fought for public utilities.

Those who fought for public schools.

Those who fought for public hospitals.

Now, ignorant, greedy, mean-spirited and self-centered individuals have captured the spotlight.

They are going to shove violence down our throats twenty-four hours a day in order to have a frightened population. Indeed, the manipulation of fear is the most treasured tool of corrupt politicians.

The great people I meet day after day cause me to say, "We're better than that." We can have a society which reflects the goodness of the vast majority of the people. But consider the toxic, so-called "defense industry." $72 billion has just been flushed down the toilet to build F-22 stealth fighters which are designed to penetrate Soviet radar. There is no Soviet radar. There is no Soviet Union.

Congratulations Butthead! Is this why we have to close public hospitals?

The mean-spirited have won for the time being. The mean-spirited have done nothing but create mean-spirited children. Of course the family must be a part of this. But families must live in an atmosphere of a concerned society. Can a policy be based on love? Of course it can. Children must be considered the new privileged class. We must make the finest schools available to them at no cost. Funds taken from the Beavis and Butthead defense budget would make this simple.

We must be in touch with our history. At one time we had a progressive income tax. It was successful. The richest paid up to 90 percent of their income in taxes and were still rich. It was excellent. Much of what has to be done in our country has a history. We are not speaking fantasy.

Before structuring a permanent and loving society we must understand that it is entirely possible. Think of this when you reflect on the fact that the death penalty has given us one of the world's highest murder rates.

The majority of the world's countries have no death penalty and they have minimal murder rates compared to ours. Ignorance is not going to cure our problem.

Think of this when you read *Driving is a privilege but not a right*. If driving were a privilege, how in God's name am I to accept gun ownership as a right? More people were killed this year by guns than by motor vehicles. We need motor vehicles, we do not need guns. Step number one is to understand that a society based on love is to everyone's advantage. It is possible. It is do-able. After we accept the logic and rightness of a society based on love, we can proceed with its construction.

U. S. Prisons

January 30, 1996

"There are currently 1.5 million people in State and Federal prisons in this country. In five years, in the land of the free, there will be 2 million people in prison. Retributive justice is based primarily on vengeance and punishment which actually perpetuates a high violent crime rate and creates a more embittered and angry nation. It is a toxic sludge in our system.

"The vicious cycle of crime and punishment followed by more crime and more punishment must be broken, otherwise society will descend into a chaotic human jungle," says Jim Consedine, who for the last seventeen years has been a prison chaplain in New Zealand. Consedine believes there is another way, a far more humane way to address the problem of crime. He calls this "restorative justice." It was introduced into the juvenile justice system in New Zealand in 1989 under the Children, Young Persons and Their Families Act, and has met with astounding results—a 27 percent decrease in young adults appearing in court.

"Many are now certain that this is the program for adult offenders as well. The prototype of the New Zealand system was conceived about twenty-five years ago by a Maori judge with the aim of restoring the social balance upset by the crime. Under this system, offenders have to admit their guilt, apologize for their crime, face up to their problems and deal with them.

"For drug addicts, violent people, and sexual offenders to face up to the causes of their problems and change, as demanded by a restorative scenario, is a lot tougher sentence than any amount of imprisonment," says Jim Consedine.

A restorative justice system follows a series of steps. Under the direction of a skilled mediator, a conference is called which includes the offender, his or her family, the victim, the victim's family (if desired) and the police. No media are allowed. Offenders that want to plead not guilty go through the normal court system; but, those who wish to participate in the restorative system must first acknowledge their guilt, apologize to the victim, and seek their forgiveness.

At the conference all parties talk about why the offense happened. This usually involves an explanation of the offenders background. Then the victim has a chance to verbalize the pain and suffering they have endured and to have their feeling acknowledged. All parties then work toward a consensus solution.

These recommendations are then taken to the judge in the case who can accept them or not. The solutions usually include financial reparation to the victim and rehabilitation if drugs or alcohol are involved. Also included is the requirement of community work by the offender and a letter of apology to the court. If all conditions are met, the offender gets a clean slate without any conviction being recorded.

The restorative justice model has the ability to heal the victim and the victimizer.

In the current retributive system the offender is encouraged to rationalize and deny guilt and responsibility. Instead of the victim being at the center of the justice system, they are on the periphery. The offender has taken the power from them and so does the law system.

Re-empowering victims facilitates the healing process. Victims need to speak their feelings, to receive restitution and to experience justice. They also need to experience forgiving the offender. Showing mercy and forgiving helps to bring about healing and a sense of closure so that the crime experience no longer dominates their lives.

Imprisonment distorts and twists the psyche and the spirit of the prisoner; for many it guarantees more serious re-offending. This means more victims and more pain. The United States now imprisons at a rate of 520 per 100,000 people. In 1970 this rate was 97 per 100,000 people.

In less than twenty-five years, imprisonment has increased 530 percent. The two men most responsible for this horrendous escalation are Ronald Reagan and George Bush, both accused of law breaking themselves. Let us go for the restorative justice plan and move out of the seventeenth century.

Liberation Theology

February 6, 1996

The *New York Times* is talking about liberation theology and its preferential option for the poor as a blend of Catholic teaching with Marx-
ist economic analysis. This theology has led to the formation of ecclesiastical base communities in which lay people and clergy analyze
religious and political issues seeking to bring about social justice.

But the *New York Times* misses the historical sequence. Liberation
theology came first. It came with the book of Exodus; Moses and the
concept that the true God liberates and false gods enslave.

Eighteen centuries before Marx was born, the teachings of the
clandestine, illegal communities of the catacombs were self-directed
and sharing.

In 312 A.D. came the Edict of Toleration of the Emperor
Constantine. What had been a capital crime, Christianity, became the
official religion of the Roman Empire.

The Chi Rho symbol of Christianity was on the Roman shield. As a
result of this imperial absorption of religion, the church became mus-
cular. The holy land was conquered in the name of God by blood-
thirsty crusaders who massacred every man woman and child of Jewish and Islamic faith. 600 years of inquisition followed with death to
heretics and the proclamation that error has no rights. While the Church
became compatible with Empire, it also became compatible with capitalism.

What is called "liberation theology" is an effort to return to the
primitive concepts of community and self-determination that marked
the first four centuries of the Church. This development may disturb
the papacy and the press. But what new idea has not? New ideas are
generally received with raised eyebrows.

What is called "liberation theology" today is the legitimate effort
to remove Roman imperial culture from ecclesiastical practice in
this post Constantinian era. The Pope is not meant to be seen as a
line officer in the military. Quite the contrary, Peter and Paul argued

about acceptable practice. Paul chided the first Pope to his face. Many bishops were elected by popular vote, not by appointment.

Imperial theology caters to political and economic power. On the contrary, spiritual power speaks the truth to the false idols of power and money. There is no compatibility of spirituality with empire— there is no compatibility of spirituality with unfettered capitalism. Those who have made their peace with the gods of power and money may hold high places in the hierarchy. They should remember the witness of Michelangelo, who in spite of the fact that he was paid by the Vatican, did not hesitate to paint members of the hierarchy in Hell. The only way to revere the past is to change. Knowledge of the past is essential, but repetition of the past is unforgivable. To repeat the past is to repeat ignorance, superstition, racism, nationalism, hatred and fanatical religious wars. Liberation theology wants to revere the past by changing the toxic conditions of the past. Authentic spirituality will never be based on definitions, dogmas and legalisms. What we call "liberation theology" is nonsectarian. Observers of conduct know that within any religious body one can identify frauds, fakes, charlatans and saints. It is never the name of the religious community that makes the difference. It is the conduct of that community and its members.

In this spirit let us promote an Atheistic, Agnostic, Islamic, Judaic, Protestant, Catholic, Hindu, Nativist, and Buddhist coalition to bring a new spirit of humanity into a toxic, twice-dead political culture whose message is an ongoing and constant lethal injection.

SICSAL
Meeting in Guatemala

February 20, 1996

I recently attended a meeting in Guatemala which was truly upbeat. I am struck by the sense of empowerment of people living in such poor and oppressive places. But part of the re-entry crisis is to once again confront the myth of powerlessness which is so common in our own country.

Nobel Prize winner Rigoberta Menchú was there, a Guatemalan human rights attorney who had been in exile as long as I can remember—and some of the world's most progressive bishops. The group is called SICSAL (*Secretariado Internacional Cristiano de Solidaridad con los Pueblos de América Latina, Oscar A. Romero*), or the International Christian Secretariate in Solidarity with the People of Latin America, Oscar A. Romero. Do not let the word Christian frighten you. This is not the so-called "Christian coalition" of the United States. This group is self-identified as macro-ecumenical, which means they are open to all perspectives on religion and non-religion. The focal point of SICSAL is solidarity with the people and especially the poor.

Bishop Samuel Ruiz Garcia of San Cristóbal de las Casas serves as president of this hemispheric organization. We were in Guatemala to identify moral and ethical problems in the hemisphere and to look for solutions.

The first moral imperative is the campaign to cancel Latin America's indebtedness to the international banks. We wish to accomplish this by the year 2000. Such debts cannot be paid and should not be continued. For every dollar invested in Latin America during the twentieth century, three dollars of raw materials have been extracted.

Second was to study more deeply the fanatical ideology which is being imposed on poor countries by an international clique of corporate capital. Alternatives to this centralized and anti-solidarity model were identified. Many of the stated alternatives are in the form of cooperatives with local decision making. Models established by the indigenous communities are excellent examples of cooperativism and communitarianism.

Opposition to the principles of neo-liberal corporate capital were clear:

No, to structural adjustment policies of the international monetary fund and the world bank.

No, to devaluation of local currencies as a condition for loans.

No, to the privatization of schools, hospitals and social programs.

No, to the use of poor countries as exporters of food while their own people go hungry.

Yes, to the removal of United States military bases from Panama, Cuba, Japan and many other countries.

Resounding support was given for displaced and migrant people with ringing opposition to California's Proposition 187 and the militarization of the United States border. Our support for the implementation of peace accords in Guatemala, El Salvador and Mexico was unanimous as was our support for indigenous autonomy.

Everyone was in their right mind. Therefore, everyone supported the elimination of the United States' ancient act of war against the Cuban people; the embargo and the blockade conducted by nine foolish United States presidents against an island of delightful people.

As usual the ideas coming from the poor express the solidarity of one family. Solidarity means we care about each other. The globalization policies imposed on us by international corporate capital are anti-solidarity, anti-people and anti-humane. We oppose them on moral and ethical grounds.

This is truly liberation theology. Such macro-ecumenical theology is not dead. It is the future of the spiritual quest of people throughout the world. What was proclaimed at the Guatemala meeting applies equally to the United States, whose great people have seen their country made into a Banana Republic by the newts in power.

Cuba

February 27, 1996

"We mourn the loss of life by Brothers to the Rescue. We ourselves are committed to peaceful, nonviolent methods of achieving change. We think Brothers to the Rescue should reflect on their methods, which continue a long tradition of invasion and violence launched on Cuba from Florida. We ask all people to understand that the Cuban people have been suffering loss of life for thirty-five years due to the United States embargo. We are distressed that President Clinton has responded to this tragedy by further tightening the United States embargo of Cuba, especially after every major church in the United States and Cuba has called for its end. The U. S. must recognize its own complicity in creating a climate of aggression toward Cuba. Until U.S. / Cuba relations are normalized, tragedies such as this will continue to fuel hatred and intolerance."

These are the words of the Reverend Lucius Walker, a leader of the Fast for Life, as he and his companions continue their fast at the border of San Ysidro, California and Tijuana, Mexico. Reverend Walker concludes his remarks by saying, "We realize that these tragic events will make our objective more difficult, but we are firmly committed to continue our fast until the 400 medical computers are released." (The computers were seized by United States Customs when the Pastors for Peace Caravan reached this border).

What are the mitigating circumstances to Cuba's action? How were the Cubans to know these planes were not armed? Armed attacks have been forthcoming from Florida for thirty-five years. The United States has been complicit in these decades of harassment, invasion, assassinations, disinformation, sabotage and disruption.

Consider the analogy of a woman who finally shoots her abusive husband after thirty-five years of mistreatment. We do not cheer her act of violence, but we understand it in the context of years of abuse and so does the court. Brothers to the Rescue have made over 1,700 such flights. Last summer they dropped leaflets on Havana encouraging the Cuban people to rise against Fidel Castro. The Cuban people are not simply expecting attacks, they have had an endless series of attacks. It was only a few weeks ago that Cubans in Los Angeles were arrested for amassing arms and planning attacks on Cuba.

In Florida, the Federal Aviation Administration had begun an investigation of Brothers to the Rescue and its founder, Jose Basulto, who is a Bay of Pigs veteran. United States intelligence officials said that at least one of the planes, the lead plane which returned safely to Florida, and perhaps all three, had violated Cuban airspace. United States intelligence also said that the air traffic control tower in Havana had warned the pilots that they were in danger.

Last month when the Cuban government protested the actions of Brothers to the Rescue as a violation of United States and International Law, it put Washington on notice that it would take all necessary measures to halt the invading aircraft. At the time they were shot down, the Cuban government said the planes were between five and eight miles off Baracoa, a western suburb of Havana. The pilot's refusal to heed Cuba's warning amounted to a provocation.

There is but one reasonable solution to this crisis: We must renew diplomatic relations with Cuba so that such matters can be dealt with by the rule of law. Cuba may not be a wife of the United States, but the level of unilateral and violent abuse from our country toward that island nation has led to this lashing out. President John F. Kennedy said it well, "Those who make nonviolent change impossible, make violent change inevitable."

The Helms-Burton bill will alienate our closest friends in Europe and Canada. It is a classically irrational piece of legislation. We must oppose it. The United States' embargo against Cuba is increasingly unpopular with the vast majority of member states in the United Nations who vote against United States sanctions by a larger margin each year. It is within our power to resume normal relations with Cuba and to stop our callous complicity in the abuse of the Cuban people.

The President of the United States can demonstrate the presidential strength that millions of citizens are longing to witness, by ending this long act of war against a small and poor nation.

A Secular State?

March 5, 1996

I have never been accused of excessive flag waving but attention must be called to the wisdom of some wealthy slave holding men who reluctantly gave us a bill of rights some two years after the Constitution. It was December 15, 1791. The First Amendment of the United States Constitution states:

> Congress shall make no law respecting an establishment of religion, or prohibiting the free exercise thereof; or abridging the freedom of speech, or of the press; or the right of the people peaceably to assemble, and to petition the government for redress of grievances.

Theocratic states do not have a future. They are condemned to perpetual war by identifying the non-believer as a second class citizen. A lack of toleration is the essence of a theocratic state. A state simply cannot be based on one religion without creating hatred.

An argument about the nature of the Holy Spirit separated the Croats from the Serbs in 1054 A.D. Neither side knew what they were talking about and the only impact of the argument was proof that such doctrinal conflicts could be manipulated into hatred by opportunistic demagogues.

Today we see an example of this in Bosnia and Herzegovina. Former prime minister Haris Silajdzic is challenging Alija Izetbegovic by running on a platform of ethnic harmony and an end to religion based politics. Muslim fundamentalists have begun accusing Mr. Silajdzic of betraying Islam. Mr. Silajdzic responds that such accusations are anti-Islamic because they put the accuser in the position of judge by violating the Muslim principle that there is no god but God. God based arguments are perpetually conflictive. Functional politics has to do with the conduct of people, and the rule of law, not a belief system.

Haris Silajdzic is doing a service for the former Yugoslavia and setting an example for other countries. While we can never prove matters relating to God, we can deal with matters regarding the conduct of a people. Confucius understood this problem well; he said we simply must live together in harmony.

With our history we have attempts of the unlettered to claim that this is a Christian country. It is not a Christian country; it was clearly designed to be a secular state where witches would no longer be burned. I think that this is the only kind of state that will remain in the twenty-first century. Would such a change end the tragic bloodshed in Israel? I think so. Look at the message of 1791. Sectarian divisions supported by the state create perpetual animosity. Religion becomes a cover for economic injustice.

What is the point? Creed and ethnicity cannot be a basis for a modern polity. Only conduct can be a basis for a twenty-first century state. But the cure is in recognition of the secular nature of the state. Here at home we must not let ignorance and fanatical light weights try to claim that this is a Christian country. It is, and will remain, a country of hundreds of religions—and be proud of it.

Instead of accusations and recriminations that begin to look like gang warfare, let us consider the structure of the states of the Middle East and the rest of the world as we seek a solution to these bloody outrages.

We have a First Amendment, and we have to fight for its implementation daily here in the United States. That amendment must now be available for export to the Middle East where it is necessary for the life of all the people. "Congress shall make no law respecting an establishment of religion . . ."

Necrophilia

March 12, 1996

Our TV set projects hundreds of fictitious murders each week and that frightens us. Our eleven o'clock news gives us a diet of real murders and that frightens us. Then a candidate by the name of Deukmejian arrives and tells us he will kill the murderers and we elect him in order to alleviate the fear. This seems to be a good campaign policy. Along comes Mr. Wilson who also promises to kill for us. Indeed, we have now found the key element to be elected; the manipulation of fear. Let us call it "necrophilia" or *love of death*. Putting to death our fears by killing.

The next near death experience is baseball or three strikes, kill them with life in prison, no matter that the majority of recent third strikes have been for possession of marijuana. What a great achievement. Life in prison for possession of a chemical substance a little less harmful than the drug, nicotine.

Historians of the future will call this the age of the fanatics. The media will keep people in a state of perpetual fear. Banal politicians who run for office will get rich. All of this creating a necrophilic and mean-spirited national environment.

Prospective district attorney's running for office on a basis of a high conviction rate (over 90 percent). I cannot think of anything less representative of one's qualifications than convicting thousands of poor people and sending them off to life in prison for possession of marijuana on their third strike. Mandatory sentencing has made our judges into robots, mannequins, non-persons. Congratulations to the judges who are protesting this nonsense.

Here comes the terrorism bill by way of the Federal government. It is called *H.R. 2768*, the effective death penalty and anti-terrorism act of 1995. More love of death; more necrophilia. The bill is a disastrous attack on the First Amendment right to dissent and an unnecessary expansion of Federal law enforcement authority and surveillance.

What is to be done? When a polity projects inclusion, that everyone belongs, we can expect the citizenry to respond by keeping the rules established for all. When a polity is based on exclusion it is logical that those who are excluded will not consider the rules as made for them. Why should I keep the rules of the club if I do not belong to the club. Inclusivity is the answer to a frightened and necrophilic society.

Of course we should be tough on crime. Rational toughness on crime would be to make the point that our society has a zero tolerance for violence. The fear factor has brought us to a point where we spend more on the new growth industry of prisons than we spend on schools. But we do not have room in our prisons for those who commit violent offenses because our prisons are filled with people who have possessed marijuana.

You cannot build a humane society on nonsense. *Biophilia*, or love of life, can replace our current environment of necrophilia, which is a love of death. Now that we are into the campaign season, let us demand of all candidates that they state their support for love of life rather than love of death. We do not need the police state that is being designed by death oriented state and federal authorities. On the contrary, we can promote a life giving and inclusive agenda by ridding ourselves of the war economy which has devastated our cities and our psyche with a death focus. The military spending binge of the last fifteen years is the major cause of our $4 trillion national debt and our crushing tax burden. We can cut this wasteful budget by two-thirds as we stop all nuclear tests and wage a diplomatic offensive for a nuclear-free world.

These issues will bring life to our society rather than the politics of death.

Christian Terrorists

March 19, 1996

Hypocrisy is often involved in the selection of words. Take the word terrorism, for example. One of the characteristics of the terrorist is an externally controlled mind. A mind controlled young person with TNT strapped to his body boards a bus in Israel killing himself and many innocent Israeli citizens is terrorism. The religion of the terrorist was Islam. The culprit is called "an Islamic Terrorist."

Fanatics in the United States blow up the Federal Building in Oklahoma City and kill scores of innocent United States citizens. This is terrorism and the religion of the terrorists is Christian. But the terrorists are not called "Christian Terrorists."

With a selectivity that Webster would never accept, the United States Air Force drops not pounds, but hundreds of tons of TNT on noncombatant Iraqis, killing over 300,000 men, women and children. This is not terrorism? Then what is it? It is terrorism of an Air Force. The dictionary accepts the fact that an Air Force can conduct terrorism. But mind controlled nationalists apparently do not. Lebanon has been attacked regularly with TNT dropped by the ton rather than by the pound and that is not to be identified as terrorism? To avoid hypocrisy most of the world's Air Forces must be identified as terrorists. We cannot exclude ground troops either. We have only to examine the role of our country in Nicaragua, Guatemala, Panama, Grenada and El Salvador.

The time has come for us to leave the adolescence of selective and nationalistic definitions. We cannot remain political infants forever.

If the bomb is carried by a suicide bomber, the act is terrorism. If it is carried by a fighter bomber or a B-52 it is still terrorism. To exempt the world's Air Forces from the word terrorist is to be mind controlled. Mind control is what creates both suicide bombers and pilots who will bomb any group of civilians they are told to bomb.

When Colin Powell was asked how many people were killed in the Iraqi holocaust, he said, "I couldn't care less." That sounds like a terrorist to me. What is this business of only mentioning one religion when we speak of terrorists? It seems the media only mentions Islam when speaking of terrorism. What kind of agenda is that?

When was the last time you heard that Christian terrorists were responsible for killing 6 million Jews, homosexuals, gypsies and alleged disloyal citizens during the holocaust of the Third Reich? Why not call them "Christian Terrorists?" The terrorist Nazis were for the most part either Roman Catholic or Lutheran. Those are the dominant churches in Germany. National identity must not include mind control any longer. Who were the terrorists killing some 3 to 6 million people in Vietnam, Laos, Cambodia? For the most part they were Christians from the United States of America. They were mind controlled by their military indoctrination.

What is the point? There are Jewish, Christian, Islamic and members of any other religion who are terrorists. But the greatest terrorism has taken place not by suicide bombers but by so-called "legitimate states."

Let us no longer tolerate the exclusivity of the phrase "Islamic Terrorist." If we are going to include the religion of terrorists, let us include all religions. Selective indoctrination is not education. There is no empirical data to demonstrate that Islamics have any more terrorists than anyone else.

Let us grow up and stop confusing nationalistic propaganda with education. Nationalistic propaganda is mind control and cult practice. Education, on the contrary, seeks that truth which hurts but which also makes us free.

Sister Dianna Ortiz

March 26, 1996

Before anyone gets appointed to a high position in government they must be subject to a security check. Well let us take a look at the guards of our security. It is always legitimate to ask, "Who is guarding the guards?"

Here is a recent statement from Sister Dianna Ortiz made before the Congress of the United States:

> "I am Sister Dianna Ortiz, a United States citizen and a survivor of torture by the brutal Guatemalan security forces. The painful account of what I will share with you today bares the truth, not just of one woman's suffering, but of a forgotten people who have been persecuted by both the Guatemalan and the United States governments.
>
> "I was abducted from the back yard of a church retreat house; I was put into a Guatemalan National Police car and taken to a clandestine prison in Guatemala City, known as "the Old Poli-technical Academy." I was subjected to heinous forms of torture: My back was burned with cigarettes 111 times. I was raped numerous times. Then they lowered me into an open pit packed with human bodies, bodies of children, women and men, some decapitated, some lying face up and caked with blood, some dead, some alive—all swarming with rats. I heard the despairing screams of people being tortured and I watched helplessly as an innocent person was tortured.
>
> "After hours of torture, I was returned to the room where the interrogation had initially occurred. It was in this room that I first met Alejandro, a fellow United States citizen who was the authority over my torturers. As my torturers were beginning to rape me again, they said, in Spanish, 'Hey, Alejandro, come and have some fun!' Alejandro responded with a crude expletive in unmistakable United States English and ordered the Guatemalans to stop the torture."

Then the CIA operative helped the Sister put her clothes on and said he would drive her to the United States Embassy. Conversing in English while driving, the United States agent said that they had tried to warn her by sending her death threats; and that she should have taken them seriously.

The United States supervisor of torture then threatened Sister Dianna Ortiz saying that she had better remain quiet because he had access to the photos of her being raped and he was sure she did not want such things released. At this point Sister Dianna jumped out of the jeep and disappeared into the jungle of Guatemala City traffic. She escaped.

Is this just one bad apple in the CIA? Hardly. The United States has designed, directed and supervised torture and murder in Guatemala since 1954. The torture and murder could not take place without United States' approval. This is in sync with United States performance in Chile, Uruguay, Brazil, Nicaragua, Panama, Honduras, El Salvador, Haiti and Vietnam to mention only a few locations.

Remember, our query at the beginning of this commentary was just who are the people that give security clearances for United States citizens? That is right, it is the very people who supervise condone and direct torture.

Actually any country practicing torture has no right to exist. Any agency condoning torture has no right to exist. We must demand the immediate criminalization of the behavior of any United States agency which directs or practices the torture of United States nuns or Guatemalan peasants.

Making Money

April 2, 1996

Holy Week and Passover; a time to think of peace and peace-making. When the cold war ended, we expected a decrease in the arms transfers to foreign governments (we might call them "foreign militias"). Instead United States transfers doubled to $15 billion per year. Now at least 85 percent of these governments have no democracy whatsoever.

Aerospace Industries Association (AIA) is the Washington, D.C. based lobby representing over fifty of the largest defense manufacturers. AIA related political action committees (PACS) have contributed $7.4 million in each of the two most recent election cycles. Some of these corporations have admitted to bribing foreign governments to purchase their weapons. They continue their foreign sales and their domestic military contracts with impunity (this of course while people in California are going to life in prison for possession of marijuana on their third strike).

Combat aircraft are sold to Indonesia; one of the worst human rights violators in the world. The victims of these death machines will undoubtedly be the people of Indonesia. If a foreign government defaults on its loans, the United States government is responsible for reimbursing the manufacturers. In the past five years our government has forgiven some $9 billion in such military loans. There is a direct relationship between these payments to corporations and the deterioration of our schools.

Aside from this sleazy effort to make money by selling death making equipment, let us take a look at how we spend money to threaten extinction of the human species. The United States is the only government capable of leading the international abolition of nuclear weapons. But instead of a program for the abolition of nuclearism, the Department of Energy plans to design, test and produce nuclear weapons far into the next century, expecting us to pay the bill and to take the consequences of a catastrophic accident. Chernobyl was simply a mild warning.

On the side of hope, at this moment antinuclear organizers from around the world are gathering in Las Vegas at the University of Nevada. They are developing a plan to oppose the destruction caused by the nuclear industry including the mining and dumping of radioactive materials on indigenous land. Their position: No mining; no testing; no production; no dumping; no nukes!

This is part of the Abolition 2000 Network; Greenpeace, Peace Action, American Friends, Citizen Alert, Western States Legal Foundation and the Japanese group *Gensuikyo*. If we have any sense of family values, if we have any understanding of what government should be, we will heartily oppose the huckstering of weapons of mass destruction to every foreign militia with the money to buy them.

We will heartily oppose the continuance of nuclearism which has the easy potential to quickly end life on this beautiful planet. The so-called "family values" hyped by incumbent politicians are simply a way to divert our attention from their rampant waste of precious resources.

In actuality, such values must include using the money we have given to them for the right to excellence in education and health care. Their death making is not compatible with family values and they know it. Our payment of taxes must be conditional and based on the humane performance of our government. The legal militias of nuclear death are far more dangerous than the illegal militias of Montana.

Police Science

April 9, 1996

Here we are in Police Science class. Here is the first question to the instructor.

STUDENT: When do police get to punish a suspect?

INSTRUCTOR: That's easy. You're never allowed to punish anyone. The laws of the United States are quite clear. You are authorized to apprehend suspects. Yes, you can arrest someone who has probably broken a law—probable cause. If you're punishing anyone, however, for any reason you are a lawbreaker.

STUDENT: What, are you telling me, I can't defend myself?

INSTRUCTOR: Police science demands the ability to understand distinctions. Any person is allowed self-defense and that includes police officers. I said you are never allowed to punish. Can you understand the distinction? Seriously, if you can't understand the distinction you should not become a police officer. Why are you looking so surprised? Police may never punish. They're not authorized to punish. This is a class in Police Science, this isn't a television show.

STUDENT: But illegal aliens don't enjoy the rights of United States citizens.

INSTRUCTOR: Yes, they do. There are no categories regarding who you can punish and who you can't punish. You can't punish anyone. It is understood that necessary force may be required in arresting a non-compliant suspect. That isn't punishment.

STUDENT: But what if I like to punish people?

INSTRUCTOR: If you like to punish people, you are a sadist and you should not become a police officer.

STUDENT: But the people who were apprehended in Temecula were undocumented.

INSTRUCTOR: The Temecula incident is a human rights issue. The abuse of frightened, hungry refugees only makes the crime against them more serious. The immigration status of the victims is merely tangential.

STUDENT: But, I understand that officers who've been involved in a high speed chase develop an adrenaline rush which contributes to a tradition of beating up the suspect.

INSTRUCTOR: What an insult to law enforcement officers. Are you trying to say that they have no self-control? And regarding traditions, we have also had a tradition of slavery and a tradition of lynching. Each and every unethical tradition must be abolished. Let me just say in passing, I get an adrenaline rush every time I hear the babble of Gingrich. That doesn't give me the right to beat him up.

STUDENT: But what about my loyalty to my fellow officers? Isn't it anti-police to want such officers punished?

INSTRUCTOR: No, my friend. You're not in a gang. Anyone who breaks the public trust deserves to be exposed. A child who's been abused by a parent shouldn't be loyal to that abuse.

It is not anti-doctor to turn in a quack.

It is not anti-lawyer to turn in a fraud.

It is not anti-family to turn in your brother if he's the Unabomber.

It is not anti-police to turn in someone who's broken the sacred public trust given by the people of California. We don't hire you to be a uniformed thug. We don't hire you to be a racist. We hire you to protect and to serve the public.

If there's anyone of you who still thinks it is anti-police not to tolerate assault and battery by law enforcement, you deserve an "F" in this class. Those who violate the trust are responsible for the uprisings of the past and the future. Don't expect society to subsidize brutality and racism. If that's your lifestyle, you should support yourself by some other means and pay your own way to join the *KKK*.

Cuba and Fasting

April 16, 1996

A long fast of over sixty days is really an annoyance. It is an annoyance because it makes us all ask what we are doing for a more humane society.

It is an annoyance because it is a challenge to all of us. The fasters hope it is also an annoyance to the Treasury Department and the president.

You might say it was bad timing on the part of the Reverend Lucius Walker? But the sixty-five year old pastor of the Salvation Baptist Church in Brooklyn follows St. Paul who said we must preach the word in season and out of season. So if it is out of season to demand that medical computers be allowed in to Cuba, so be it. Let the computers in.

On January 31, 1996 and again on February 17, 1996, an army of United States Treasury agents seized 400 low tech used computers destined for the churches of the Cuban Ecumenical Council. Cuban pastors were to oversee the distribution of the computers to a Cuban online medical information system sponsored by the United Nations and the Pan American Health Organization. Timely medical information saves lives.

Our government has now spent over $1 million to stop the shipment of this medical aid to Cuba. Join the thousands of citizens who are calling President Clinton, Treasury Secretary Robert Rubin and Secretary of State Warren Christopher to demand that this humanitarian shipment be permitted.

You might say a fast is self-destructive and not the best thing to do. Smoking is self-destructive and so is overeating but neither one is effective in calling attention to a crime. If this is not the perfect thing to do, why do you not suggest a perfect alternative? Of course it is not the perfect thing to do. Perfectionism is simply an excuse for nonaction. Waiting to do what is perfect is a formula for doing nothing. This perfectionist trap is frequently used by organized religion. But not so for Pastor Lucius Walker, Lisa Valenti, Brian Rohatyn and the Fast for

Life. Mary McGrory calls it "High noon between the Treasury Department and the Pastors for Peace."

Fasting is an ancient, mysterious and powerful ritual. Ghandi fasted. Jesus fasted. The annoyance we feel regarding these fasters is a goad—a spur to all of us.

Let us look at the United States policy toward Cuba over the past 143 years. First there was the *Ostend Manifesto*. In 1853 President Franklin Pierce instructed the United States Ambassador in Spain to buy Cuba; offering a top price of $130 million. The bottom line was, "We'll either buy Cuba or take it by force." The document created so much international ridicule that Washington quietly dropped it.

Then there was the Platt Amendment of 1902 to 1934. This clause was placed in the Cuban Constitution by the United States giving our country the right to intervene for any reason and so we did. The world looked on the Platt Amendment with disbelief.

Now we have the most blatant document of all time . . . The Helms-Burton legislation as signed by President Clinton. This document is an out of control flailing at our closest friends, "If you try to sell us Swiss chocolate made with Cuban sugar, we will punish you . . . We will get even with you." Our international tantrum has led Canada and England to ask for legal relief as we bash them to strike out at Cuba.

The logic of Reverend Lucius Walker is far more focused than the logic of Ostend, the Platt Amendment or the Helms-Burton legislation. Let the computers go on to Cuba and let us end 143 years of irrationality towards a small and beautiful country.

Necrophilia

II

April 30, 1996

Once again the state will practice premeditated murder. The children of this state and the rest of the country will receive the message very well. If you have a problem . . . Kill it. Do not try to solve the problem, do not make any concessions, just kill. Kill with malice and aforethought. Kill in a cold-blooded way. So much for the education of our children. This education is called "Capital Punishment." But, you might say, "This is the biblical injunction of an eye for and eye and a tooth for a tooth." Very well, let us do it. How about plucking out eyes and knocking out teeth? What is the matter, no courage? We should also stone people to death for practicing adultery . . . What would that do to our political incumbents? A frightened state tells a frightened people, we will protect you by killing for you.

In the practice of capital punishment we should not ask the question of how many times it has been wrongly used. On the contrary, we must ask if it has ever been rightly used. I certainly doubt that it has. Just think how useful this custom is for a corrupt state? It makes everyone feel powerless, and that is just what corruption wants. A powerless people who will do what they are told by public servants who really want to be public masters.

But you might say, "The vast majority of the people support the death penalty." Why do so many people support the death penalty? Because we live in a death culture. We not only think we can solve the crime problem by death, we think we can solve any political or economic difference by death. 3 million people in Indochina received the death penalty for simply living in Vietnam, Cambodia and Laos. War is just one more example of indiscriminate capital punishment. We do not like Manuel Noreiga so we blow away an entire section of Panama City in order to see if someone knows where he is!

Just think of how many counterproductive and incompetent people have been elected by supporting death. All they had to do was play

36

into the hands of a dead culture. What to do? People who are a danger to public safety must be locked up whether they are politicians or street thugs. This does not mean they have to be tortured. They can be locked up, study, work, and lead productive lives. They can even be paid the minimum wage and that wage can go to their victims or to their families as the court may see fit.

Death vengeance is an admission of defeat. Rehabilitation is our goal. If rehabilitation fails, the convicted would have to spend the rest of their lives in custody.

As society becomes humane, the message will be clear. We do not tolerate violence in our society. If you practice violence we will isolate you and we will not allow you to walk our nonviolent streets.

Do not vote for anyone who supports the death penalty. Most of those who do are simply catering to a dead culture. By eliminating supporters of the death penalty, we are supporting *biophilia*, or love of life. We can isolate dangerous people including politicians.

It is hard to speak of humanity when I think of the people who killed KPFK reporter Michael Taylor. I would hope that such people be lovingly placed in confinement and, if not rehabilitated, remain there without parole for the rest of their lives.

Socializing Costs

May 7, 1996

The cost of gasoline is socialized. We are one big team working together and all of us are members. Each and every one of us will pay higher prices for gasoline. But wait—with these socialized costs we all pay together as one big family. One little thing seems to be lacking; how did we ever miss this small detail? While the costs are socialized, the profit is privatized. That is right, we all give together but only a few receive the goodies. It may be better to give than to receive, but it seems to me that should be a matter of choice.

Let us get serious now and consider the fact that the corporation takes the risk. Does it now? I do not think so. I think the employees take the risk. Investors are generally playing with disposable dollars but workers are investing their disposable lives.

We are obliged to redesign the blueprint of the corporation.

1. The essential capital of the corporation must be the people working in and for the corporation.

2. One person, one vote must be the law of the corporation.

For the first time the corporation will be democratic. Votes will no longer be by the number of shares held by nonworkers but by the individuals who have dedicated their lives to the entity. These are the risk takers. Employees risk and sometimes lose their lives while working. They are at risk from chemicals, underground labor in mines and poor quality of air in sick buildings. The children who work our fields are at risk. Pesticides are nerve gases, which places all the farm workers at risk.

Then there is always the risk of losing one's job.

The corporation must spotlight a new subject of risk, the worker's risk. Investors are rarely at risk, they eat well if the corporation lives or dies. So the corporation of the future will no longer be able to hire someone as an irrelevant thing . . . As a commodity. The corporation is obliged to demonstrate its relevance to the common good. What is manufactured and why? What service is being performed? In short, the corporation must demonstrate distributive justice. Granting CEOs 150 times the salary of the average worker is a criminal matter. The current corporate model is a worn out relic of the nineteenth century.

What an amazing recommendation bubbling from congressional witchcraft. Cut the gasoline tax in order to lower the price per gallon. But lowering the taxes in this era of deregulation only gives the oil companies an excuse to raise prices even higher. Unless the corporations are rigidly controlled they will simply continue to take the money and run.

Today's thoughts are not meant to be an exercise in fantasy. United Airlines is a major corporation currently engaged in employee stock ownership. This marriage between workers and management is the only hope of viable future corporations. In the future, an ESOP, which stands for Employee Stock Ownership Plan can be exclusively worker owned.

We have here a direction, a beginning of the end of capital's historic oppression of labor.

I now pronounce you man and wife, no longer owner and serf, no longer exploiter and exploited, no longer a money-grabbing monster. Welcome to the dawning age of cooperativism, the common good and distributive justice.

Cuba and Fasting
II

May 14, 1996

President Bill Clinton would like to be re-elected and his chances appear to be quite good. The presumption of victory can be dangerous; however, and here is one area where his political antennae seem to be missing signals. He is allowing a small organization in Miami to make United States policy on Cuba. That group is called the "Cuban-American National Foundation." The group does not represent the people of Miami or the people of Cuba. It represents only the self-interest of its wealthy members.

We had hoped he would understand the religious, spiritual and humanitarian message of Pastors for Peace in their effort to deliver computers to the Cuban Ecumenical Council for distribution to Cuban hospitals.

On February 21, 1996, after being violently stopped by United States authorities, Pastors for Peace began their fast in San Ysidro, California. On April 3, 1996, the fast moved to Washington, D.C.. Today is the 84th day of the fast. But in view of President Clinton's inability to get their spiritual message, let us just look at the political implications. That is a language he surely understands. I believe the president is going to lose a great many votes by catering to Miami Republicans. They are not going to vote for him under any circumstances, but they are very successfully manipulating him.

The president can say, "The Reverend Lucius Walker and his companions don't have to die. They can give up their fast now." But their fast is a direct result of the absence of humanity our Cuba policy. The United States is the most isolated of the world's nations on this question. The entire world opposes our position. We have offended our closest allies to the point where they are accusing us of violating the GATT agreements. The president's recent support for the Helms-Burton legislation was the last straw. Our friends who do business with Cuba are being severely punished. On this matter, the United States appears to the world as a wounded monster slashing at everything in sight.

There are people in this state and in this country who are on the fringe of leaving the Democratic Party and the Clinton campaign. Not a single vote will be won by letting the Reverend Lucius Walker and his companions die. What can the president lose?

I have some letters with me and a three page, single spaced list of the religious leaders throughout the United States which include:

- The National and World Council of Churches, who are leaders of the national Protestant denominations representing 51 million believers.

- Leaders in the Cuban-American community who are in full support of Pastors for Peace and who regularly join their delegations to Cuba.

- The African-American community in support of an African-Latin Nation called "Cuba."

I also have a list of Democratic members of the House of Representatives who are willing to personally deliver the computers to Cuba.

So as a result of ignoring these fasters, the President could lose California and even lose the election. I wish we could simply discuss this matter on moral terms, but that seems out of the question. Therefore let us continue our demands for the release of these used computers which would be considered outdated by our standards but which will serve the Cubans as well as their 1958 Chevys. One of the fasters, Brian Rohatyn, a Canadian, has gone to San Ysidro, to witness the transfer of the Canadian computers to the Mexican side of the border. He will end his fast once that matter has been verified. But the fasters who are United States citizens are still being ignored.

Mr. President, let the computers go to Cuba.

$1 Trillion Missing

May 21, 1996

Exactly ten out of ten of the largest weapons contractors have admitted to or been convicted of fraud between 1980 and 1992.

Under the Clinton administration, United States weapons sales have increased dramatically. A stunning 90 percent of the countries receiving United States weapons are documented human rights abusers. These weapons will supply the new and ever more irrational ethnic wars. What does it take to start such a war? Michael E. Brown of Harvard's Center for Science and International Affairs has completed his book, *The International Dimensions of Internal Conflict*. Of thirty-four major internal conflicts in recent years, twenty-three have been deliberately triggered and engineered by political leaders inside the countries involved. In short, all that is needed is a huge arms supply and some corrupt and manipulative political leadership. This formula applies in Bosnia, Rwanda or the United States by supplying the arms for such easy to start wars. We bear much of the blame for the devastation of these wars.

This year tax payers will spend billions guaranteeing corporate profits by subsidizing arms exports and then spend billions more in defense to protect us from the terrorists who have openly purchased our products.

According to an audit by the General Accounting Office, the Pentagon cannot account for $1 trillion in assets. This is one-third of the national debt.

The ugliness of which we speak is not simply in the sale of arms. The ugliness is in the sale of torture through the School of the Americas which is based at Fort Benning, Georgia. The use of torture is taught and promoted as an interrogation technique. It is not enough that torture is taught, but the United States citizen military teachers actually join their students in countries like Guatemala for on-site instruction and direction as leaders of torture and death squads.

While the arms merchants admit their guilt and go free, while the schools of torture remain open, those who demonstrate their opposition to such crimes are in federal prisons.

I had always thought that prisons were places for people who are a danger to public safety. But today we have the guardians of public safety going to prison for pointing out the disaster of our run away military madness. I am speaking of convict Father Roy Bourgeois of Maryknoll and his twelve convicted companions. We are proud of these prisoners and we look forward to the day when such former prisoners will be governing this country just as former prisoner Nelson Mandela is governing his country. Both Republicans and Democrats have proven themselves incompetent or unwilling to correct these abuses. Therefore it is necessary to build a new political movement with a view to popular power, a movement for rational people who can affirm insanity of our cult of militarism and restrain the corporate power that has channeled our tax money for their private greed.

Cancer

May 28, 1996

Discernment is the key to a critical mind. We are surrounded by hype, con and cult. How do we discern the charlatan from the legitimate and authentic?

When your child has a burst appendix removed by the rapid drugging and cutting of western medicine, you know that a life saving procedure has been performed and you give thanks for such technology. Then there are the alternatives to western medicine. They are truly exciting. When acupuncture is used effectively, when ancient herbs are identified as healing, we take note and study. But we are accosted by half-truths, fallacies, poor logic and downright nonsense.

If someone tells you that having a better attitude can help you to avoid cancer, your discernment may affirm that insight with certain reservations. If someone says that if you have a "loving heart," you will have a healthy body, you may affirm that with reservation. But if the same guru fails to recognize that 90 percent of cancer is environmentally caused, please realize that you are dealing with someone who is either poorly educated or a phony.

Let us go a step further, if anyone gives you the idea that your cancer is your own fault, you are dealing with a charlatan. You are dealing with someone completely in sync with the world of advertising. In reality, you got cancer by virtue of the water you drink, the air you breathe and the food you eat. None of these things are your fault. Even if you are a food freak, vegan or vegetarian, you can still get cancer from the environment. The only way to avoid it is to either leave the planet or humanize the political system. What we are dealing with here is the old, "You have no one to blame but yourself" axiom which has been used so well to blame victims for centuries.

Some guru may tell you that you get sick because of an unresolved issue in a past life. I do not get anything but hype from such comments. Why do you not tell that five year old who has cancer, because of corporate pesticide spraying, that the cancer is caused by the child's attitude? I think Dow Chemical would pay you to write the book.

Let us get some discernment into our lives. I will die. You will die. We should not allow commercially driven soothsayers to tell us anything to the contrary. The body ages and lives in time. It is not ageless or timeless. It is temporary and it wears out as any material thing.

Does life go on after this body wears out? I think it does. *Vita mutatur non tollitur*, says the Latin Mass; "At death, life is changed and not taken away." Socrates said, "You can kill me but you cannot hurt me." I understand these sayings. But let us have the discernment to recognize commercial oracles, diviners, past life hucksters, and necromancers, who simply divert us from the work to be done. Those who ignore the commercial environmental causes of disease and would direct us to spend the rest of our lives staring at our navel.

Population

June 4, 1996

One of the great excuses for war is the myth that there are too many people on the planet and we must do something to stop this population bomb. A book by that title was written by Paul Ehrlich and published in 1968. The book is rightly called "a trash thriller" by Chase Madar writing in a recent issue of *Nation Magazine*. Madar identifies a new book titled *How Many People Can the Earth Support?* by Joel Cohen as a continuation of the Malthusian Myth.

Population hysteria got to the point that some were saying it was a greater threat than nuclear war, and that is just what military industrialists wanted. War is a wonderful solution because it helped us to defuse the population bomb. All of this was part of the rebirth of the ideas of Augustinian Monk Thomas Robert Malthus, who invented the idea of overpopulation in 1798. His views were thoroughly discredited but were renewed by math teachers and the military industrial academics of the 1960s. There is a connection between the diversionary tactics of new age fanaticism and population hysteria. Both turn us away from the reality of political and economic exploitation. Both turn us away from the over consumption of the affluent nations.

Why would those concerned about human population fail to deal with the run away cattle population? Perhaps the reality of mad cow disease will help us to understand that we do not need the cattle at all. These bovine perpetually eating machines destroy some of our best farmlands, drink excessively and dirty up the planet far more than human beings. Is it not curious that the Rockefeller Foundation is more concerned about excess people than excess cattle? What does that tell you about their family values?

Regardless of their religion, or lack of religion, people who are in misery will have as many children as they can as a sort of a security apparatus. Perhaps one or two of the children will be living when they are old and can take care of them.

When the state develops a certain humanity and concern for social justice and human rights, people have less children. When education becomes the objective of the state and people become educated in all areas such as literacy and family planning. With an infrastructure of humanity, the population will stabilize.

We read of population ravaging Indonesia, but we do not speak of population ravaging the Netherlands, which has a human density three times as high as Indonesia. The major famines are a result of the military machinations. Mass starvation in Ethiopia during the mid-1980s was caused by the two existing superpowers pumping the country full of guns and goading rival factions into a civil war. During the collapse of civil society in Ethiopia, the small amount of available land was used for growing export crops. Exporting food is the last thing that any poor country should do. Military industrialism looks upon any uncontrolled people as the enemy. But the logic of humanity looks upon people as the inheritors of the planet. The logic of military-industrialism will make this planet look like the moon with no population whatsoever. The logic of humanity will stabilize space ship earth into a garden. There is no scarcity of food. Per capita, food production has increased steadily for fifteen years. There exists, however, a poor distribution of people, a poor distribution of food and a poor distribution of money. Our task is not to demonize the poor of the human race as so-called "surplus population," but to demand distributive justice.

A New Cathedral

June 11, 1996

There has been a great deal of discussion about the building of a new Cathedral in Los Angeles. Some say it should be built in the same spot, at 2nd and Main. Some would have it be constructed in the San Fernando Valley. There is discussion about who will be the architects. There is even the legal matter regarding the destruction of a historic landmark.

But the theological issue includes none of the above. The theological issue is why build a Cathedral at all? Serious Catholic intellectuals are discussing the end of the parish system.

The old Cathedral is situated in the heart of homeless country. Each night hundreds of people spread out their mats in the area and sleep in the street near the Cathedral of St. Vibiana.

Is there any message in this? Jesus said to read the signs of the times. Well those signs tell us that 80,000 people have no place to sleep at night in Los Angeles. This includes many children.

Just what kind of issue was homelessness to Jesus? It was so important that he made it the stuff of his judgment mandate. In a powerful word picture Jesus describes what he wants us to think of as we consider our moral choices.

Here is the text:

The ruler will say to those on the right, "Come, you blessed of my Abba God! Inherit the kingdom prepared for you from the creation of the world! For I was hungry and you fed me; I was thirsty and you gave me drink. I was a stranger and you welcomed me; naked and you clothed me. I was ill and you comforted me; in prison and you came to visit me." Then these just will ask, "When did we see you hungry and feed you, or see you thirsty and give you drink? When did we see you as a stranger and invite you in, or clothe you in your nakedness? When did we see you ill or in prison and come to visit you?" The ruler will answer them, "The truth is, every time you did this for the least of my sisters and brothers, you did it for me." (Matt. 25:34-40, *The Inclusive New Testament*, Priests for Equality, Brentwood, Maryland, 1996.)

Now in this current era of mean-spirited greed and the creation of the prison State of California, would it not be theologically correct to build a welcoming shelter for these homeless people? This could include a chapel for all to use together with living quarters. There are more than adequate funds to do this (the $45 million should cover everything).

I would suggest that such a chapel be available to Catholics, Jews, Muslims, Buddhists and any other religion or spiritual path. Political and ecclesiastical sectarianism is dead. Now is the time for a macro-ecumenical movement. Unfortunately religious institutions are often behind the cutting edge of society.

Jesus did not recommend the construction of buildings from his message. His people were citizens of the catacombs; the cemeteries of Rome. It was only after the beginning of imperial religion, the era of Constantine the Great (Fourth Century), that cathedrals were designed.

Cathedrals represented imperial religion, religion of the inquisition and religion of the conquest. This is not a meaningful time for Cathedrals. This must be an age of service to the people. The intrinsic value of one homeless person is of more spiritual importance than all of the world's Cathedrals put together. Why can we not put our $45 million into such solid theology and build a church of flesh and blood?

To Work and to Home

June 18, 1996

Kitchen, children and church. Does that not sound warm and homey? What could be better for society? Just one slight problem, this was one of the favorite slogans of the Nazis. Fatherland, liberty and family. Sounds patriotic and moral, right? This was the slogan of the dictatorship in Chile from 1973 until the recent elections. God and country. Sounds excellent. But the confusion between God and country led many of our finest young people off to die as the enemy in places where they were not wanted.

The billboards in the dictatorship of Argentina during the dirty war of the fascist generals read "To Work and to Home."

Do you get it? A free translation of the billboard is, "Do your job, go home and shut up." For centuries dictatorial regimes have used a facade of family values as a control mechanism. They have used religion and religiosity as a cloak for malice, whether they were killing Indians or burning African-American churches. What are authentic family values in a democratic society? We must begin by viewing society as a family. If we want family values; then we insist on an international family wage.

Certainly a functional family would never blame its problems on the weakest or sickest members. But wolves in sheep's clothing want you to do just that. Hypocrisy and corruption promote disfunctional family values isolating and separating the community into a zoo of conflictive identities. If I were a classic fascist I would use every bit of my strength to urge straights to fight gays, whites to fight African-Americans and Latinos, women to fight men and the young to fight the old. With such identity wars, I could easily control the entire society.

The authentic family societal questions; however are, "Do you love one another? Do you care for one another?" A civil and familial society promotes excellent schools instead of a prison state. A civil and familial society promotes health care for all of its members instead of "we don't cover that" insurance companies.

What kind of a family builds cages for its members? An insane family? That is correct. Now we are beginning to catch on. Do you know that each dollar that is used for prisons is taken directly from education? That is not an estimate. That is not a guess that is the budget of the prison state of California. The information comes directly from the Controller of the state of California.

The most common third strike in the prison state of California is possession of marijuana. The practice is clinically insane . . . Unsound. Do you understand? That means twenty-five years to life for having grass in your possession. It would be more logical to imprison people for having Draino in their possession.

It seems that illiteracy is a requirement to maintain a prison state. Educated people might revolt at what is being done. In terms of narcotic addiction the war on drugs is an absolute and international failure. In terms of creating a pre-fascist prison state with the elimination of the Fourth Amendment, it is a great success.

We can have a familial democracy and harmony in society or distorted Disneyland non-virtues reflected in the slogans of historic fascism. It is our choice. But we must do our homework.

A Slight Change
in the Military Budget

June 25, 1996

We hear the word "cyber" frequently these days. It comes from the Greek *kybernetes*, the pilot of a ship—the one at the controls, the tiller, the Governor. If you have ever been at the tiller of a sailing ship you know how making slight changes is the art of sailing. If you have not piloted a sailing ship you know that the slightest movements of your steering wheel are the essence of good driving. Slight changes are trifles. Michelangelo said, "Perfection is made of trifles and perfection is no trifle."

There is a group of business leaders from an organization called "Business Leaders for New Priorities." They wanted to talk about a trifle so they purchased a full page in last Sunday's *New York Times* to say the following: "It's time America's last sacred cow shared the burden of budget cuts."

They followed that headline with an open letter to Bill Clinton and Bob Dole. Here is some of that letter:

> As the two American leaders most responsible for setting our national agenda, we strongly urge you to put the Pentagon back on the table when considering cuts in next year's budget.
>
> Deep cuts are proposed for education, nutrition, and medical programs for poor children. But the Pentagon, which represents over half of discretionary funding, may get $14 billion more than was asked for by the military. . . . We spend more today in inflation adjusted dollars than President Nixon spent in the 1970s at the Cold War's height. . . .
>
> We are deeply troubled that America has the highest child poverty rate in the industrialized world, and the lowest, per capita, spending on poor children.
>
> Building a truly strong America requires insuring that children get a fair start, with adequate medical care, nutrition and education. . . . Surely,

giving poor children the hope of lifting themselves out of poverty would solve many other national problems.

The Government Accounting Office reports that the Pentagon departments cannot be audited for lack of even "rudimentary bookkeeping." Conservative Senator Charles Grassley warns of "financial chaos," and the National Reconnaissance Office has discovered $4 billion in misplaced funds.

We ask you both to lead the fight to reduce this wasteful Pentagon spending that threatens America and to support programs providing every American child with a fair start.

Sincerely,
(*Signatures of a host of corporate CEOs follow*)

The keynote message of this full-page ad is a quote from General and later President Eisenhower from April 16, 1953.

"Every gun that is made, every warship launched, every rocket fired signifies, in the final sense, a theft from those who hunger and are not fed, those who are cold and are not clothed.

"This world in arms is not spending money alone. It is spending the sweat of its laborers, the genius of its scientists, and the hopes of its children."

A slight change in the military budget will mean a drastic change of direction in the *ship of state*. No more nonsense about a lack of funds for schools, no more nonsense about a lack of funds for social security and Medicare and no more silence about this massive military production of useless trash. Drop $40 billion as a trifle step number one, and watch the people insist that another $40 billion be dropped as trifle number two.

Perfection is made of trifles and perfection is no trifle.

Report Clears CIA
of Abuses in Guatemala!

July 2, 1996

Headline from the *Los Angeles Times* for June 29, 1996:
"Report Clears CIA of Abuses in Guatemala!"

This is like saying the holocaust of the Third Reich never happened. No report can clear the CIA of its abuses. The abuses are history, The abuses are the essence of the CIA. The abuses are ongoing and continue to this day.

The CIA is not an island, it is the instrument of United States foreign policy. That policy is historically marked by having no human rights component. The United States has even refused to sign the Universal Declaration of Human Rights of the United Nations.

Therefore the CIA is either an illegal rogue government or it is doing what it is told to do. Because of its fifty years of performance, it becomes clear by induction that the CIA is doing what it is told to do.

Never have all of these issues come together more clearly than in the case of Sister Dianna Ortiz an Ursuline nun and United States citizen. A group of humanoids tortured, raped and terrorized this nun in every imaginable fashion. Then a gringo operative threatened the Sister telling her that everything was on tape and that she had better shut up or the tape would be released showing her involved in forced sex and forced murder.

Let us look at some history:

- The overthrow of Guatemala's democratic government in 1954. Here was a government modeled on the New Deal of Franklin Delano Roosevelt. It had existed for ten years with the approval of the Guatemalan people. It was destroyed by the CIA with the approval of President Eisenhower.

- The use of Guatemala as a base for the invasion of Cuba in 1960-1961. That action was the occasion of the current insurgency. A group of progressive military officers objected to this use of their land by a foreign power; thus began the rebel movement known as the 13th of November which has continued under various titles for the past thirty-six years.

- From 1962-1996 the CIA has participated in the relentless genocide of the Guatemalan indigenous people. The agency has shown no more concern for the rights of these indigenous Guatemalans than General Custer showed in his savage military ventures.

These have been years of unadulterated terror . . . Rebels, students, labor leaders and professionals are jailed, tortured and killed. The embassy and its CIA staff are no strangers to this terror.

On this matter, I speak as a witness. The CIA was all over Guatemala during my tenure in that country. They were approaching religious personnel with a simple question: Do you want some CIA money?

I asked a former officer of the agency if he could identify one constructive action by the CIA. He answered in the negative. The agency needs to be abolished. For the first time in history, human rights must become a functional component of our foreign policy.

We will no longer have to expect comments like those of Anthony S. Harrington, chair of the four-member panel reviewing recent events in Guatemala who said, "The human rights issue simply was not factored into the system." The time has come for the United States to sign the Universal Declaration of Human Rights, adopted and proclaimed by the General Assembly of the United Nations, December 10, 1948.

Ralph Nader

August 20, 1996

In the age of glib sound bites we have heard one of the most substantive acceptance speeches in American history. It is doubtful that many journalists will recognize this any more than Lincoln's Gettysburg address was recognized at the time he gave it. We hear the most banal of conventional wisdom day after day and become addicted to form over content. But Ralph Nader's acceptance speech was content, content and content.

Public citizens will never consider voting as the measure of their citizenship. Voting is a small act done once every few years. Citizenship is our daily involvement in the community, local, national and international.

Nader was speaking on behalf of issues that the vast majority of United States citizens want. Unfortunately, some people will not understand this. TV has numbed their minds to the point where they cannot distinguish between orange juice and Coca Cola. There is a lack of discernment. Were this not so, citizens would quickly understand the huge surplus of tax money available for such programs as universal health care, superb schools and care for over 20 percent of the children in the United States who are living in poverty. That surplus is daily flushed down the toilet of government gifts to corporate greed and unnecessary militarism.

The greatest single myth in our current culture is that of powerlessness. But we are not powerless. We must understand with Daniel Webster that the great work of human beings on earth is to deliver justice. The good stuff in our entire history is a record of citizen action. Consider: The Women's suffrage movement, the abolitionist movement, the organization of small farmers, the labor movement, the civil rights movement, and now the movement for the abolition of the war system.

Citizen action is being hindered by a person without a body to kick and without a soul to cast into hell. That person is called a "corporation." Did you know that GE made $6 billion in profits / year and paid no taxes?

As result of this obscenity, rich people on welfare are eating us out of house and home. The upward shift of income and wealth is bankrupting our nation, and none of the corporations are more confiscatory of United States wealth than the military and industrial monsters.

Did you hear the reference to TV as an electronic child molester? Do you see the full page ads urging children to see the latest movie about mass murderer, torture and revenge? Do you understand that Channel One is corporate interference with education in our schools?

We must control that which is ours, namely: The airwaves; public lands; parks; pension plans; civic institutions; libraries; national parks. There must be no user fees, we paid for these things with our tax money. The philosophical component of Ralph's talk was equally rich. People who strive for justice are the happiest people on earth. To strive for justice is to be truly alive. Civic life is the best social life. Let us look for content rather than form. Let us become alive citizens inside and outside of the workplace as we commit our time to being public citizens—Unleashing our talents, our knowledge and our good will. Thanks, Ralph!

The CIA
and the Cocaine Connection

September 3, 1996

Under the watchful eye of the Central Intelligence Agency, a San Francisco Bay area drug ring headed up by Nicaraguan Contra Leader Oscar Danilo Blandon, wholesaled tons of cocaine to the Crips and the Bloods gangs of Los Angeles. The gangs then retailed the drugs and made Los Angeles the crack capital of the world. The gangs were able to purchase sophisticated weapons to extend their drug sales throughout the United States. Millions in profits were funneled directly to the mercenary Contra Army which was directed by the CIA.

Try to follow:

1. The CIA, in conspiracy with the DEA, acts as the Board of Directors. The agencies want money for their illegal and clandestine wars.

2. Military planes from the United States fly arms to El Salvador. The CIA directs Colombian cocaine as cargo for these aircraft on their return flights to the United States.

3. The CIA owned Colombian cocaine is entrusted to Nicaraguan operative Juan Norwin Meneses Cantarero and Oscar Danilo Blandon who work under Contra Leader Adolfo Calero. Think of these men as Managers under the board of directors.

4. Ricky Donnell Ross, of South Central Los Angeles, is located as a district manager and receives tons of this cocaine at bargain basement prices. The cocaine is boiled into crack. The crack floods Los Angeles and soon floods the rest of the United States. Assault weapons are purchased for the domestic sales people.

5. The board of directors, that is the CIA, uses the profits from the cocaine to purchase more weapons for the Contras and to pay for private charters to bring guns to the Contras and to return with cargoes of cocaine.

6. President Reagan declares himself a Contra and then denies any connection with these Iran / Contra crimes.

7. 40,000 Nicaraguans are massacred.

8. Thousands more die in our cities as a result of the domestic drug wars.

Now, is this a single case example? The crimes uncovered by Gary Webb of the *San Jose Mercury News* are not the work of a few bad apples. This is criminal policy! Such criminality requires restitution. We must rebuild the cities that have been destroyed with the funds that will be available by abolishing these agencies.

What about some documentation?

The Report of Senator John Kerry, April 13, 1989—The Senate Subcommittee on Terrorism, Narcotics and International Operations which is a subcommittee of the Committee on Foreign Relations (Call Senator John Kerry's Office for the report). The media was very quiet about it.

The story reported by the *San Jose Mercury News* is similar to the CIA involvement in Southeast Asia as it contributed to the heroin epidemic of the late '60s.

Far from considering the drug network their enemy, United States intelligence organizations have made it an essential ally in the covert expansion of United States influence abroad.

Nothing can be more aggravated than for the shepherds to mislead and butcher the flock they were set to defend and feed! And the guardians of the public interests, to turn traitors and assassins to them that raised them to their high places. (Samuel Webster, 1777)

The Iraqi Drive-by

September 10, 1996

One of the great drive by shootings of all time. Billie Clinton must prove he can draw blood. It is apparently a requirement for heading up his gang. But he does not want to blow away his good friends who are on the payroll in Northern Iraq so he drives by southern Iraq and lets go with some big ones. This is a payback—he is somewhat confused by the different groups. There is the PKK (Turkey's rebel Kurdistan Workers Party), which he has allowed Turkey to attack day and night with impunity.

There is the PUK (Patriotic Union of Kurdistan), which Iran is funding to work its way back into Iraq. There is the KDP (Kurdish Democratic Party), which he thought was on his side—he paid Barzani just as his predecessors had paid Saddam—is there no appreciation?

Then there was the $20 million deal to neutralize Saddam Hussein. Apparently that was not enough. He could have gone to organized crime and had the job done for bargain basement prices.

Let us get serious . . . Mrs. Kathryn Porter (President of the Human rights Alliance and wife of Republican Congressman Porter), has been communicating with the various factions of Kurds. She came up with a proposal to have formal peace talks and set the price at $2 million.

Remember JFK.

We will never negotiate out of fear. But we will never fear to negotiate. She was not negotiating out of fear. She was negotiating out of personal courage. But the government turned her down . . . $ 2 million was too much to spend for negotiations among the Kurds.

So we are spending billions to create an international conflict without end! Think how great that will be for the arms trade. We can sell to all three Kurdish factions and perhaps create some new Kurdish factions. We can sell to Iran and then sell to Iraq. And then watch everything go bang.

Then look what happened:

King Fahd, can we use your bases to kill Iraqis again?

No, you cannot. I'm about to lose my kingdom because of my selling out to the United States.

King Hussein of Jordan, can we use your bases to kill Iraqis?

No, my people are in revolt over the price of bread and they are fed up with my concessions to the United States.

Well, how about our old friend Turkey. Surely we can use Incirlik. Right?

No, You may not.

We dare not ask Iran. They would say "yes!"

How about Wake Island? That's a good place. Okay, we will strike out on Wake Island. Where is everyone? Do they not see what a great thing we did? We have opened the way for Iran to work its way back into Iraq. We have opened up a space for Turkey to attack Iraq. We have canonized Saddam Hussein among his people. Not as we intended with two "n's," but on the contrary with one "n" as in canonization. Here is the suffering servant of the Iraqi people, agent of the CIA, invader of family dictatorships. It would be hard to find a moment in history when we had more enemies among our allies.

What do we have here? An illegal attack on a sovereign state. The entire matter should have been submitted to the United Nations. China opposes—Russia opposes—*It's Unilateral.*

Illegal attack—The new International Criminal Court should be called into session on this one. Bill Clinton may get through Whitewater. I do not think he would make it through the International Criminal Court without conviction.

We have gone through a qualitative mutation after the Vietnam holocaust. Bush was up to 90 percent popularity during the Iraq holocaust. Blood, blood and more blood. Mr. Netanyahu likes the drive by. How touching. Absolute noncooperation with such, malicious ignorance. Sorry Bill, you've lost my vote, you do not get any points for a drive-by shooting. You have given a great message to our youth; "Just drive by and blast 'em any time you think you are not getting what you want."

Sorry, kid, you can go back to Arkansas as far as I'm concerned— I couldn't vote for you.

Us and Them

September 17, 1996

Identity is a matter for childhood and adolescence. Maturity implies that identity has been achieved and one is ready to serve the common good. Plato may have been extreme when he directed that no one should teach or rule until reaching the age of fifty. His concern was to have mature people in these fields. I have seen mature people of thirteen; however, and infants of sixty-five. Haven't you?

White is good, black is bad. Black is bad, white is good. Latino is good, white is bad. Latino is bad, white is good. Gay is good, straight is bad. Straight is good, gay is bad. Is it not pathetic to make morality a matter of identity? Like many, I have always wondered what I am going to do when I grow up. But a life long focus on identity creates nothing but a stagnant pond.

After station identification we generally get on with the program. But some people intend to spend the rest of their lives in station identification. "I'm a vegan. I'm a vegan. I'm a vegan. I'm a vegan." Thank you very much what else do you do?

Ethnic identity is necessary and important. We must know what our roots are. Hopefully we will love our ethnic identity. But to romanticize our identity or to think for a moment that our ethnic identity is an exclusive source of justice, truth or beauty is a trap.

If I were Bob Dole, and I wanted to divide progressive forces, I would do everything possible to break them up into conflicting groups of straight, gay, lesbian, black, white, Latino and oriental. The ancient tool of divide and conquer will have won again! Keeping people in political adolescence is a marvelous way to maintain the status quo.

Men who hate women need psychological counseling. The same may be said of: Women who hate men. Straights who hate gays. Gays who hate straights. Whites who hate blacks. Blacks who hate whites. Must I go on? Is it not obvious to any logical person that your identity group is not homogeneous. No one speaks for all in an identity. Any attempt to do so is wasted time. Paul says in 1 Corinthians: "When I was a child, I used to speak like a child, think like a child, reason like a child. But when I became an adult, I put childish ways aside."

Let us identify ourselves ethnically, sexually, religiously, nationalistically or in any other way we wish. After this necessary childhood and adolescence of identity, we can move into the pursuit of the common good. We can put aside staring at the navel of our identity and enter into a broader world pursuing human rights, social justice and international harmony. We can make love into a system. For centuries philosophers throughout the world have agreed on one thing: Those who see relationships are wise. Those who fail to see relationships are unwise. There is one race on this planet. It is called the "human race." What the philosophers proved by centuries of induction, Einstein proved in physics, mass and energy are eternally related. In relativity is wisdom. Isolation is stupidity. 200 dinky little nation states under the guidance of self-seeking demagogues will fight with each other forever in the ignorance of their mythological identities. Indeed, isolation by identity is not the answer to anything. It is the problem.

The Battle for History
is the Battle for Truth.

September 24, 1996

This week the PBS series called *The West* told us about some indigenous massacres in the nineteenth century. How ready young children are to hear such truth. But we continue to destroy children with the treachery of falsehoods. A minister created the story of George Washington not being able to tell a lie and we have told the minister's lie to children ever since, lying to children so they will not tell lies.

The problem is not with resilient capable children. The problem is with adults who cannot stand the ring of truth. The birth pangs of truth hurt but the truth makes us free. We are not free if we live a lie.

Buffalo Bill was great at telling stories . . . But the stories were not true. His Wild West Show pictured our citizens as simply defending themselves from hostile indigenous tribes. That is not what happened.

Buffalo Bill became the political public relations model for twentieth century misinformation:

- The School of the Americas trains its students in torture. Those who practice the torture are free. Those who denounce the torture are in Federal Prison today.

- Guatemala has been ruled by sheer terror from 1954 to 1996. Our intelligence agency initiates and maintains the terrorism. Anti-terrorist laws are then written in the United States.

- Agencies of government are in the drug business. Our prisons are bursting with citizens who have been victims of agency drug pushing.

Shall we tell the children? Of course. It will make them less apt to go off and die as the enemy in a place where they are not wanted. It will make them critical thinkers capable of effecting change. We do not need cheerleaders. We need conscious citizens.

Conventional wisdom is ignorance. Conventional wisdom thinks that what is positive is negative. It is positive to tell children the truth about sex and about history. Children who know the truth about sex and history are not apt to be molested by demagogues or by sex offenders. It is negative to tell children lies in place of history. It is positive to tell them about the holocaust in the Americas. It is positive to shout at someone who is about to step off of a cliff and to warn of impending doom. It is negative to say, "Have a nice day" as you see someone about to step off that same cliff.

The nineteenth century included the religion of Manifest Destiny which considered it right for us to exterminate. The twentieth century gave us the bravado of gunboat diplomacy. After World War II, there began the clandestine policies of overthrowing governments secretly. The longest lasting of the covert actions has been Guatemala from 1954 to the signing of the Peace Accords in the '90s.

What component is missing in the battle for history? What is missing is a regard for the component of human rights and social justice. The battle for history is quite simply the battle for truth. History is generally written by the conquerors. But truth crushed to the earth will rise again. That resurrection is now taking place.

Prosecuting a Noncrime

October 8, 1996

Danger lurks in our alleys. Right here in our city, evil aliens are looking for aluminum, glass and paper. Now these aliens are taking this paper, our personal waste and they are selling it. That's right they are selling it. They receive money from these sordid sales and are actually using the profits to purchase food for their children. This crime is happening here and now. But rejoice with me, fellow citizens, our courts are hard at work prosecuting these criminals. Judges, lawyers, prosecutors, public defenders, bailiffs, secretaries and translators are all working hard to send these people to jail. Perhaps the Governor will propose the death penalty.

"What are you in for?"

"Oh, I was picking up aluminum cans in an alley."

Just think how this kind of prosecution is going to help our society. It is turning our courts into a nonfunctional bureaucratic sinkhole of mean-spirited stupidity. It is saying to people "You can't glean as the Bible says you can and should. You can't take any portion of the trash of the affluent."

Never mind that these industrious people are taking a burden away from the city. Never mind that they are carefully helping to recycle by their micro-enterprise of small business. Never mind that they are trying to earn a few cents per hour to feed their kids.

But in an intellectual, spiritual and moral stupor we are spending millions of dollars to convict and jail the poorest of the poor. Call your City Council Members and ask them to remove such embarrassing and self-condemning drivel from the civil code. We make fools out of ourselves by jailing the most industrious people in our society for trying to sell our trash.

Ten percent of bank robberies are from people who enter the bank from the outside. Ninety percent of bank robberies are from people within the bank. Would it not be better to place the attention of our prosecutors, judges and jailers on the internal bank robberies that continue on a daily basis? Let us demand an end to the prosecution of the gleaners and let us praise these gleaners for their industry, self-reliance, ecological correctness, responsibility and concern for their children as they attempt to earn a few dollars a day.

In the book of Deuteronomy (chapter 24:19-22), we read:

> When reaping the harvest in your field, if you have overlooked a sheaf in that field, do not go back for it. Leave it for the stranger, the orphan and the widow, so that Yahweh your God may bless you in all your undertakings.
>
> When you beat your olive trees you must not go over the branches twice. Let anything left be for the stranger, the orphan and the widow.
>
> When you harvest your vineyard you must not pick it over a second time. Let anything left be for the stranger, the orphan and the widow. Remember that you were a slave in the land of Egypt. That is why I lay this charge on you.

This is called "gleaning" and the Good Book tells us to practice it.

Put a sign on your aluminum cans, bottles and papers. *This is my personal property*. It is not the property of this city. This property is here for industrious workers in private enterprise to take and to sell for their benefit and the benefit of their children. I am donating this personal property to the stranger, the orphan and the widow.

"and to our petrified leaders; stop prosecuting this non-crime . . ." Purchase a backbone at the backbone store and start prosecuting bankers who steal our money from banks.

Nobel Peace Prize

October 22, 1996

The news of the Nobel Peace Prize for José Ramos-Horta and Bishop Carlos Filipe Ximenes Belo of East Timor was especially thrilling to the Office of the Americas. This year we were asked to introduce the nearly unknown José Ramos-Horta at two small gatherings in Los Angeles. After all, who wanted to hear about East Timor?

Let us look at the situation in historical context.

1957: the CIA began its most sophisticated program. Tens of thousands of rebels were armed and equipped by the United States Army. The United States Navy put Indonesian troops ashore with communications equipment. Weapons were dropped deep into Indonesian territory. CIA pilots took to the air bombing and strafing civilian targets. But the CIA failed in this hearty effort to unseat the Sukarno government. In 1958 President Eisenhower denied any United States involvement.

In 1965 there was a second attempt to overthrow Sukarno, the leader of the nonaligned and anti-imperialist movements of the Third World. This attempt succeeded as it took the lives of 500,000 Indonesians.

Indonesians of Chinese decent were considered to be "communists," a word which for decades meant "Okay to kill." The *New York Times* called it "one of the most savage mass slaughters in history." Former Deputy CIA Station Chief in Indonesia, Joseph Lazarsky and his boss Edward Masters confirmed that CIA agents contributed in drawing up death lists.

One third of the Indonesian general staff had United States training as did almost half of the officer corps. At the time of the coup to overthrow Sukarno, 1,200 Indonesian officers, including senior military figures, had been trained in the United States. Who was the United States' choice to follow Mr. Sukarno? Mr. Suharto of course. Mr. Suharto had been at the service of the Dutch Colonialists and the Japanese invaders. Suharto's behavior in taking over Indonesia included a government run protection racket, jails overflowing with political prisoners, torture as routine, death squads roaming at will killing alleged subversives and suspected criminals by the thousands.

In the wake of losing the war in Indochina, President Ford and Henry Kissinger went to Jakarta. Suharto wanted them to support his efforts to take over East Timor. Ford gave his approval on December 6, 1975. The UN immediately condemned the act as international aggression. Amnesty International estimated that Indonesian troops had killed one-third of the population of East Timor; 200,000 people out of a population of 600,000. Unlike the United Nations and the European Community, the United States has consistently supported Indonesia's claim to East Timor. Omnipresent United States military advisers, training, weapons, helicopter gunships and all the other instruments indispensable to counterinsurgency warfare continue to flow into the hands of the Indonesian military. East Timor reports United States advisers directing and even participating in combat. Sound like El Salvador? It should. The same CIA is directing the operation. Just three days after sharing the Nobel Prize, Bishop Belo condemned Indonesia's military rule of East Timor and called for a referendum on autonomy to end the twenty-one year conflict. Bishop Belo suggested that the United Nations sponsor talks between the East Timorese, Indonesia and Portugal. Now we must demand of President Clinton that he cease and desist in his effort to sell more F-16 military jets to Indonesia.

Proposition 209

October 29, 1996

Affirmative Action is a very successful transitional program. The transition will be complete when people realize there is only one race, the human race and that women must never be submissive to men.

I have witnessed the abuse of affirmative action. I have seen poorly qualified minorities wrongly selected over better qualified white males. That is an abuse of affirmative action. If and when such an exceptional abuse takes place the matter can be taken to court. Proposition 209, however, is designed to destroy affirmative action. Our poorly graded Governor is once again attacking victims.

Governor Wilson, his attorney general, Dan Lundgren, and his trusted Regent, Ward Connerly, want to eliminate: Tutoring and mentoring for minority and women students; hiring and promotion of qualified women and minorities; outreach and recruitment programs which encourage applicants for government jobs and contracts; and programs which encourage women to study and pursue careers in math and science.

The independent, nonpartisan California Legislative Analyst gave the following report on the effects of proposition 209: The measure would eliminate a variety of public school and community college programs such as counseling and tutoring, student financial aid, and financial aid to selected school districts, where these programs are targeted based on race, sex ethnicity or national origin. Proposition 209 claims it will eliminate quotas, but there are no quotas. The United States Supreme Court has already made two decisions declaring quotas to be illegal. Proposition 209's real purpose is to eliminate affirmative action equal opportunity programs for qualified women and minorities. Proposition 209 permits discrimination against women. It changes the California Constitution to permit state and local governments to discriminate against women, excluding them from various job categories.

Ward Connerly (a member of the University of California Board of Regents) has already used his influence to get children of his rich and powerful friends into the University of California. 209 reinforces the "who you know" system that favors cronies of the powerful.

We need affirmative action until such time that our people acknowledge the reality of one human race and there are no special categories for men over women.

Office of the Americas Honorees

November 12, 1996

The Office of the Americas has chosen honorees for this, our thirteenth anniversary because each personifies our mission.

Father Roy Bourgeois personifies our conviction that the war system can be abolished. He has identified step number one by his heroic efforts to close a school of torturers and assassins known as the School of the Americas. The culture of militarism which has marked the twentieth the most violent of centuries, must be mutated into a culture of peace. We must be the instruments of that peace. Father Roy is the only honoree who will not be with us on November 16. He is currently in the Federal Prison at Atlanta, Georgia for a protest of nonviolent civil disobedience at Fort Benning, Georgia. Those responsible for the massacres, he and his companions were protesting, have not served one day in prison. Another protest will begin today.

Sister Dianna Ortiz personifies how the seemingly powerless things of the world can confound the strong. She has shaken the very foundations of a corrupt and counterproductive spy agency that is responsible for destroying millions of lives while creating an international propaganda machine in search of enemies and fueled by secrets and lies.

Reverend Lucius Walker personifies the relentless persistence for nonviolent change in Latin America. He brings the methodologies of Dr. Martin Luther King to an international level. He has called the world's attention to the punitive and vindictive blockade of Cuba imposed by our country for over three decades. He has also directed hundreds of tons of medical and food aid to Mexico, Central America and Cuba.

In spite of any electoral defeats here at home or in Nicaragua, the Office of the Americas will continue to work for peace by working for justice. The Zapatistas in Mexico have not selected state power as their objective. On the contrary, they demand honest government pursuing the common good and social justice.

On this day of our anniversary, there is a commemoration of the Jesuits murdered together with their housekeeper and her daughter in El Salvador. The murderers were graduates of the School of the Americas. The commemoration is taking place at the School of the Americas in Fort Benning, Georgia.

On this day there are ongoing and irreversible denunciations of the toxic legacy of the CIA. On this day the nations and the churches of the world have denounced the anti-democratic efforts of our country to punish its friends for their trade with Cuba.

Deceptive Advertising

November 19, 1996

The *Los Angeles Times* has done a recent series on Los Angeles Gangs. Upon analysis, such organizations can be identified as cults. Why? It is the nature of a cult to recruit, to win over, to seek out and then to degrade the new member into total submission. The successfully recruited new member will place his or her will in the hands of the leadership. The member will then prove loyalty by attacking or killing on command. Another characteristic of the gang is the fact that one is not free to leave. Some gangs retain their members by threat of death, others permit departure after a large monetary payment.

The gang is a miniature of a culture of militarism. For centuries kings have recruited peasants to fight their battles. Kings have developed a mystique of honor, and religiosity generally stating that God is on their side. Kings preside and the peasants die.

Militarism, like gangs, is not simply a culture. It is a cult. In our country some $2 billion of our tax money is spent every year in advertising for recruits. The deceptive Pentagon advertising stresses money for college.

Two books can help you more than the recruiter:

1. *You Can Afford College* (Kaplan, 1996).

2. *Fund Your Way through College* (Kirby, 1994).

The deceptive Pentagon advertising stresses job skills and training. But your local community college can train you far better than the military in computer repair, graphic design, medical technology and many other fields.

The deceptive Pentagon advertising stresses travel and personal growth. But if you want to meet people far from home you can do it without first being trained to dehumanize them. In addition to the Peace Corps there is Peace Brigades International and an entire booklet produced by Global Exchange titled *Alternatives to the Peace Corps.* Our stalwart former Defense Secretary Cheney put it well, "The reason to have a military is to be prepared to fight and win wars . . . It's not a jobs program."

There is a myth of military economic opportunity. But actually veterans earn less than non-veterans. Researchers Bryant and Wilhite found that veterans averaged only 1.78 months of training in thirty-one months of active duty. Magnum and Ball, Ohio State University researchers who received funding from the military found that only 12 percent of male veterans and 6 percent of female veterans made any use of skills learned in the military after going into civilian work.

To become eligible for the GI Bill, enlistees have to pay a non-refundable $1,200 fee. But only 35 percent of the GI's receive any benefits at all. The Army has taken in $720 million more in fees than they have paid out in GI Bill benefits. The military estimates that one-third of the homeless people in the United States are veterans.

Joining the military is hazardous to your health. It is hazardous to women. It is hazardous to people of color. It is hazardous to your education. It is hazardous to your civil rights. It is hazardous to the environment. It is also hazardous to the so-called "enemies" that are created by a busy propaganda machine.

We believe that the cult of gangs and the cult of militarism can be abolished. This is why we oppose the growing intrusion of Junior ROTC into our school system. Quite simply we believe the war system can be abolished internationally. It is the role of the world's strongest nation to take the first step!

Bill,
the Doer of History

November 26, 1996

Bill, now that you have been reelected, it is time for some decisions. You can be a good-old-boy lame duck friend of Newt, or you can have a well-deserved place in history.

I would suggest the following program for you to become all that you can be:

1. You have insisted that welfare people get jobs where there are no jobs. What to do? Establish a Federal Jobs Program. Your Democratic predecessor FDR did it by way of two extremely effective and successful programs, the CCC and the WPA.

2. Insurance companies are fighting to pocket profit from the trillion dollar a year medical business. Rather than see your citizens continue to die of insurance company "we-don't-cover-that" policies, remove the sixty-five year age requirement on Medicare and you have a single payer health plan that is available to all who want it.

3. Your weapons sales are directed to any dictator, thug or murderer who puts cash on the barrel. Stop this corrupt industry in the streets of the United States and in the nations of the world. Foster gun control at home and abroad.

4. The United Nations in full operation has the potential to abolish the war system. Instead of the mindless and wasteful multi-billion-dollar project for the United States to produce tritium to enhance nuclear weapons, pay your dues to the United Nations and work internationally for the elimination of all nuclear weapons.

5. The so-called "War on Drugs" has been the greatest assault on the Fourth Amendment in United States history. Overseas this drug war is simply counterinsurgency run wild. Drug dealing armies in Mexico, Guatemala, El Salvador, Honduras, Colombia, Peru, Bolivia and elsewhere have been heavily funded with military equipment and money. They have used this money to fund death squads which are killing people who are in pursuit of social justice and human rights. Direct the currently wasted billions into programs of rehabilitation for nicotine addicts, alcohol addicts, cocaine and heroin addicts.

6. Declare a zero tolerance for violence in the United States people who are a danger to public safety must be locked up for life if necessary. Those who are not a danger to public safety can receive alternative punishments, which are cheaper and more effective.

7. Deal with the sacred cow which every citizen is called to worship. It is the military / industrial / prison and gun lobby. This cow is to receive 54 percent of the 1997 budget. Exactly what enemy do you see out there? We do not need $200 billion for a new model jet fighter and we do not need to sell the used ones to Indonesia. Your citizens live with constant insults to their intelligence as they hear a babble about no money for Social Security, no money for schools and hospitals. Pentagon waste is destroying our cities and our nation. Every weapon manufactured wreaks destruction on our cities.

And Bill, abolish that fifty year old death squad called the "CIA." The legislation to do so is on Senator Moynihan's desk.

With your second inaugural, Bill, you have the opportunity to be a doer of history, a doer of the will of God on earth . . . Or to waste away your life as just another of the many political hacks that have preceded you in office.

Fit to Print

December 10, 1996

Certain stories are not hard news. Why should fluff and pudding be found on the front pages of our great newspapers? Remember the motto of the *New York Times*, "All the News That's Fit to Print?" Obviously, some news is not fit to print. Take the case of a Four Star General who served as Commander in Chief of the Strategic Air Command and who was responsible for all the nuclear weapons of the Air Force and the Navy. Suppose he has a conversion? Suppose he wants to abolish nuclear weapons?

What is news about that? What does it have to do with the O.J. case? O.J. is news and will be news for the next hundred years. But a Four Star General who is speaking for Admirals and Generals in seventeen militarized countries and fostering the abolition of nuclear weapons, where is the news in a story like that? Madonna had a baby. That is news. But ending nuclear weapons could probably be bad for business. What is bad for business is bad for Christmas. Some people do not think anything is sacred.

Here are some of the General's words:

> "We military professionals who have devoted our lives to the national security of our countries and our peoples are convinced that the continuing existence of nuclear weapons and the armories of nuclear power and the ever present threat of acquisition of these weapons by others constitutes a peril to global peace and security and to the safety and survival of the people we are dedicated to protect."
>
> —Gen. Lee Butler, Former Commander in Chief of the United States Strategic Air Command speaking on behalf of generals and admirals of seventeen countries at the National Press Club in Washington, D.C..

I have not seen a word in the *Los Angeles Times* or the *New York Times* about this monumental statement, have you? But we must save space for real news like the elephant's birthday.

We have had such bad luck with Generals by the name of Butler. Here is another one, Gen. Smedly D. Butler, who reflected on his career back in 1935:

"I spent thirty-three years and four months in active service as a member of our country's most agile military force, the Marine Corps. I served in all commissioned ranks from a second lieutenant to a major general. And during that period I spent most of my time being a high-class muscle man for big business, for Wall Street and for the bankers. In short, I was a racketeer for capitalism. Thus I helped to make Mexico and especially Tampico safe for American oil interests in 1914. I helped make Haiti and Cuba a decent place for the National City Bank to collect revenues in . . . I helped purify Nicaragua for the international banking house of Brown Brothers in 1909-1912. I brought light to the Dominican Republic for American sugar interests in 1916. I helped make Honduras 'right' for American fruit companies in 1903."

These are the words of Gen. Smedly Butler in 1935. Now, sixty-one years later, we have the words of Gen. Lee Butler. I wonder if they are related.

What we have here is a case of media censorship. Failure to spend money on nuclear weapons would mean that too much money might be available for schools. Money for schools could lead to the formation of critical thinkers. Critical thinking might create even more General Butlers. Then who would be left to protect CEOs who pocket $100 million a year and foster international misery?

Economics

December 17, 1996

Christmas is a time to consider economics. The mother of Jesus reflected on the economic conditions of the coming Messianic Era and prayerfully said:

> You have shown strength with your arm, you have scattered the proud in their conceit, you have deposed the mighty from their thrones and raised the lowly to high places. You have filled the hungry with good things, while you have sent the rich away empty.

But how can economics become a science that is not dismal? It is dismal now because economists are hired guns, like lawyers. They fight for their clients with the jargon of privatized knowledge. They sanctify unintelligible formulae to confuse and to mystify that which is really quite simple.

Here are two basic economic terms that must be altered:

Cost: In the dismal economics of the past, cost refers to monetary cost. Enlightened economics of the future cost must include ecological factors. What does this venture cost in terms of ozone layer and atmospheric sewage . . . Formerly called "smog?" What is the cost to the world's people of allowing run-away cattle production to interfere with the corn, beans and rice that are needed to end world hunger?

Demand: The key economic word of the past must be translated into the word "need." Need can be determined by the practice of economic democracy. Need can replace the outworn concept of demand. By the way, there is a great demand for $35,000 watches this Christmas. There is absolutely no need for $35,000 watches. Get it?

The new language of economics must first of all be ethical including the balance of distributive justice. It must also be systemic and mathematical. We are talking about evolving from economics to ecology. The physical limits of economics must expand beyond the bounds of companies or nations and encompass ecology in its entirety.

Economics must no longer have the time span of the daily hype of Wall Street attention deficit disorder. The time span must include the future of the planet.

Wealth must no longer be confined to material goods. It must include cultural enrichment, ecological balance, the end of basic wants and respect for diversity.

Value must include nature and collective cultural assets. The free market is simply not an effective instrument for raising up a civilization founded on and governed by ethical values. The conventional values in traditional economics must be reversed. This means that the ethical values of distributive justice will be first, social objectives will be second and economic technology will be third.

Only the taste for intellectual adventure will end the dismal cynicism of contemporary economics. The global scope of the ecological dimension must be in the forefront. That monstrosity we refer to as "Gross National Product" or GNP has nothing to do with a better quality of life. If we engage in planetary destruction by way of nuclear war, the GNP will go up . . . That is until we all perish.

The only gauge worthwhile, is the Gross Social Product. An economics based on Gross Social Product will end the reign of Ebenezer Scrooge known as "corporate capital."

The United States Must Restore Normal Relations with Cuba

December 20, 1996

The international diplomatic community is conscious of the fact that the United States intransigence on the matter of Cuba is punitive, vindictive and oppressive. During the worst moments of the Cold War, the United States and the Soviet Union never broke relations.

Diplomatic relations do not necessarily imply approval. Such relations merely open the way for dialogue, trade travel and transportation.

The history of U.S. / Cuba relations is one of endless abuse by the more powerful country. When Spain angrily refused to sell Cuba to the United States for $130 million in 1853, President Franklin Pierce issued the *Ostend Manifesto*, which stated that the United States would either buy Cuba or take it without the consent of Spain.

The United States co-opted Cuba's independence (1898-1902) by appointing Gen. Leonard Wood Military Governor of Cuba. In 1901 the Platt Amendment was placed in the Cuban Constitution, giving the United States the right to intervene for any reason and establishing a United States military base at Guantanamo. The United States militarily intervened in Cuba in 1906, 1912 and 1917.

And in recent decades:

- The United States broke relations with Cuba in 1961; B-26 bombers with CIA paid pilots attacked Cuba and a CIA trained force of 1,200 invaded the island.

- In 1962, United States and the Soviet Union were in crisis over missiles based in Cuba.

The Cuban Democracy Act of 1992 expanded the impact of United States economic measures on third country relations with Cuba. The

General Assembly of the United Nations has condemned this law on a yearly basis ever since it was passed. There is virtually no international support for and there is vehement international opposition to the Cuba Democracy Act.

This aggressive United States policy has included direct military intervention, the threat of nuclear annihilation, countless acts of sabotage and efforts to assassinate Cuban leaders (see United States Senate Select Committee to Study Governmental Operations with Respect to Intelligence Activities, Alleged Assassination Plots Involving Foreign Leaders, *Senate Report 465*, the Congress, 1st Session, 1975).

The Helms-Burton legislation, signed by President Clinton in 1996, is clearly the most outrageous and internationally illegal document in a century and a half of oppression of Cuba. The entire hemisphere opposes this legislation. Our closest allies in Europe and Canada are deeply angered by our interference in their affairs. Helms-Burton is a direct violation of the GATT and NAFTA Agreements.

It is time for the United States to repent of its abuse of Cuba and to reestablish normal diplomatic relations.

The Human Spirit

January 7, 1997

The most beautiful experience we can have is the mysterious. It is the fundamental emotion which stands at the cradle of true art and true science.

These words were written by Albert Einstein in *The World as I See It*. The presence of awe, the sacred attentiveness of wonder is at the center of authentic spirituality. The current international heresy of fundamentalism is simply a form of psychic death. Our culture gave birth to a long reign of fundamentalism initially known as "Manifest Destiny." In the twentieth century manifest destiny congealed into the fundamentalist religion of anti-communism. This ruthless ideology led to the killing of millions of innocent people because they lacked the "truth" which we allegedly possessed. Fundamentalists are people who have lost their sense of wonder, the essential hallmark of our species and the central feature of the human spirit.

Dr. Melvin Konner, a United States physician, anthropologist and writer, is attempting to break through the stifling of wonder which has been such a toxic part of our educational culture. As we look in awe at creation, we must recognize that we are the only creature that understands evolution and that can alter its very course. We will lose that possibility by pride, ignorance or laziness.

We need the full reinstatement of the sense of wonder in relation to nature and humanity. We must try to experience the human soul as soul and not just as a buzz of bioelectricity. We must recognize the human will as will and not just a surge of hormones. The human heart is not just a fibrous, sticky pump, but the metaphoric organ of understanding. We need not believe in these organs as metaphysical entities, they are as real as the flesh and blood they are made of. But we must believe in them as entities; not as analyzed fragments, but as wholes made real by our contemplation of them, by the words we use to talk of them, by the way we have transmuted them to speech. We must stand in awe of them as unassailable, even through they are dissected before our eyes.

As for the natural world, we must try to restore wonder there also. We could start with that photograph of the earth taken from space. We are the first generation to have seen it and the last generation not to take it for granted. It is up to us to try to experience a sense of wonder before it is too late. If we cannot, we may do the final damage in our lifetimes. If we can experience that sense of wonder we may change the course of history, and consequently, the course of evolution, setting the human lineage firmly on the path toward a new evolutionary plateau.

We must choose, and choose soon, either for or against the further evolution of the human spirit. It is for us, in the generation that turns the corner of the millennium, to apply whatever knowledge we have, in all humility, but with all due speed, and to try to learn more as quickly as possible. It is for us, much more than for any previous generation, to become serious about the human future, and to make choices that will be weighed not in a decade or a century, but in the balances of geological time.

Thank you, Dr. Melvin Konner.

The History of Mutiny

January 14, 1997

The history of mutiny is a history of consciousness. The study of mutiny is far more instructive than the study of imperial victories. But history is written by the victors so students suffer from the boredom of unrestrained triumphalism.

Mutiny in the civil war was massive on both sides. Yankee immigrants who did not have $300 to buy their way out of the draft were resentful. Many left their ranks to seek meaningful employment. Mutiny was massive in World War I. General Pershing ordered his officers to execute the deserters. Pershing's officers did not comply. General Eisenhower approved the desertion execution of Private Slovick in World War II.

Mutiny is punished by death in absolutist structures. It is simply the doctrine of infallibility as applied to the state. The mutinous and deserters of the Korean War may still be found in various parts of Asia.

The mutiny in Vietnam was an indelible rejection of United States policy. Orders were ignored, officers were assassinated by their own troops. A mutation had taken place in the concept of a soldier as a robot. Soldiers became conscious of how they were being used.

Why have we deprived students of the history of mutiny? It seems we are afraid they too might break from an absolutist obedience to tyranny. Mutiny is a substantive component of world history. It must not be ignored. A sharp example of mutiny took place before the Civil War. It was the Mutiny of the San Patricio Battalion in the 1846 War with Mexico. The war was a vicious conquest of Mexico, not by Spain, but by the United States. Abe Lincoln opposed the war with Mexico saying that our troops were killed on Mexican soil as "aggressors." Ulysses S. Grant described the war with Mexico as, "The most unjust ever waged by a stronger against a weaker nation." Robert E. Lee expressed similar sentiments.

President Polk was full of fundamentalist *manifest destiny* and dreamt about taking everything down to Mexico City. The war ended in 1848 with the United States generously taking only half of Mexico.

The Irish immigrants who fled the potato famine in their country came to the United States and were quickly inducted into the United States Army to vanquish Mexico. But United States Captain John Riley, formerly of County Galway, analyzed the situation and determined that this was a war of aggression against the Mexican people. He saw in the Mexicans the same love, the same hospitality and the same Church he had left in Ireland. Why should he fight these beautiful people? He brought his battalion to the Mexican side and fought against the invading gringos. Mexico honors the San Patricio Battalion every year. Ireland honors the San Patricio Battalion every year. We will honor them once we prefer critical thinking to absolutist conformity.

The history of mutiny is a reflection of the history of consciousness.

Filmmaker Mark Day has directed and produced a superb documentary (*The San Patricios*) on the San Patricios and revealed the history of a few brave men who abandoned a conquering army to follow their consciences.

Mutiny is not the tragedy. The tragedy is that we feed our young people an endless diet of triumphal garbage and allow them to be deprived of a truth that hurts and liberates.

Human Rights
and United States Policy

January 28, 1997

Human rights and social justice must become part of United States domestic and foreign policy. Currently human rights are not a component of either domestic or foreign policy. On the contrary, we have allowed civil liberties to become a cloak for the absence of human rights. Everyone is allowed to speak, but some people are not allowed to eat. Everyone is allowed to assemble, but some people are not allowed to have shelter. People are allowed their religion but many are not allowed to have medical care.

There is a difference between human rights, social justice and civil liberties.

The Universal Declaration of Human Rights of the United Nations adopted and proclaimed on December 10, 1948 states in section 25:

> Everyone has the right to a standard of living adequate for the health and well being for self and for family, including food, clothing, housing and medical care and necessary social services, and the right to security in the event of unemployment, sickness, disability, widowhood, old age or other lack of livelihood in circumstances beyond one's control.

Motherhood and childhood are entitled to special care and assistance. All children whether born in or out of wedlock, shall enjoy the same social protection. And in Article 26:

> Everyone has the right to education. Education shall be free . . . Higher education shall be equally accessible to all on the basis of merit.

But money has become an end in itself rather than a means to an end. A culture of profiteering becomes a threat to human rights and home and overseas.

Let us just look at some examples this week:

According to today's *Los Angeles Times* a salary of $13.00-$17.00 per hour is required for a mother with two children . . . But in violation of human rights we tolerate a minimum wage that will not even cover minimal rent.

Under the current dispensation, the purpose of health care is to make money. Thousands of bright young eager MBA's and ancient entrepreneurs have discovered gold. They have $1 trillion a year to play with. Let us get rich on the nondelivery of health care.

The greed merchants have now discovered that they might also make a similar windfall by taking over the welfare system. Just think of all the funds out there. What we have learned from the military industrial complex can now be applied to welfare, prisons, schools and health care. Public funds will go directly to private hands and those hands will take the money and run.

Congratulations are due to the people of the United States. With all the hype, with all the lies, they have seen through it. They know there are tens of millions of children and adults with no health care at all.

The *Los Angeles Times* reports that ordinary people increasingly view doctors, hospitals and insurance companies as profiteers. The National Coalition for Health Care has completed a poll after a survey of 23,000 patients. Over two-thirds of the people interviewed expressed no confidence in our health care nondelivery system. There is a simple solution proposed by some members of Congress. Take the existing Medicare program and remove the requirement for the recipient to be sixty-five years of age. Simply apply the system to everyone who wants it.

Human rights and social justice do not represent a problem, they represent a solution.

Torture

February 11, 1997

How do we get information? One way is to do our homework. There is another way to get information. It is called "torture." Torture requires moral and mental perverts in positions of authority. They, in turn, must recruit obedient and non-critical robots who are willing to become sadists. The sadists are then turned loose on helpless and generally innocent people who are intentionally maimed, physically and psychologically, for life.

Wimps who design torture know very well that they can never get accurate information this way. Then what is the motive? Torture is really not about information, it is about silence. It is simply a form of terrorism designed to stifle popular opposition.

Thank you *Baltimore Sun* for releasing the material on the *Kubark Manual* published in 1963 and used in Vietnam. Thanks also for releasing the *Human Resource Exploitation Training Manual* of 1983.

A review of the alumni records of the United States Army School of the Americas shows that Honduran military officers implicated in the 1983 disappearance of Father James "Guadalupe" Carney were trained at the notorious school of torture and assassination known as the School of the Americas. Father Carney was tortured and then flung out of a helicopter by a member of Honduran Army's Battalion 3-16. Witnesses say the execution of Father Carney was ordered by Gen. Gustavo Alvarez Martínez, commander of the armed forces, who created Battalion 3-16, an elite Honduran Army death squad. Alvarez Martínez, a graduate of the School of the Americas, was awarded the Legion of Merit in 1983 by President Ronald Reagan for promoting "democracy." United States Army documents declassified last September confirmed the School of the Americas used training manuals advocating the use of torture, false imprisonment, sodium pentothal and assassination.

This growing library of torture manuals has come from a corrupt, decayed, dishonest, death centered, clandestine organization paid for by hard working citizens who have no idea of the misusage of their faithful funding. "Keep the subjects naked, blindfolded in windowless dark interrogation rooms that are sound proof. There must be no toilet." Tell the subject, "we know your mother and your brother and if you do not cooperate we are going to bring them in . . . Rape them . . . Torture them and kill them." This was done.

"Conduct an examination of all body cavities." Now what psychopath put that in the text? These are people you intend to kill, just what are you looking for? The United States School of the Americas began in Panama where it taught torture techniques using homeless people for experimentation. The moral cesspool was moved to Fort Benning, Georgia in 1984. Article 5 of the *Universal Declaration of Human Rights* states: "No one shall be subjected to torture or to cruel, inhuman or degrading treatment or punishment."

Germany repudiated Naziism and developed a successful nation by denouncing its past horrors. The time has come for the United States to abolish its criminal agencies and their fiendish practices. Together with German citizens, we can say, "We're better than that!"

Corrupt members of government and business must get out of the way so *The International Declaration of Human Rights* can be applied to both our foreign and domestic policy.

Themes from a Meeting
in Panama

February 18, 1997

Since last here in the studio, I have been in Panama meeting with the legacy of Archbishop Oscar Romero of El Salvador. The archbishop was assassinated while celebrating Mass on March 24, 1980. He was killed under the direction of graduates of the School of the Americas. He clearly and definitively took the side of the poor in their conflict with the Salvadoran military and he became the voice of the voiceless.

Many people throughout the world are irreversibly committed to continuing the mission of Archbishop Romero.

Here are some of the themes of our recent meeting:

1. First, the agenda was macro-ecumenical which means inclusion of all people of good will in the struggle for peace and justice. Matters of dogma have generally only served to divide people of good will. There was no bickering about doctrinal matters at this meeting.

2. Second, the organization opposes militarism. The plethora of United States bases are an annoyance to people from Japan to Guantanamo. These bases are a drain on the treasury of the United States and a threat to world stability. While the gathering was in process, a group of Panamanians arrived with a petition. They asked us to join them on the following day for a demonstration at Fort Howard in the Canal Zone. At first I thought our leadership would decline the Panamanian request because our agenda was clearly set. On the contrary, the group unanimously accepted the invitation to take part in the demonstration. The protest was a moving experience for me because from the very same location, the main gate of Fort Howard,

we began the International March for Peace in Central America eleven years ago.

Aside from a constant military threat, these bases represent a major source of environmental contamination and a generator of AIDS. The Panamanians want to use the facilities for civilian purposes.

3. A third major theme was the globalization of the economy, which places international decision making in the hands of a tiny clique. The situation demands the globalization of solidarity on the part of the rest of the world including labor, church and civic organizations. The beginnings of that international solidarity are already evident.

The group is called SICSAL which are the initials in Spanish for *Secretariado International Cristiano de Solidaridad con el América Latina; Oscar Romero* or the "International Christian Secretariat in Solidarity with Latin America; Oscar Romero." This year's focus was directed to the needs of the people of Colombia and Cuba.

A Jubilee Year is planned for 2000 including a plan for cancellation of international debts.

It is unfortunate that many humanistic liberals are not disposed to work with progressive church people. Theistic humanists and atheistic humanists have the common ground of the one human race. Together they have a powerful weapon against the fanaticism of money and power.

Panama is the country that Mr. Bush attacked, bombed and invaded during the Christmas Season of 1989.

Here is a translation of one of the hymns sung in memory of that massacre:

No, No, No . . . It is not sufficient to pray. There are many other things necessary to win peace.

The pilot who boards his plane to bomb the children of San Miguelito is praying . . .

But, No, No, No . . . It is not sufficient to pray. There are many other things necessary to win peace.

Drug War in Mexico

February 25, 1997

As of today, Mexico could lose its status as a country that fully cooperates in the United States war on drugs. But President Clinton is still planning his trip to Mexico on April 11 and 12. If Mexico cooperates with our so-called "drug war," we will send more arms. If Mexico is removed from our drug war, we will send more arms and more advisers.

The reason for this apparent contradiction is that the arms were never really directed at a drug war, they are directed at social and political revolutionaries. Rather than dealing with the social conditions that led to the rise of the Zapatistas and seventeen other armed groups in Mexico, our president is prepared to repeat the failed savagery of our policies in Central America and Vietnam.

Clinton's largesse began in November of 1996 with $50 million in weapons including four C-26 reconnaissance planes, 73 Huey helicopters, made famous by genocide, and 500 armored personnel carriers. In addition there is $10 million in night vision devices, together with command, control and communications equipment. Of course there is the radar and spare parts for 33 helicopters given to Mexico over the past seven years and also machine guns, semiautomatic rifles, grenades, ammunition, flame throwers, gas masks, uniforms and rations. Evidence from our own General Accounting Office has demonstrated that the Mexican government is using this equipment to suppress insurgency. In his generosity with our tax money, former President Bush had already sent $212 million worth of military hardware to Mexico under the pretext of fighting a drug war.

Now the Army General who headed Mexico's national drug agency, Gen. Jesus Gutierrez Rebollo, who was chosen by President Zedillo to take over Mexico's drug program and who was canonized by General McCaffrey is now being held on charges of cocaine trafficking. There is simply no learning experience here. The empire is condemned to self-destruct because of its belief that might making right and its rejection of human rights and social justice.

One-third of Mexico's army, 60,000 troops, are now stationed in the state of Chiapas. Encampments of 500 troops are surrounding indigenous villages of 300 people. The Mexican army brings in its prostitutes, its AIDS and its drug abuse. Alcoholism has increased as well as rapes. Indigenous villages suffer continual harassment, intimidation, house raids, land evictions, and forced labor. People are denied freedom of movement and the right of peaceful assembly. Human rights workers, teachers, social workers and journalists have all suffered attacks and threats.

The coming war in Mexico can be averted if we can alter our history of racism, ignorance, violence and greed. In short, if we do not behave as a decadent empire. Only three things are required; all of them are cheaper than the repetition of our failed military adventurism:

1. Respect for the dignity of the indigenous people of Mexico. This can be demonstrated in a concrete way by restoration of Article 27 of the Mexican Constitution of 1917.

2. Potable water. It is tragic to observe people drinking water from highway gutters in Chiapas. Mexico is the world's largest consumer of soft drinks. Could it be that potable water might interfere with the sale of Coca Cola just as more doctors might interfere with the sale of medical attention in the United States?

3. The third requirement is electricity.

Respect, water and electricity are much cheaper than a war which will bathe Mexico in blood and similarly disrupt the country to the north of the Rio Grande.

Dialogical Thinking vs. Competitive Thinking

March 4, 1997

Do you ever get tired of hearing the word "competitive?" I hear the word "competitive" about fifteen times a day in the jargon of conventional wisdom.

This competitive formula would pay hospitals not to train doctors so fewer doctors can receive, not earn, more money. With this greed based logic we should pay universities to train fewer teachers, and pay nursing schools to train fewer nurses. Let us pay our city and state governments not to train so many professionals in police and fire protection.

I do not think Nobel Prize winners are competitive. They are generally people on fixed incomes who have pursued excellence. Income was simply not the motivation for their excellence. More often than not, excellence is not competitive, it is cooperative.

Competitive thinking is adversarial thinking and this is the motor force of our current society. Competitive thinking when applied to international relations means warfare when things do not go our way.

There is a better way, dialogical thinking is the opposite of competitive thinking. Dialogical thinking observes truth through its perspective and listens to other perceptions of truth. By so doing dialogue can give birth to new cooperative concepts. These are win-win concepts.

But competitive thinking would have us criminalize everyone and everything that does not foster the god of profit. In this environment we have seen children become the enemy together with strangers. The poor become the enemy together with the sick and disabled. But can we have a cooperative society? Of course we can. The best things in our society are already cooperative. Every program established to fill a need for the common good has been effective.

Police, fire, public schools, public utilities, forest rangers, and civil servants who make the government, run as vapid elected officials come and go. They go hand in hand with community infrastructure, sewers, highways, national and local parks, social security and Medicare, not to mention the already destroyed Aid to Families with Dependent Children.

Our courts can also become dialogical instead of adversarial. Rather than look for a 99 percent conviction rate, local DA's can seek out cooperative solutions including a zero tolerance for violence together with rehabilitation. Hollywood studios are highly competitive but they seem absolutely incapable of producing anything of culture and beauty. On the contrary, they grind out hundreds of competitive turkeys each year. Competition does not create excellence. Most works of culture and substance are produced by independent film makers who want to make films of culture and substance. They are not competing with anyone. But, what about sports? They are competitive, but they are regulated by a level playing field. Capital is not regulated in a similar fashion. Free trade is not fair trade.

We can have a cooperative future. It will be like that low-income family you have seen which sends all of its children to college by the cooperation of all members. This family value of cooperation must become a societal value. This is how there will always be enough loaves and fishes to feed the multitudes. This is how we can live without destroying each other and this is how we can save the planet.

Cooperation, *yes*.

Competition, *no*.

The Computer is Mightier than the Sword

March 18, 1997

The computer is mightier than the sword. This week the highest command of the Colombian military, headed by General Bonnet, came to the city of Apartado, in the northwest of Colombia, to tell the Mayor of that city, Gloria Cuartas, to order the Colombian Support Network of Madison, Wisconsin to take their page out of the internet. The page was created in 1996 to provide news to the world about the repression by the Colombian military and their paramilitary allies against the civilian population and about Mayor Gloria Cuartas who had a million peso bounty on her head. The page has helped to prevent the death of the mayor.

Gloria Isabel Cuartas, the Mayor of the City of Apartado in northwest Colombia, was recently in the United States speaking about the violence and repression in her country. Upon her return, a bomb exploded in her city killing twelve and injuring sixty people. The generals are now blaming her for the bomb attack. The charge is both treacherous and outrageous. But it sends a clear message to paramilitary death squads that she should be killed.

We, who want peace, are asking for the immediate removal of General Rito Alejo del Rio. Since he took command of the battalion near Apartado, Colombia, paramilitary violence has increased greatly. His former second-in-command, Colonel Carlos Alfonso Velazquez, even complained to the high command of the Colombian military that General del Rio was making no attempt to curtail paramilitary violence. Another example of disinformation was quite clear this week as we heard columnist Georgie Anne Geyer make the bizarre allegation on National Public Radio, that no one says the Colombian police or military are dirty. Indications are quite to the contrary. The same clandestine United States agency that ran wars in Nicaragua, El Salvador and Guatemala is apparently hard at work in Colombia promoting the same dirty behavior.

We fully agree with former Attorney General Ramsey Clark that we should not seek a new leader for the CIA. It should be abolished. But if the moribund agency is to continue against our will, we must ask our representatives to begin an investigation into the link between the spy agency and the Colombian military.

History Lesson for March 25, 2020;

The United Republic of the Middle East

March 25, 1997

History lesson for March 25, of the year 2020.

The present government of the United Republic of the Middle East was formed after much unnecessary pain and suffering. The cause of fifty years of war was identified as an outdated attempt to manipulate politics under the banner of religion. Separatism in an age of globalization was counterproductive to any hope of human rights and social justice. Palestinians formed a nonviolent interreligious unity among their Christian and Islamic people. Israel identified its fundamentalists as an obstacle to unity comparing them to both Christian and Islamic fanatics. Israelis of Peace now became a majority movement denouncing their nuclear weapons and militarism as clearly suicidal. Israel joined the Republic together with Palestine. If demagogical religious manipulation continued, it was clear that Sunni would fight Shiia forever so Iran and Iraq became part of the United Republic of the Middle East. Jordan was quick to join the union as was Lebanon with its mix of Byzantine Catholics, Islamics and Druse. Syria did not want to become an international ghetto, so it joined the union as did the sordid family states of the former Saudi Arabia and Kuwait.

The momentum for this change began in 1997 when peace talks between Palestine and Israel deteriorated. Fanatics were making negotiations impossible. Religious states simply cannot be the basis of a functional polity. History tells us that such attempts lead only to inquisition and violence. Non-Zionist Jews rejoiced in the realization that they would no longer be marginalized from their ethnicity by a failed nineteenth century ideology. Nonreligious Jews, Islamics and Christians rejoiced to know they would no longer have their lives curtailed by religious taboos. Millions of Islamic, Jewish and Christian women celebrated their new-found equal rights with men.

The constitution of the United Republic of the Middle East is no longer based on disputed sacred texts. Separation of Church and State became a reality which protects the practice of all religions:

> The parliament shall make no law respecting an establishment of religion, or prohibiting the free exercise thereof; or abridging the freedom of speech, or of the press; or the right of the people peaceably to assemble, and to petition the Government for a redress of grievances.

The new republics borrowed the First Amendment of the Constitution of the United States of America. Another component was borrowed from Article Six of the Constitution, Section Three; ". . . No religious test shall ever be required as a qualification to any office or public trust under the United Republic of the Middle East."

Modern polities must be based on social justice and human rights. Ideological states are now history. Public policy is properly derived from sociology, not religious doctrine. What about the Holy City of the three Abrahamic religions: Islam, Judaism and Christianity? Jerusalem remains as an international shrine in celebration of the separation of church and state. Just think, only twenty-three years ago, in 1997, the Middle East was absorbed in the politics of terror and hysteria. Today it is a functional and prosperous United Republic of the Middle East, which rejoices in religious freedom and tolerance. If this new Republic had not been visualized, it never would have become a reality.

Mind Control

April 1, 1997

In spite of recent cult murders, there are still therapists who know nothing about mind control and who even think mind control is a First Amendment right. Such professionals are tragically misinformed and could be contributing to the expansion of groups like Heaven's Gate. Mind control is the submission of a slave to a psychic master. Mind control is not brain washing. Brain washing is a physically coercive methodology used against detainees. Mind control does not require such physical restraints. It is sometimes referred to as "Svengeli hypnosis."

When a friend or relative joins a group like Heaven's Gate we are tempted to say, "She is over twenty-one and should be free to do whatever she wants." But such comments do not apply to mind controlled people. They are held as psychic captives and if we care about them, we must take appropriate action. In short we must seek out exit counseling. Exit counseling includes consultation with cult experts who may know something about the group in question. In Los Angeles, I would surely recommend the fine work done by Jewish Family Services.

Should we physically intervene in cases of mind control? That question must be answered on an individual basis. The cult, or its victims, might accuse rescuers of kidnapping. That risk is willingly taken by some exit counselors. This difficult and dangerous work requires professional know-how and has liberated thousands of people who would have spent the rest of their lives chasing comets or selling roses for such inspired leaders as the Reverend Moon, Jim Jones, David Koresh or Marshall Herff Applewhite.

People who are forcibly removed from mind controlled slavery often come out of their condition after three or four days in a safe house. An estimated 20 million people have joined cults in the United States over the past twenty years. Some 5,000 cults are hard at work recruiting new members. The manipulators now dealing in captive minds and bodies must be regulated before they walk off with the souls, and savings of your family members.

Mind control requires active and aggressive intervention. It requires a new body of law and new requirements for therapists. We needed food and drug laws when patent medicines were killing people at the turn of the century. Now we need new laws to protect people from the mind control of destructive cults.

The legal rubric for eliminating mind control is that of undue influence. Self-centered charlatans have no right to psychically enslave unsuspecting people. These destructive cults may be found under the banner of religion, politics, psychotherapy, commerce and education. There is no First Amendment right to mind control. Find an exit counselor. Rescue the victim and end the charade. Let the victim freely return to normal life. Thirty-nine victims in California represent only some of the deceased. The living dead are all around us in cults of a similar nature. This is not freedom of religion, it is psychic captivity leading to slavery and murder. Well before the recent disaster in California, Dr. Margaret Singer concluded her book *Cults in Our Midst* with the phrase ". . . let us not call these deaths suicides."

Let us view them for what they are: The sad, lonely, dreadful ending of life for people who trusted too much, followed too long, and could not get away from a self-serving and murderous leader.

JROTC

Junior Reserve Officers Training Corps

April 8, 1997

*What a great day it will be when the schools are fully funded
and the military has to have a bake sale to survive.*

Nearly 5,000 students in the Los Angeles Unified School District are
currently enrolled in the Junior Reserve Officers Training Corps program in twenty-six high schools from East Los Angeles to Hollywood
High.

According to Ted Nelson, Budget Director of the Los Angeles Unified School District, the net cost of JROTC to the school district, after
the Pentagon's contribution, is $1.3 million per year for twenty-six
JROTC units. Such funds would be better spent in the nonviolent sector; the humanities, conflict resolution and leadership training. Instead our most promising low-income students are being channeled
into the hands of military recruiters. This is called a "poverty draft."
At the very time we are trying to get guns out of our schools, the
JROTC is teaching students how to aim, shoot and kill.

JROTC is sold to school districts as a "dropout prevention program." But to qualify for JROTC students must maintain a C average
and stay out of trouble with the law or school authorities. At-risk youth
are thereby excluded from the program. The military is not going for
potential dropouts, it is going for the best and the brightest. Over 50
percent of JROTC graduates join the military directly after high school.
They deliver themselves over to the hype, con and false promises of
recruiters who speak of college funds and technical training. Military
recruiters behind on their quotas will call local JROTC programs saying, "I need four or five more to make it this month."

The recruiters fail to mention that aside from battlefield deaths,
there are other occupational hazards in the military: One-third of the
homeless people in Los Angeles are veterans, the government's historical rejection of veterans is traceable from the revolution of 1776
to the Gulf War, which massacred the people of Iraq and sent United

States troops home with Gulf War Illness. Veterans currently suffer the results of our own weapons which used depleted uranium. The government continues to deny what the medical profession can verify, these troops were victims of chemical warfare and medical experimentation.

In spite of the reality of history and maybe because of it, the JROTC program is an ongoing sales pitch for military service. It would correctly be classified as a dead-end job in a racist, sexist institution whose very mission is violence. Instead of recruiting our children into the military these funds could be used for all of the students, especially those who are at risk.

The Pentagon has far more money than it needs. The military budget is a sacred cow which politicians continue to worship to affirm their misguided religion of war-making. Of all the nonsense that the Los Angeles Unified School Board has approved over the past decades, including sixteenth century corporal punishment, this is the most obnoxious. Millions continue to be paid into the Pentagon by the Los Angeles Unified School District to support the Heaven's Gate Cult of military recruitment. We oppose this cult in our midst and we oppose the manipulation of our children into its membership. Congratulations are due to the Central Committee for Conscientious Objectors for making this abuse known to the public.

Tax Day

April 15, 1997

Secretary of Defense Cohen has an important message for the North Korean people on this tax day, "You folks are spending excessive amounts of money on your military and that is leading to malnutrition for your children."

Secretary of Defense Cohen has an important message for the South Koreans, "Please buy our perfectly good surface to air Patriot missiles rather than spending your billions on Russian SA-12 missiles." But Cohen forgot to mention the impact of this purchase on South Korean malnutrition. The military budget not only brings malnutrition to North and South Korea, it brings malnutrition to 20 percent of the children of the United States as well.

Currently, your tax money is being worse than wasted. It is used to destroy the minds of those who spend it and the bodies of those who are victims of it. The wasteful $254 billion military budget is bankrupting our society. Last year Congress was willing to shut down the entire Federal Government in their debate over which social programs to cut. But the military budget was increased with virtually no debate (by $7 billion increase in 1995 and an $11 billion in 1996.) Congress people were paid $10.5 million in campaign contributions from the weapons industry to buy this budget. As we glory in being number one in military spending, we are rapidly falling behind the rest of the world in health care, child nutrition and education.

We continue to lead the developed world with the percentage of our citizens in poverty and prison. The gun business is destructive at home and abroad. Our message to is to end welfare programs for the arms industry. *Arms exports alone have been subsidized to the tune of $7 billion in a single year.*

Our message is to ratify the Comprehensive Test Ban Treaty.

Our message is to abolish nuclear weapons.

In fiscal year 1997 we will continue to spend our taxes on the Trident II nuclear missile (at a total cost of $28 billion), the Seawolf nuclear submarine takes $13 billion and Stupid Star Wars takes $100 billion. Now, sixty-one generals think we can abolish nuclear suicide and have joined Generals Lee Butler and Andrew Goodpaster saying, "Nuclear weapons are a peril to global peace and security and to the safety and survival of the people we are dedicated to protect." But these generals cannot put as much money into the pockets of Congress-people as can the arms manufacturers.

Our message is to stop arms sales to human rights abusing nations. Seventy percent of our arms sales are to nations recognized as human rights abusers. Forty-five of fifty of the world's current conflicts are conducted with United States weapons. The overwhelming number of casualties are civilians.

Our message is to end military aid to repressive governments. We are currently arming governments like Turkey, Indonesia and Mexico. We provide equipment such as electric cattle prods which are used to torture humans. We are defending corporations like Nike and Disney so they can pay pennies a day to their workers.

Our payment of taxes must always be conditional. If our public servants are good stewards, we will continue the process. As it is now, however, our hard-earned money is being used to foster international crime. Forty-five wars are currently being conducted with our weapons.

The people of the United States are great people. We deserve more than to see our treasury used in this disgraceful and immoral fashion. Taxation without representation is tyranny.

A Progressive Ghetto?

April 22, 1997

What is holding the progressive movement back? There is the axiom that "the ideas of every age are the ideas of the ruling class." But the majority of our people do not really agree with the politics imposed on them. They simply lack the ability to change the control of the many by the few.

Small private corporate cliques make public policy for the United States. Small private corporate cliques also make international policy. We are actually dealing with paper tigers. Rather than fear the tiger, we must enter a phase of non-cooperation.

Why should we cooperate by eating food from countries where people are hungry? Why should we support wage slavery at home or abroad? Why should we accept fear as is the motor force of society? The rash of new and mean-spirited laws are based on our fears, our fear of life and our fear of death. We should also include our fears of our family and friends together with the fears of the alien from outer space and the alien from Mexico, in short, the fear of life. To take a hold of life completely we must put aside such fears. Perfect love casts out fear.

When Martin Luther King was asked what made it possible for him to develop a national movement for civil rights he said, "When I put aside my fear of death."

For progressives to bring their hopes to fruition requires religion. I do not mean any particular religion, I am referring to the need for a mystique of community and family. How often the egghead progressive sounds sterile and academic. Such intellectuals are out of touch with their mother and their children. The stereotype I am thinking of will know the GNP of the Netherlands, but will not know that his or her child is contemplating suicide.

To observe the kind of community organization needed for a progressive future, I suggest putting aside our prejudice and participating in Sunday Services. You will find community, you will find something for everyone, the babes in arms, the preschoolers, the elementary and high school students, college age and all phases of life thereafter. But you will say, "I can't stand the message from the pulpit." Do not worry no one else can either. People do not come for the message, they come for the community. What about our own message? How many people does it draw? Government is not necessarily the solution to every problem. But cooperation is the solution. Once we take a family view of society we will be able to put aside the manipulation of fear which is the motor force of corrupt politics.

We must get out of our progressive ghetto and take a look at the community organizing done by the churches. The progressive movement lacks enthusiasm. Think of that dull professor you had who could not get excited about the material taught. Dullness is not a requirement for the hard sciences. I remember a professor in organic chemistry who was so excited about the truth he taught that the students became excited as well. The progressive movement must put aside its fundamentalism and welcome enthusiasm and personal concern.

Peru

April 29, 1997

Unjustly imprisoned people are held in newly designed terrorist cells. They are tortured and some are executed. The judiciary of Peru is not functional. In its place we see faceless thugs who are called "judges" and who make decisions based on unfounded accusations. The Spanish Inquisition allowed the accused heretic to defend his or her position. Contemporary Peru does not.

Autocratic President Fujimori designed an auto-coup and subjected himself to military review of each administrative action. Some call this being "tough." Upon observation, it is simply being a wimp. Tell the military they can do no wrong; then they might continue to let you act like Napoleon. Fujimori created a Goliath to terrorize the suffering majority in Peru. For better or worse, a small group of young men and women took on the perilous role of David and stood up to Goliath. They did not, as David, decapitate their victims, they held the power of Peru in their hands for some months and were actually gracious to their victims. Japan wanted to deal with the hostage takers in accord with their very successful methodology of negotiation. But the United States opposed the Japanese strategy and from day one trained commandos for an intervention. One of the unjustly held prisoners in Peru is a United States citizen, Lori Berenson. Lori is not a member of the *Movimiento Revolucionario Túpac Amaru* (MRTA), but as many Peruvian citizens, she was accused of being a member and slammed into a terrorist cell after an accusatory episode with a hooded non-judge. The rebel leadership asked for her release because of the accusation, not because of her membership in their organization.

Secretary of State Madeleine Albright has sent congratulations to President Fujimori. He can easily interpret her letter as saying:

Congratulations on having a de facto military government in Peru.

Congratulations on your terrorist prisons.

Congratulations on your absence of a judiciary.

Congratulations on your ongoing practice of torture.

Congratulations on ignoring the humane advice of the Japanese.

Congratulations on the mutilation, assassination and disappearance of the bodies of the accused.

For over a century, now, the United States has supported a policy of internal military dominance in Latin America in support of friendly local oligarchies. The poor of both the United States and Latin America clearly understand the message coming from their governments.

As we commemorate five years since the greatest urban uprising in United States history, we might remind those in power that the misuse of government funds for military purposes will not be solved by a half hour a week of volunteer work. Money has been taken from our checks for the common good. It is then misdirected to oppress people in Mexico, Central and South America.

The diversion of hundreds of billions of dollars to our glutted military establishment is not going to be resolved by President Clinton and Colin Powell painting walls for thirty seconds on camera. I would prefer that money collected from our taxes be used for urban renewal in Lima and Los Angeles.

Gross Social Product (GSP)

May 6, 1997

There are people in Mexico who have the answer to the problem of Mexican / United States relations. They are the Mexican homeless who are demonstrating in front of the United States Embassy in Mexico City. Mexican teachers trying to join the group were stopped by the military some blocks from the embassy. Unbelievably, IMF (International Monetrary Fund) World Bank policies forbid loans for social spending. Therefore no money can be loaned to Mexico for the establishment of consumer cooperatives. But such programs as consumer coops and employee owned enterprises have the potential to end the horrible mal-distribution of wealth in both the United States and Mexico.

Twenty-first century economics must include gauges and practices which make cooperative justice possible. Such a gauge is the gross social product in contrast to the currently useless gauge of gross national product. Instead of squeezing billions of dollars out of hungry people to make the glutted rich of Mexico and the United States richer, a focus on gross social product would create an equilibrium in society making insurgency unnecessary, promoting international tranquility and terminating the counterproductive drug wars.

Gross social product does not look at money as an end in itself, on the contrary it looks at people as an end in themselves. Gross social product is driven by distributive justice and thereby is peace oriented rather than war oriented. Unlike the useless gauge of gross national product, gross social product looks at the ability of the economy to improve housing, literacy, health care and cultural education.

As President Clinton lays a wreath at the Monument of The Boy Heros, Niños Heroes, in Mexico City, I can only hope that his handlers will remind him of the monument's origin. In 1847, a United States invasion force was fighting its way toward Mexico's capital in a war engineered by President James K. Polk. Over 50,000 Mexicans were killed, Irish immigrant soldiers drafted to serve in the United States Army, mutinied against their Protestant leaders and went over to the side of Catholic Mexico. Abe Lincoln was outraged by the United

States intervention. One of the main obstacles to Lincoln being elected president of the United States was his opposition to the war with Mexico. Abe Lincoln, just as Bill Clinton, was accused of being a "peacenik" and thereby unfit to govern our country.

In the final battle of the war, United States troops stormed the military academy and bayoneted its last defenders some fourteen teen-aged cadets known as the Boy Heros. (Perhaps the fourteen teenagers murdered in Peru last month will be remembered in a similar fashion).

The United States took California, Arizona, Nevada, Utah, New Mexico, Texas and a good bit of Colorado in 1848. The Mexican people were in their own country and instantly they were declared foreigners.

We must demand a new and meaningful focus on the gross social product of Mexico and the United States. Such an effort will create political equilibrium and end the need for insurgency in Mexico, Central and South America.

Torture in Israel

May 13, 1997

Humane Israelis have identified a pathology in their nation and have attacked it with professional vigor. Dr. Ruchama Marton is a practicing psychiatrist. She is founder and chairwoman of the Association of Israeli-Palestinian Physicians for Human Rights. A conference was held in Tel Aviv on the international struggle against torture and the case of Israel. Dr. Marton and Neve Gordon documented the results of the conference in their book titled: *Torture, Human Rights, Medical Ethics and the Case of Israel* (Zed Press, 1995). Something very toxic, even suicidal, is going on in Israel. After Israeli physicians identified and documented torture as policy, the practice has now become legal, making Israel the only western democracy where torture is lawful. This week, the *New York Times* told the story of George, one of thousands of Palestinians who have been victimized by Israel's legal torture. He was kept sleepless in contorted and excruciating positions with a stinking bag over his head, he was beaten and subjected to violent shaking until he became unconscious. This obscene sadism went on for seventeen days.

As Israel's Supreme Court continues to condone the practice, the United Nations Committee against Torture summoned Israel for an extraordinary hearing to face accusations that its practices violate international conventions against torture. Amnesty International, the International Committee of the Red Cross and various Israeli human rights organizations say the Shin Bet's methods are indisputably torture as defined by international law. The conventions prohibiting torture exist precisely to protect detainees in extraordinary times, even in war. Lea Tsemel, a veteran defense lawyer and a founder of the Public Committee Against Torture in Israel says, "This is not some brute in the secret service beating up on a prisoner. It is done in the open. There is a quiet legitimation by high ranking commission and government ministers." Human rights organizations estimate that about 5,000 Palestinians a year were subjected to some combination of ill treatment or violent methods in the years before the signing of the peace agreements between the Palestine Liberation Organization and Israel in 1993. By all account the practice has continued unabated since.

Factual information has never been obtained by torture. Torture is a form of terrorism designed to create a culture of silence. Theocracies have traditionally used torture. The Inquisition in the Catholic City State of Rome questioned Galileo and told him he was about to be tortured if he did not repent. He quickly lied, said the sun went around the earth as the bible says . . . In free translation concluded, "Now let me out of here!" Torture is not fact-finding, it is simply terror. Personally, I do not think there will be any remaining theocracies in the twenty-first century. The science of politics has evolved from Thomas Jefferson and the enlightenment to the present with one clear message, "the state must be secular and there must be no laws regarding the establishment of religion." It is hard to imagine anything worse than to make religion the basis of a political system. Such failures are clear in Iran, Afghanistan and Saudi Arabia. They should be equally clear in a state that purports to be a western style democracy.

Atheists at Prayer

May 20, 1997

Do atheists pray? Of course they do. When? Whenever they feel like it. Many atheists are actually non-theists; that is, they cannot bear to retain their early descriptions of a deity because such descriptions were so very irreverent. How are theists more irreverent than atheists? Theists lack all reverence if they purport to comprehend God, if they start telling us what God will or will not do, if they confine God to some dinky sect and if they maintain exclusivist or fundamentalist concepts declaring those outside of their narrowness to be devils. Such theism is a monument to irreverence not to reverence.

I once sat at the feet of Eric Fromme in Cuernavaca, Mexico. As a priest, I was concerned about his alleged atheism. He said he was from the ancient Hebrew tradition that did not take the name of the Lord in vain—His theology was impressive. He was not speaking of contemporary swearing and cursing, he was speaking of not using the name of God as if we knew what we were talking about . . . In other words, *in vain*. Such a mystery is not to be tossed around flippantly, not to be manipulated for profit, not to be comprehended, but to be reverenced. Taking the name for Fromme was to claim comprehension. He preferred to stand back in awe of the mystery and referred to himself as a non-theist. Atheists who pray are not hypocrites. They are entitled to lift up their hearts and minds to the unknown. They are entitled to reach out to the great spirit of wisdom, understanding, fortitude, peace, patience, joy, love, goodness, kindness and endurance.

They are also in sync with the Buddhist tradition of seeking consciousness, of being truly awake and practicing non-self. Atheists who pray are not hypocrites. When Jean Paul Sartre expressed his views on the meaninglessness of the universe, he was accused of having no moral compass. No moral compass? Because I consider meaning to be absent, it is imperative for me to create as much meaning as possible. The meaning that exists is the meaning we create. Hypocrites are military brass suffering from missile envy who want to throw stones at a woman who can fly their B-52. Hypocrites are people who spread

AIDS all over the world, foster child prostitution and promiscuity of all kinds and then attack a woman who has achieved what they have reserved for men.

The adultery was to create the B-52 in the first place. The adultery is to attack the first woman who knows how to fly it. The adultery is the legal action against her. A carpenter from Nazareth speaks to the group of hypocrites ready to throw stones at an alleged adulteress and says, "Let the person among you who is without sin throw the first stone at her." The audience drifted away one by one, beginning with the elders. May the military hypocrites and elders responsible for this adulteration of justice quickly drift away as well.

ESOPs and Unions

June 1, 1997

The questions asked by Karl Marx in the nineteenth century have not been answered. Marx was struck by how the owners of the means of production simply appropriated the wealth created by workers. Today, the individual worker creates more wealth than his nineteenth century counterpart and the distribution of wealth is worse than ever. Marx is dead, but two solutions to this problem remain. One is unionization, and the other is the ESOP or *Employee Stock Ownership Plan*. Some argue that the days of unions are over and that we must only have employee stock ownership plans. It seems to me, however, we need both.

Unions are established to protect the rights of workers, hours, wages, working conditions, health programs and employee stock ownership programs. As unions become effective in demanding stock ownership, the adversarial relationship between management and labor will mellow. Workers will finally be recognized as what they are, the essential stock holders of the company, the essential risk takers of the company and the producers of the company's wealth.

This is not a theoretical discussion. Take the case of the McKay Nursery in Waterloo, Wisconsin. Since 1984 all of the company's stock is in an employee stock ownership plan. At the McKay Nursery employees are required to sell their stock to the company when they retire. After thirty years the lowest paid worker can cash in for $100,000. Some small businesses like the McKay Nursery are 100 percent employee stock owned in contrast to larger firms like United Airlines, which are only partially owned by employees. In California, members of the United Farm Workers Union with the best contracts, enjoy medical, dental, and vision benefits as well as paid vacations. Add to these union benefits a full share in worker ownership and we will have finally answered one of the questions which Marx asked, "How can workers share in the wealth they create?" The answer is, by effective unionization leading to complete stock ownership of the corporation. Unlike the present order, workers who build a home will then be able to live in it. Workers who put food on our tables will then be able to buy it. Unions are the proper mechanism for creating an ESOP future.

What is called for here is *discernment*. The beginning of a peaceful economic revolution leading to distributive justice simply requires our consciousness. The richest 1 percent who control most of this nation's wealth should even be able to understand this. But if they cannot, let us remember that working people are far more than a majority. Are white collar workers real workers? Of course they are. Their participation in unions and stock ownership programs can help them to regain the job stability they once had. There is more to all of this. Once the employees own the company, they can evaluate the ecological impact of what they produce. They can evaluate the need for what they produce. They can evaluate the meaning of what they produce. They will no longer be a commodity but decision making human beings. And Marx will turn over happily in his grave.

Geronimo Pratt

June 9, 1997

Justice delayed is justice denied.

Orange County Superior Court Judge Everett W. Dickey ruled that Geronimo Pratt's 1972 conviction was heavily influenced by the testimony of an informant whose infiltration of the Black Panther party was unknown at the time of Pratt's trial. The judge added that the prosecution wrongly suppressed information about the informant, Julius "Julio" Butler, and that this suppressed information could have swayed the jurors to affirm Pratt's innocence. A thirteen page decision by Judge Dickey concluded that the evidence withheld about Julius Butler and his activities could have put the whole case in a different light and failure to disclose it undermined confidence in the verdict. There is joy in this release. It is similar to the joy at the release of Nelson Mandela. It gives us hope of a new era in the United States.

The corruption of class justice must be reversed. At the base of the pyramid, unknowns are getting life sentences for stealing pizza on their third strike. At the top of the pyramid, George Bush can massacre one million Iraqis and that is okay. The corruption of which we speak is institutional. We must not simply look to the obvious weakness of Mr. Garcetti. The problem is deeper than that. The corruption of the District Attorney's office, the corruption of the FBI are rooted in conditions of class and race.

Living in a war culture, militant peace advocates are seen as the enemy, Dr. King and Panthers are assigned to insider death squads. By comparison, some of us are treated mildly by simply having our academic careers destroyed. Some are killed in cold blood. Some receive decades in prison. Are we conspiracy theorists? Please, do not give in to glib conventional put-downs. We are not conspiracy theorists. We are people who have hard data. J. Edgar Hoover's psychotic hand is clear in the hard copy of my freedom of information files. This is not theory. It is history. Investigations must begin to uncover the lies, manipulation, racism, and corruption of these agen-

120

cies. We have reason to suspect the same agency that framed Geronimo Pratt was responsible for the murder of Dr. King. Let us get on with the liberation of the least known of the falsely imprisoned in the United States as well as Peru. The ghost of J. Edgar Hoover must rule the agency no longer.

I look at hundreds of pages of my own Freedom of Information files and see similar false information written by government agents who have security clearances. Just what are they trying to secure? I cannot help but think that I have suffered so little by losing some twenty-seven years of academic employment and Geronimo has lost twenty-seven years of his life. But has he? His contribution will help us to force the worms out from under the rocks where they hide and conspire. His contribution will lead us to identify the sin against the spirit which shall never be forgiven. Those who look into the face of the truth and have chosen a lie. Thanks for the sacrifice you have made Geronimo. I remember you, and I think you remember me. In the wake of your being framed, you can help government to understand that it is not enough for our agencies to stop the corruption. Police agencies must become instruments of dialogue.

The very people who have been brutalized in the past have within themselves the answers to society's problems. Free all political prisoners throughout the world.

Mumia Abu Jamal . . . Leonard Peltier . . . Lori Berenson . . . We will not forget you.

Colombia

June 17, 1997

Suppose you contributed money to a cause with the intention of aiding flood victims. Upon examination you determined that the money was not being used to aid the victims. It was being used to kill them.

This analogy reflects the impact of our current Drug War in Colombia. Violence in Colombia claims about 35,000 lives annually. Conventional corporate wisdom in the United States claims that the slaughter is rooted in drug trafficking. But the Andean Commission of Jurists estimates that less than 2 percent of Colombia's violence has anything to do with drugs, while 70 percent is the work of Colombia's army, police and paramilitary death squads. In the past decade, over $1 billion in military aid has been given to Colombia by the United States allegedly to fight the drug war.

Human Rights Watch reports that our tax money and CIA officials restructured the Colombian military's intelligence apparatus setting up "killer networks" of paramilitary soldiers to murder suspected leftists. "The paramilitaries have increasingly become the chosen tool of the Colombian military for suppressing political dissent" writes Robin Kirk and Anne Manuel of Human Rights Watch. But political dissent is not drug dealing.

In sync with Human Rights Watch, Amnesty International gave documentation of the Colombian military using its gifted weapons against unarmed civilians who were not connected with the drug trade.

Dr. William Schultz, Director of Amnesty International in the United States, said at a recent press conference, "Almost every unit highlighted by Amnesty for murdering Colombian civilians was in fact receiving United States supplied arms and other equipment." In other words United States weapons that were ostensibly intended to fight drugs were actually used to equip thugs in uniform who murdered people inconvenient to the Colombian government.

In the United States, the war on drugs has served as a rationale for surrendering civil liberties including random searches, increased wiretapping and lengthy prison sentences. In Colombia the stakes are higher.

Mayor Gloria Cuartas was speaking to an elementary school class in Apartado, Colombia as part of a "peace week." Her lesson was on conflict resolution. As she spoke, two death squad members ran up to the playground outside and grabbed an eight year old boy César Augusto Rivera. One of the men chopped off César's head and threw it into the classroom at the Mayor and the children. Is this a war on drugs? We have seen the fraud of our so-called "drug war" for too long. It is disrupting civil society in the United States, in Mexico, in Peru and in Colombia.

A Code of Conduct

June 24, 1997

For the first time, a code of conduct with criteria for determining who can buy American arms has passed the House of Representatives. The British government says it will adhere to an even stronger code, and support is growing in the European Union for a code that would apply to all members. Together the United States and Europe account for 80 percent of the world's arms trade.

The code passed the House last week with no one in opposition. Where is the opposition? Certainly not from Dana Rohrbacher, a conservative California Representative. Rohrbacher sponsored the bill together with progressive Cynthia McKinney of Georgia. The opposition to this moderate and watered down legislation comes directly from the Clinton Administration and the aerospace industry. Why do we say "watered down?" Because if the Administration wanted to sell arms to a country that does not meet the criteria, it could propose a waiver in the interest of national security. Congress would then have eight months to block or condition the Administration's request.

Currently, about one half of United States arms sales go to countries that are correctly classified as "dictatorships." We must remind the president of how United States weapons have been turned against our own troops in Somalia, Panama, Haiti and Iraq.

Nobel Laureate, Oscar Arias, points out that eighteen of the world's poorest countries spend more on their militaries than on education and health combined. Arias, who has led the effort for the Code of Conduct internationally, would like to see the money once spent on weapons, go to demobilize armies instead. While most governments will not unilaterally renounce modern arms, many will be happy to join in a ban that applies to their rivals as well. At a recent conference at the Carter Center in Atlanta, fifteen former and current Latin American heads of state joined former presidents Carter and Ford in endorsing the code. The Code of Conduct must be mutual among the major weapons-exporting nations. Countries denied arms must not be able to look elsewhere. Here is another case where the United States with its international hegemony, can lead as it must. The same principle applies to land mines, nuclear weapons, chemical warfare, dues for the United Nations and closure of the School of Assassins at Fort Benning, Georgia. Rather than a morbid focus on the alleged sex practices of the president, we must shame him out of his marriage, to the sleaze merchants of arms.

The movement to develop a code of conduct on arms is being firmly built from the base by small organizations.

Nothing grows from the top down. The banning of arms to dictators must include all of those façade states where demonstration elections are held and the military rules. If we are to continue to call such nations democracies, we are surely going to lose our own. Before long we will not even be aware that the president is only tolerated by the military industrialists. Why would any intelligent person like Bill Clinton kowtow to them were he not controlled by them? Our support for the Code of Conduct is a clear indication that we have moral principles, family values that we and the rest of the world would like our president to practice. We do not need any cynicism. All we need is solidarity in action for peace and justice.

Growth Industries

July 22, 1997

Dustin Hoffman received advice suitable for a graduate in the film of the same name. The advice was Plastics! Today, in the same spirit, the growth industries are "WELFARE, WARFARE, PRISONS AND HEALTH CARE." These are the new sites of windfall profit.

The purpose of health care in this setting is to make a profit. $1 trillion a year is available. The less money used for health care delivery, the more gravy available for private profit.

But is this true of welfare as well? Lockheed, the company which has been on government welfare for decades, and often has government as its sole customer, wants to make a profit on the welfare. How is that done? The formula is the same as for the privatization of health care. Deliver as little as possible of the block grants to the poor, take the rest of the money and run.

How is the military being privatized? Military mercenary ventures, like the famous Iran / Contra scandal, are now legally outsourced to private industry. Retired officers can form their corporations to train such democratic forces as those of Saudi Arabia and Colombia. Congress will not interfere in such private enterprise.

What we see here is the corporate take-over of the United States using the World Trade Organization, WTO, model. But take heart, the trend can be reversed.

There is an academic field of public administration. For years experts in this field have identified areas that are principally appropriate for the public sector rather than the private sector. From the founding fathers insistence on the public welfare and the common good to the New Deal of FDR, Public Administration has become a science.

I think our domestic public sector spending has been quite effective. I am thinking of national parks, city parks, public libraries, public health facilities, public schools, public assistance to the sick and disabled, rehabilitation programs for addicts, safe highways and public utilities. None of these effective public sector programs were designed to make a profit.

Countries of the developed world put aside some of their treasury for those who fall through the cracks. It is not fitting that such funds be made available for private profit.

The profit sector in a developed society must be reserved for such enterprises as small businesses which seek investors and pursue legitimate entrepreneurial goals. At this time, however, corporations which have been unable to sustain themselves without government subsidy are attempting to raid even more of the public treasury.

Privatization is the process by which the responsibilities of government are transferred to unaccountable corporate hands. There is no fantasy here. These trends are in force and must be reversed. You have already seen the greed of the so-called "Health Maintenance Organizations" which profit on your illness. Currently welfare is seen as the hottest area in the United States for privatization. Lockheed Martin and other firms are competing for a government contract in Texas to administer the state's welfare program as well as parts of the food stamp Medicaid and unemployment programs. Just as city governments have outsourced many functions to minimum wage contractors, so now state and federal government is outsourcing health care, welfare, warfare and prisons in a similar fashion. We can turn this around this counterproductive trend by demanding that funds which we have placed in the common treasury for the common good be administered under government supervision rather than for private profit. Continuing the fanatical and greedy rush to privatization will ultimately destabilize both the United States and the world economy.

"Where your Treasure is, There your Heart will Be"

July 29, 1997

As a society we manifest what we treasure.

The richest city in the richest state in the richest country of the world cannot, will not, provide sufficient books for students in our schools. The duty to provide such books is a mandate of the Constitution of the State of California.

Is this because the money is lacking? No.

Is this because we cannot afford such luxuries? No.

Then what is the problem?

The Governor and our school administrators are apparently collecting their salaries and not doing what they are hired to do.

How to solve the problem? When state law is violated by failure to provide texts to students, there should be an immediate state of emergency declared in the school district. Each and every off- campus administrator should receive no salary until all required textbooks are provided.

We must continually make the point that the schools are here for the children. When a school system fails to deliver essentials such as texts, it appears that the schools are simply a mechanism for enriching administrators. But teachers and administrators are hired solely because there are students to teach.

If anyone should say, "We don't have enough money!" Let them be anathema. We have enough money to give tax cuts to the richest people in our country as the Congress is now doing. There is absolutely no merit to the lack of money argument. But there is a lack of will to deliver. Behind that lack of will is race and class prejudice.

Old and rotten racial and class prejudice must give way to new thinking. Such new thinking will identify children as the privileged class of society. Failure to deliver adequate texts must be categorized as malfeasance of office.

Governor Wilson presides over a state that is now 47th in expenditures for texts. Both the Governor and the United States Congress are far more interested in giving money back to glutted and overstuffed citizens than in educating children. But we cannot exempt the guardians of the schools system. Did they know nothing about this crisis? Did they purposely remain silent and thereby approve of the situation? After the administrators, the responsibility falls on the teachers. Such a crisis is worthy material for a teacher's strike. No books . . . No classes! Comply with the constitution of the state of California and do not continue to insult our intelligence by telling us that the richest state in the richest country in the world cannot afford books for students.

Where your treasure is, there your heart will be. Just what do we treasure? If, as a society, we do not treasure children, what is our problem?

Che

August 5, 1997

Jon Lee Anderson has completed a definitive volume on Che Guevara titled *Che* (Grove Press 1997).

Che represents the paragon of revolutionary zeal, total dedication, and political sainthood. Nothing in this volume contradicts the image. His mother once said, "He had always lived trying to prove to himself that he could do everything he could not do, and in that way he polished his amazing will power." His mother teased him for being intolerant and fanatical saying that he was motivated by the necessity for totality and purity. He became the most puritanical of the western revolutionary leaders. While the myth of Che will remain as the personification of revolution, the reality of Che must be subject to critical analysis. Jon Lee Anderson does this well.

Che believed in the armed struggle. As a youth he did not participate in demonstrations. He wandered Latin America as a freeloader looking for his role in society. He saw the horror of the CIA intervention in Guatemala in 1954 and was revolted by the failure of Jacobo Arbenz to resist the invasion.

Che met Fidel Castro in Mexico and became the key military leaders in the overthrow of the government of Fulgencio Batista. Without ever denying Che's dedication and unfettered zeal, Anderson demonstrates the negative factors in the doctrine of armed struggle. First there is summary justice. I recall the signs on the trail going up the Sierra Maestra to Che's command post reading, "If I am leading, follow me. If I am falling behind, push me. If I am holding you back, kill me."

And so it was. The large number of executions within the ranks of the rebels has never been so well documented as in Anderson's book. Second there is the matter of identifying one's own agenda as the agenda of the people. Peasants are not eager to enter the armed struggle as Che discovered in Cuba and in Bolivia. Third, the armed struggle gives the incumbent military free reign to eliminate all suspected opposition. We have seen this reactionary military violence in all parts of the world.

Anderson's work on Che Guevara projects the life of a guerrilla who had a vision of social justice and who was willing to personally kill anyone who interfered with the program. As most of history, this model of armed struggle does not bear repetition.

Che, as King David, will be remembered as a warrior for the people. But his warrior methods, like those of King David, are not for repetition. Those up for imitation in the years ahead are people who have identified instruments of change which are powerful, effective and humane. Such tools as have been presented to us by Cesar Chavez, Dr. Martin Luther King and Mahatma Ghandi are more effective than the ancient and outdated armed struggle.

It is our task to utilize these humane and effective tools and to modernize them.

Colombia

II

August 12, 1997

Since the end of July of this year, I have been in Colombia in search of answers some questions. Here are a few of my observations:

Approximately half of the thousand municipalities in Colombia are held by rebel forces. These forces are called "narco-guerrillas" by our press. This implies that war on the rebels is a war on drugs. Actually, the rebels are not in the drug business. It seems, however, that the ethical standards of the rebels have deteriorated because they do tax the growers of coca just as they tax the growers of corn and beans. Small farmers grow coca in order to survive. But the drug lords who pay for the coca are part of the political-military power of Colombia.

Some 200 paramilitary death squads are identifiable. Unbelievably these organizations are listed under a legal entity called *Convivir* (to live together). The Colombian army told us that they are opposed to these killer groups. But we saw the paramilitary controlling the town of San Jose in Uraba and the military ignored them. The general in charge simply shrugged his shoulders when we asked him why they did not confront these death squads. There is a legitimate political party which could pull together all the opposition forces of Colombia. It is a popular third force known as the Patriotic Union. The oligarchy dominance is maintained; however, by way of an eternal pendulum swing between liberals and conservatives which has dominated Colombian politics as a status quo for over a century. While the Patriotic Union offers a legal avenue of reconciliation and social justice, there is a problem; the power structure of drug lords, military and feudal oligarchs have presided over the killing of 5,000 Colombian leaders of this party. Active membership in the Patriotic Union has become a virtual death sentence. There are some 35,000 violent deaths in Colombia each year. While visiting the Colombian Government's Office of Human Rights, we were told that their representative just visited

Guatemala to get advice on the Guatemalan Civil Patrols. Apparently the Colombian government would like to unite the 200 diverse paramilitary squads into similar units.

This conflict has created 1 million displaced Colombians. We visited the African Colombian refugees from Choco who are languishing in the stadium of the city of Turbo. Their storehouse was empty. They were sick and tired. Their lands were bombed and they were told to get out immediately. They walked for days looking for refuge. When we asked the General how the paramilitary death squads could get helicopters to bomb Choco, he said they might have rented them.

While children in Los Angeles are illegally being denied schoolbooks, our government has poured over a billion dollars into Colombia's genocide in the name of the war on drugs. Some 2,000 Colombian military and police officers have been trained in the United States. 100 of the 246 Colombian Officers charged with human rights violations received training at the United States Army School of the Americas at Fort Benning, Georgia. Colombia is the largest recipient of United States military aid in this hemisphere since 1989.

The most prestigious legal organization in Colombia, the Andean Commission of Jurists, estimates that less than 2 percent of Colombia's violence has anything to do with drugs while 70 percent is the work of Colombia's army, police and paramilitary death squads. Our country is simply funding the feudal system of Colombia which was the cause of the revolution in the first place.

What is the answer? We met at length with Almudena Mazarrasa Alvear who is the director of the Office of the High Commission of the United Nations for Human Rights in Colombia. It is her opinion and ours that the only hope is to establish a United Nations negotiating team in Colombia. Almudena said that the only way this will happen is for the President of the United States to pressure Colombia to permit such a process.

Therefore, I ask you to help us by calling writing and faxing the President, asking him to stop all military and drug war aid to Colombia together with his support for a United Nations negotiating team for peace in Colombia.

Big Bang

August 19, 1997

The purpose of the Comprehensive Test Ban Treaty is to halt the development of new weapons of mass destruction by imposing a global ban on nuclear explosions. President Clinton signed this accord in 1996 and the United Nations endorsed it. The treaty has been signed by 146 nations including Russia, China and other declared nuclear powers. The United States Senate has yet to ratify this document. While looking for support last year, the Clinton administration stressed that the ban would rule out all new weapons and would end the nuclear arms race.

As 150,000 disabled children lose their federal benefits, $4 billion a year is going into a deadly and formerly secret project of "modernization." We can thank the Natural Resources Defense Council for obtaining this previously classified information. Our government is working hard to redesign the heart of the hydrogen bomb, that is its atomic trigger. Such work is in direct opposition to a treaty that was intended to stop innovations on weapons of mass destruction. 25,000 people are involved in this Department of Energy program. The Energy Department says these are not new weapons. This is simply the modernization of old weapons. But this work is enhancing the power of nuclear weapons.

What is at stake here? Walking mummies of the cold war are arguing and nit-picking about how they are not breaking the letter of the treaty. As usual, they have missed the whole point. It was St. Francis of Assisi who said, "Preach the Gospel, and if you have to, use words." Such a simple message of leadership. When the most powerful nation seeks even more power and demonstrates less leadership, we can be sure our regressive action will be imitated. We want a bigger bang. China will want a bigger bang. The leader has spoken, not by words but by dumb, repetitive and destructive action. Russia will also want to modernize and the Nuclear Test Ban Treaty becomes null and void.

To carry out the spirit of the Comprehensive Test Ban Treaty we might send a few of those 25,000 Department of Energy employees around the world to inspect the compliance of other nations.

The Comprehensive Test Ban Treaty was forty hard years in the making. Its goal was to halt the manufacture of nuclear weapons. We currently have over 10,000 warheads. What areas of the world are in the greatest danger as a result of this euphemistic modernization? In the light of the near irreversible damage that has already been done by the nuclear arms business, I think the greatest potential danger from this secret, subversive and destructive activity would be the demise of such cities as Chicago, Minneapolis, Los Angeles, Boston, New York, San Francisco and anything in between. We must demand an immediate halt to this rebirth of the nuclear arms race and insist on the letter and the spirit of the Comprehensive Nuclear Test Ban Treaty.

Idolatry

August 26, 1997

While flying recently, I was reading the *Apocalypse*. It proved to be very timely:

In Chapter ten we read: *The rulers of the earth joined in the idolater's sin and the earth's buyers and sellers grew rich because of their idolatrous greed.*

Let us try to identify some of that idolatry.

The Cassini Idol:

On October 6, 1997 NASA plans to launch a most perilous mission. At the bargain basement price of $3.4 billion, it will blast 72.3 pounds of plutonium on top of a Titan IV rocket allegedly to explore the planet Saturn. But this military industrial idol is toying with all life on earth. While in the earth's gravitational field this monstrosity could disintegrate and shower plutonium into the earth's atmosphere. According to Dr. Ernest Sternglass, Professor Emeritus of Radiological Physics at the University of Pittsburgh, the death toll could reach from 30 to 40 million people because of plutonium exposure. NASA's own environmental impact statement concedes that should an inadvertent reentry happen, "approximately five billion people will be exposed to the plutonium's radiation." Thanks to Mike Wisniewski and the Catholic Agitator for this information. Thanks to the Florida Coalition for Peace and Justice for spearheading the opposition to the Cassini Probe.

The B-2 Bomber:

This idol is very delicate, like the wicked old witch, it dissolves in water but it also blisters in the sun and chips in the cold. It really does not fly well at all. Its major mission has been to risk the lives of everyone in the Rose Parade on January 1, 1997 by attempting to fly over without dissolving. Its radar cannot distinguish between a rain cloud and a mountain.

That is right folks, we are talking about the B-2 bomber. But the idol was never created to defend us from anything so do not be concerned that it cannot fly, it was designed to transfer our tax contributions from the public sector to the most incompetent sectors of private enterprise.

Representative Jane Harman and Senator Diane Feinstein consider the B-2 a jobs program. How about jobs programs that create public transit, low cost housing, schools, child care, assistance to needy children and the right to medical care. Breaking large rocks into small rocks would be a much more useful jobs program than the massive $45 billion waste of the B-2 bomber program. Our enemies can rejoice that this junk aircraft does not work. Our friends and our citizens can live in terror. They may try to fly the thing over another parade.

Do the people of the United States need the Cassini Probe? No, they do not. Do the people of the United States need the B-2 bomber? No, they do not. Together we can strive for the establishment of a democracy. That democracy will be identified by utilization of the resources of our country for the needs of the people who live here and not for the greed of parasitic corporations structured to siphon our treasury into a cesspool of their own making.

Israel

September 9, 1997

Ms. Albright, you are going to Israel. Here are some thoughts for your trip.

There is a question of just who is to be excluded in Israel. A small group of Orthodox Jews in Israel have excommunicated non-Orthodox Jews including Conservative, Reform and Reconstructionist.

In the United States we may be inclined to read intra-Jewish squabbles and the Israeli-Palestinian clashes as unrelated. Actually, they are aspects of one systemic problem. The solution depends on communication between Palestinian Muslims, Christians and non-Orthodox Jews discussing and recognizing common interests.

For non-Orthodox Jews, the problem is a monolithic definition of Judaism that excludes plurality. For Palestinians the problem within Israel and the Occupied Territories is a monolithic definition of Israel as a Jewish state where non-Jews are a negligible minority who cannot challenge Jewish majority rule. These two problems are allied and converging. Visitors to Israel report a frequent comment, "I am not Jewish, I am an Israeli." The problem is exclusivity. Orthodox Jews who control the rabbinate in Israel and their allies among Orthodox Jews around the world are identifying non-Orthodox Jews as non-Jews.

The next step would be to make non-Orthodox Jews second class citizens in Israel, above Palestinian Israelis, but below Orthodox Jews and full citizens of what would become an Orthodox Jewish State ruled by an Orthodox reading of Jewish Law. This effort has caused a great deal of alienation among non-Orthodox Jews in America and elsewhere. But as every crisis, it is an opportunity. Now is the time to prepare for the twenty-first century demise of any kind of ethnic-religious exclusivity. It seems that the world's states will either move to the past with increasing fundamentalism and self-destruction or move to a future with open pluralism and multiculturalism. Palestinian Israelis want Israel to be defined as a pluralistic state religiously and ethnically so that it will no longer make second class citizens of Palestinian Israelis but can truly be a democratic state of all its citizens, equally embracing all kinds of Jews as well as non-Jews.

The logic of a monolithic ethnic-religious definition of Israel means exclusion of Palestinians on the one side, but also an increasing exclusivity toward non-Orthodox Jews on the other. It is time for non-Orthodox Jews to talk to Palestinians to recognize areas of common ground and common action.

This is your mission, Ms. Albright. Do not confuse the issue by attempting to make it a merely personal conflict between Mr. Benjamin Netanyahu and Mr. Yasir Arafat. If that is your mission, you will have wasted your time. The problems of Israel and Palestine are not personal. They are structural.

By the way, Secretary of State Albright, you might suggest something like: "There shall be no law respecting an establishment of religion, or prohibiting the free exercise thereof."

Repentance

September 23, 1997

The German nation has acknowledged the genocide of their holocaust. They have a few "crazies" still ranting and raving about the good old days, but as a nation they have both recognized and repented for the international crimes of the Third Reich, which took a minimum of 6 million innocent lives.

In the case of the United States, there is a problem. In the fifty years that have followed the holocaust, our country has been responsible for the death of more than 6 million innocent people. The killing agency in our case is the CIA which for fifty years has purportedly done the bidding of each sitting president. According to law, this secret agency operates at the discretion of the Commander in Chief.

Let us take a case in point: The Guatemalan Truth Commission began its work on July 31, 1997 and has only one year to carry out its mandate. This commission needs documents which are currently stored away in the archives of the CIA, the agency which overthrew the legally elected government of Jacobo Arbenz in 1954. This treachery became a model for our Latin American policy and was repeated in Cuba, Guyana, Chile, the Dominican Republic, Nicaragua, El Salvador and elsewhere.

What we need at this moment is an executive order from the President for the release of all files on human rights violations in Guatemala since our infamous invasion. The President tells us that many documents have already been released and that is true. "Many" refers to 1 percent of the documents being held by the CIA at this time. Some documents concerning abuses against individual United States citizens have been declassified but little meaningful information has been made public.

Many documents are so heavily blacked out that they are unreadable, some are simply blank sheets of paper while others are copies of letters sent by CIA supporters to their representatives and official form letters sent in response. Some documents regarding the 1954 coup against President Arbenz were made public in May of 1997. But there has been no release of information pertaining to the 200,000 official death squad murders and disappearances since 1980.

To achieve a lasting peace, the people of Guatemala need to know the truth about what happened in their country from 1954 to the present. Given the history of interference in Guatemalan affairs, the United States has a moral obligation to help in this search for truth by providing documents, memos, cables, military and intelligence reports and electronic intercepts. These documents are indispensable to the Truth Commission in clarifying the history of violence against the Guatemalan people. President Clinton can order this release of these documents with the stroke of a pen.

Failure to declassify is an obstruction of justice on the part of the United States government. The United States played a key role in eliminating Guatemalan democracy in 1954 and has maintained that beautiful country as a military police state ever since. We have the moral obligation to help the Guatemalan people confront their history, establish accountability and end the cycle of impunity.

This can be the beginning of our repentance. Without repentance our country will continue as a serial killer unable to say, "Stop me before I kill again." We must take a lesson from the people of Germany.

"The Only War We've Got"

September 30, 1997

A war system must have a war. Speaking of the drug war, an officer at the United States Southern Command in Panama said, "This is the only war we've got." We taxpayers have provided nearly $290 billion for the war on drugs, yet cocaine and heroin are more readily available and at cheaper prices than ever before. Personally, I doubted the accuracy of that figure, $290 billion. But the amount was confirmed in our most credible journal on the Americas, *NACLA* (North America Congress on Latin Americ); "Report on the Americas," September / October, 1997. The article is written and documented by Coletta Youngers, Senior Associate at the Washington Office on Latin America. In action reminiscent of the agent orange defoliation in Vietnam, the United States supplied turbo—thrush spray aircraft take off on a daily basis to drop a potent herbicide on fields of coca in the Guaviare region of Colombia. The coca will be dead within four hours. We do not know how much longer it takes the herbicide to poison people. As they watch their fields wither away, small coca farmers who are paid a pittance by the drug oligarchy have two options: They can go deeper into the jungle to grow more coca or they can join the ranks of Colombia's largest insurgency, the Revolutionary Armed Forces of Colombia (FARC). The local bishop, Belarmino Correa says, "The people fear that if they stop growing coca, they will die of hunger." Such a drug policy perpetuates coca production. As the Cold War faded, the drug war was born as a convenient rationale for continued engagement with Latin American militaries for training, assistance and joint operations. Such assistance has skyrocketed over the past year, with devastating consequences for the countries where the drug war is being waged. In the Andean region, the United States is forging ever closer ties with abusive police and military forces. In Peru and Colombia, Washington is providing assistance to military and intelligence services that are among the worst human rights violators in the hemisphere.

In various forms, United States intervention has marked this entire century in the Americas. This new model of intervention called the "drug war" has completely failed to stem the flow of illicit drugs into the United States. There is a glut as never before of both cocaine and heroin. The United States demand for cocaine can be met with just 14 percent of the world's coca crop. The *Washington Post* claims that a year's heroin supply for United States users can be made from poppies grown in just twenty square miles of farmland. A year's cocaine supply for the United States can be stashed in thirteen truck trailers.

Coca has been part of the Andean culture for 5,000 years. The leaf is a mild stimulant and is used in tea and a host of legal substances. The chemicals necessary for transformation of coca into cocaine are generally imported. There appears to be little or no control over these chemicals without which cocaine cannot be produced. President Clinton's current Drug Czar, General Barry McCaffrey, announced that the Administration would eliminate worldwide illicit coca production within the next decade. Such a claim smacks of cult leadership, it has no basis in reality. Unfortunately we do not have the luxury of laughing at the general, this kind of propaganda could be used as a justification for future military interventions. The supply side approach to controlling drug abuse defies all logic. The centerpiece of our government's effort must be to decrease demand through treatment, education and rehabilitation. Let us not waste another $290 billion on the drug war fraud.

A Letter
to General Barry McCaffrey

October 21, 1997

Dear General Barry McCaffrey:

We have read the reports on your recent visit to Colombia. It seems that speaking to the Colombian military and the government of Colombia leaves one almost completely misinformed regarding the actual reality of that country since 1947.

We read your comments printed in *El Tiempo*, the Bogotá daily for October 12, where you say the United States is ready to enter a new phase in the war against illegal drugs by joining the fight against Colombia's rebels.

General, if the rebels of Colombia are completely destroyed together with every one of their sympathizers by way of an all out war, with napalm, white phosphorous, agent orange, 1,000 pound bombs, carpet bombing, summary execution of leaders, interrogation by torture, massacre of noncombatants and atomic weapons, there will be little or no impact on the drug business. The drug business, sir, is in the hands of the Colombian oligarchy, the Colombian military and the Colombian paramilitary. There is no question at all about the rebels taxing the growers of coca. They do that. They also tax the growers of rice, beans, and corn. If you were quoted correctly by *Reuters*, you asserted that the rebels are not politically motivated. That is an amazing statement. Just what might their motivation be?

You mention the involvement of the paramilitary in the drug trade and that is correct. It is essential to understand that the paramilitary are in-sync with the Colombian military just as the death squads of El Salvador and Guatemala were in-sync with the armies of those countries. I do not know of any nongovernmental organization or human rights organization in or outside of Colombia that doubts this relationship. The marriage between the paramilitary and the military has been consummated by the formation and legalization of Convivir.

You certainly are aware of Amnesty International's documentation regarding the diversion of our Drug War aid to counterinsurgency operations. General McCaffrey, $290 billion of our citizen's hard earned money has been wasted on the drug war. The result of this waste is seen in a dramatic increase of cocaine and heroin on our streets at increasingly lower prices. If this "war" is ever to be won, it will be won by rehabilitation of addicts. We must stop using the drug war facade as an excuse to fight wars against the poor domestically or internationally.

There is an answer to this violence of Colombia. The new United Nations Human Rights Office in Bogotá made it clear to us on our recent visit, that their agency could establish a peace negotiations team. They added such a venture, for the United Nations would only be possible if President Clinton puts the necessary pressure on the Colombian government and military to accept such a team. Please encourage the President to use his good office to end this fifty year old conflict by engaging a United Nations negotiating team.

Homies Unidos

October 28, 1997

The war against gangs has been about as effective as the war against drugs and by that I mean that both wars have failed.

Of all the factors contributing to gangs and their epidemic of violence in Los Angeles, none is more significant than the staggering rate of unemployment. Unemployment and per capita income are more closely associated with the city's gang homicide rate, than race or education. This study is reported into today's *Los Angeles Times* and will be presented today at UCLA.

Once young people receive a clear message that they are excluded from the club of middle-class society, they will form their own clubs. Call them "gangs" if you will. The effort must not be to destroy the association of young people but to include them in the club of the larger society. This demands available work.

We are currently learning a great deal from gang members who have been deported to El Salvador. Some seventeen years ago, young families came here from El Salvador when their villages were being bombed under the command and control of the United States. As part of an excluded under-class, many of the youth joined the Eighteenth Street and Marasalvatrucha gangs.

Now, in the nineties, some of these young people have been identified as undocumented and have been deported to El Salvador. But because of living most of their lives in Los Angeles, they know little about their own country and for self-protection they reconstruct their gangs in El Salvador. But there is some good news. An approach has been taken toward the Los Angeles gangs now in El Salvador which is so effective that it should be adopted by law enforcement and social services in the United States.

Magdaleno Rose-Avila, a U.S. citizen with years of experience in Amnesty International and the U.S. Peace Corps, has developed Homies Unidos or Home Boys and Home Girls United as a bridge between gangs in Los Angeles and El Salvador. His unique approach is not an attempt to destroy the gangs but to calm the gangs. Calming means taking on a nonviolent life style. Magdaleno wants to first take the tattoos off of their hearts before taking the tattoos off their bodies.

In El Salvador, the revolutionaries of the National Liberation Front of Farabundo Marti (FLMN), have also found a calm and nonviolent approach to political change. Members of the FMLN are working with the gangs now in El Salvador and directing their attention to human rights and social justice. They are in frequent dialogue with the Salvadoran police, the government and the people in general. The dress and appearance of the gang members is not the central issue. The issue is their conduct. As they come under the leadership of Homies Unidos, they change into the new and calm life style. Those who violate the discipline of this new direction lose their good standing until they prove themselves calm.

With the cooperation of the INS, calmed members of the two largest gangs will continue to communicate between Los Angeles and El Salvador. This approach does not attempt to destroy the style of dress, or the gang itself but to calm behavior by directing lives away from vengeance and toward social justice, human rights and employment.

Iraq

November 4, 1997

Both the *Los Angeles Times* and the *New York Times* have given their approval for a renewed attack on Iraq. This means that some savage act of retaliation has been sanctified.

What is Iraq asking? Simply that U.S. citizens not be members of the inspection teams. Compliance with this request would not be difficult. An agreement declaring that the inspections will be carried out by citizens of any of the other states of the United Nations would suffice. This is really not too much to ask. In a spirit of "might-makes-right," our nation has taken over 1 million lives in Iraq, most of them noncombatants. It is truly touching to see the piety of these great papers. Where were they when the highest body of the United Nations, the International Court of Justice ordered the United States to pay $17 billion in retaliation to Nicaragua for war crimes during the devastation of the Contra War? Our country simply ignored the order and thereby devastated the jurisdiction of the World Court.

Our attack on Iraq was also a war crime. George Bush could have been brought before the new International Criminal Court if it existed in 1991. How do we know that? Our former Attorney General Ramsey Clark conducted hearings in twenty United Nations countries and thirty cities in the United States. This was the International War Crimes Tribunal regarding U.S. conduct in the Gulf War. On Saturday, February 29, 1992 in New York, the tribunal's international panel of judges concluded that President George Bush was guilty of nineteen charges brought against him by the Commission of Inquiry.

Here is charge No. 10: *President Bush obstructed justice and corrupted United Nations functions as a means of securing power to commit crimes against peace and war crimes.*

The evidence supporting this charge was overwhelming. It included both bribes and threats.

These same newspapers which published today's bloody editorials refused to cover the decision of the International War Crimes Tribunal and thereby were guilty of a breach in their professional responsibility to the public. The foreign press covered the Tribunal as an important news story and was present as an international panel of twenty-two judges, gave the pronouncement of guilt before an audience of 1,500 people in New York.

The 5,000 to 6,000 deaths caused monthly by the combination of bomb damage and United Nations sanctions are a continuing crime against humanity. The sanctions are killing infants, children, the sick and the elderly. Actually there was no war in Iraq there was only a merciless slaughter by 110,000 aerial sorties dropping 88,000 tons of explosives. 93 percent of those explosives fell freely on a defenseless country.

Have we forgotten that our country supported Iraq against Iran for ten years in one of the major wars of this century? But the power of unrestrained corporate petroleum capital demanded that their representative do their bidding.

What about Saddam's threat to shoot down the U-2 spy planes? Such surveillance can be conducted by the Air Force of any other United Nations Member. The decision to comply with Iraq's request must be made in the light of a criminal holocaust conducted by our country against that nation.

Let us continue the inspections and leave the Yankees at home.

The International War Crimes Tribunal

November 11, 1997

On this Veteran's Day let us remember the victims of Gulf War Illness and seek the maturity to be more than a cheering section for the lies and devastation for which our nation is responsible.

The Third Reich acknowledged its unspeakable horrors and Germany has developed into a productive and peaceful nation. We have not gone through that catharsis and its seems that the time to do so is now.

The history of the U-2 gave us the mother of all lies. It was May 1, 1960 and Gary Powers was flying his U-2 spy plane over the Soviet Union; he was shot down. President Eisenhower denied any such flights. Six days later Khrushchev produced the U-2 and Gary Powers. President Eisenhower then admitted the lie. Within a week what we had called an unthinkable falsehood was transformed into a sovereign right.

The continuation of inspections in Iraq and the rest of the world including the United States is very much in order. All Iraq is asking at this time is for some balance in the make-up of the inspection teams. But the corporate war mongers who own and censor our media are salivating for more blood, for more Gulf War Illness and another 250,000 dead Iraqi children.

With the same clarity and intensity of the Bertrand Russell Tribunal on the Indochina War, former Attorney General Ramsey Clark conducted his tribunal on the Gulf War in twenty nations and thirty cities of the United States. I was in Baghdad, in January of 1991 and served as one of hundreds of witnesses leading to the judgement of February 29, 1992 in New York. Here is a summary of that judgement:

President Bush intended to draw Iraq into a conflict which would be used to justify U.S. military action and lead to permanent U.S. domination of the Persian Gulf. The president acted to prevent any interference with his plan to destroy Iraq economically and militarily.

President Bush obstructed justice and corrupted United Nations functions as a means of securing power to commit crimes against peace and war crimes. The United States was guilty of the following:

- Intentionally bombing and destroying:
  - ▶ Civilian life
  - ▶ Commercial and business districts
  - ▶ Schools
  - ▶ Hospitals
  - ▶ Mosques
  - ▶ Churches
  - ▶ Shelters
  - ▶ Residential areas
  - ▶ Historical sites
  - ▶ Private vehicles
  - ▶ Civilian government offices

- Intentionally bombing indiscriminately throughout Iraq.

- Intentionally using excessive force, killing soldiers seeking to surrender, unarmed and far from any combat zone.

- Using prohibited weapons capable of mass destruction and inflicting indiscriminate death and unnecessary suffering against both military and civilian targets.

- Intentionally attacking installations in Iraq containing dangerous substances.

- Waging war on the environment.

These are but a few of the crimes identified by the International Tribunal. In view of the context of its crimes against Iraq, the United States has lost any moral authority to dominate inspections of that country. I suggest that we pay our dues to the United Nations, assist the organization with necessary technical support and let the inspections continue without the threat of further war crimes.

Goodbye Thomas Robert Malthus

November 25, 1997

Thomas Robert Malthus, you may now rest in peace. Your flawed theory of 1798 stating that growth of population always outruns the growth of food production is twice-dead.

Thomas Robert Malthus became a professor of history and political economy at the East India Company's college in England. He was a close friend of David Ricardo who gave us the so-called "Iron Law of Wages." This quack theory has been preserved to the present to promote the idea that wages must be kept at the lowest level possible to maintain a proper political economy. The social basis of Ricardo's thinking is Thomas Robert Malthus. If there are too many people, we must make it as tough as possible on them, this will lead to less of them and will also maximize profit for the owners of property and production. This kind of talk might still be used to promote a tenured position at places like the East India Company's College. But the twentieth century was to be the Century of Progress and progressive academics ruled out Malthus as a myth for the first fifty years.

After two massive world wars and endless imperial wars, East India-Company style scholars began to see real value in digging up Malthus once again. They called it "overpopulation." Self proclaimed experts began to think they knew how many people the earth could support. They considered petroleum and cattle as essential for human existence. Instead of saying we have too much petroleum in the atmosphere and too many cattle on the soil, they determined we have too many people. Actually alternative sources of energy abound. We do not need petroleum and we do not need cattle. We need energy and food.

The very economic powers that gave us the East India Company revived the Malthusian theory. At their highest point of hysteria, population explosion theorists claimed that overpopulation was a greater threat than nuclear war.

The population bomb theory helped to justify war, to justify low wages and to give a rationale for the pollution of the globe. But population is not responsible for these problems. Unbridled pollution is the result of deregulation.

Let us try to reason. There certainly is a very poor distribution of people on the globe. Too many people live in large cities. They can be given financial inducements to move to rural areas. The world's population is now about 5.7 billion people. Barring the very real possibility of nuclear accident, by the middle of the next century, the population will stand at about 9.4 billion.

Recently leading demographers from around the world met at the United Nations to study a new concern: *Will there soon be too few of us?* Joseph Chamie, director of the United Nations population division which organized the conference states that by 2015, 67 percent of the world's population will have a fertility rate below the replacement level. Surely, people who are in misery will have as many children as possible for self-protection and security. Religion does not seem to have much to do with it. Italy has the world's lowest fertility rate followed by Spain. As education expands, women become liberated and the population will continue to implode. To replace the existing population couples must average 2.1 children. The only reason the population of the United States is increasing is immigration. Without the blessing of immigration we would be a declining population. And a population decline is on the chart in the very near future.

Goodbye for the second time Malthus. May you rest in peace and may the East India Company rest with you.

Remember Pearl Harbor

December 9, 1997

Do you remember Pearl Harbor? I do. On that day of infamy the United States became united as never before. We were one family, determined to stop an aggressor and willing to do whatever it took to defend our cities and nation. We sang happy songs and made sacrifices joyfully for victory over fascism.

Our intelligence agencies should have made a note at that time saying, "Nothing unites a people more completely than to be bombed by a foreign power." The British went through this unifying experience even before we did.

So we developed the cry, "Remember Pearl Harbor!" But we have failed to remember the essence of Pearl Harbor; no matter how many differences a nation has internally, an external attack will bring national unity.

How could we forget this message so quickly? Instead of remembering Pearl Harbor, we forgot it. Had we remembered Pearl Harbor, we would have understood how our bombs unified the people of Indochina. Had we remembered Pearl Harbor we would have understood how our bombs have unified the people of Iraq.

Our forgetting Pearl Harbor reached its apex this week. Our leader has given an ultimatum to the world; *the United States will not reject nuclearism*. As a matter of fact, the President has declared that we will retain a psychotic policy of first strike. If for example, we invade a small nation, and if that nation attempts to defend itself with something we choose to call "chemical weapons," we are now committed to using nuclear weapons against them. In complete disrespect for language, our policy implies that nuclear weapons are not chemical weapons. If nuclear weapons are not chemical weapons, just what are they?

Trying to translate Pentagonese into simple English we read, "If you do not allow us to invade your country unmolested, we will annihilate you."

Now do we understand why our State Department has to warn U.S. citizens that it is not safe for them to travel abroad? Must our citizens become the victims of an international revulsion created by our foreign policy?

What is the answer? Seize the moral leadership. Lead in abolishing nuclear weapons worldwide. It is now technically possible to do so. If we fail to take the moral leadership, it is only a matter of time before some terrorists from Oklahoma or elsewhere take out their rage on us with nuclear suitcases.

Mr. President, we demand moral leadership and not threats of massacre. What your new policy says to every other nation is, "Prove to us you don't have chemical weapons, prove to us you don't have nuclear weapons and if you don't comply, we will destroy you." You will have done nothing by this policy but make our country an isolated and indefensible pariah to the world. Why should we be exempt from the conditions you are placing on other nations?

Our militaristic policy is uniting the world in opposition. According to today's *New York Times*, bitterness toward the United States has led Egypt to join the Islamic Conference currently being held in Iran. Even more surprising, Vice President Taha Yasin Ramadan of Iraq will attend the Iran gathering as the highest ranking Iraqi visitor to Iran since the bloody war of 1980-1988. Let us remember the essence of Pearl Harbor.

Money

December 17, 1997

Concern about the stability of the international monetary system has even reached the mass media. What is surprising about such a system is that it works at all. Monetary instability has been identified as causal of previous wars. The avoidance of armed conflict requires a new look at international economics.

An impossible jungle of jargon and questionable formulas is not necessary to identify some problems with the current international monetary system.

We must not continue to have only seven, eight or nine nations at international economic summits. Every nation with a currency must be admitted. The exclusion of the majority of the world's nations from economic summit meetings clearly gives undue influence to nations which are already dominant. Money is not a constant. The variable in any society depends on just what services can be removed from the money economy. If we follow the lead of the Universal Declaration of Human Rights of the United Nations we would understand the wisdom of removing health care and education from consumer concerns. Health care and education belong in the realm of international infrastructure, not as commodities. By removing these two items from the money economy, we will have defused the importance of money and thereby limited the potential for crime.

Nothing demonstrates the immorality of unrestrained capital more clearly than limiting the access to health and education. The terrorism of denying emergency care to the indigent and the greed of sending sick people home rather than continuing needed hospital care must be terminated. The mantra "We don't cover that," designed by profit hungry insurance companies has no place in a humane health care system.

Regarding education; Jonathan Kozol has described the Savage Inequalities of our educational system in his book by the same name. Education must be part of an international infrastructure just like highways and streetlights. Nothing is sadder than to meet a person who is obviously a genius and to know they will never have access to the education they deserve.

It is time for our insular, protected and deprived economy to observe the success of nations where carefully regulated capital has given the lie to David Ricardo's Iron Law of Wages.

Perhaps it is the endless corporate drivel on TV that makes workers in the United States unaware that countries now delivering health care and education as part of their national infrastructure also offer two months paid vacation to their workers. Indeed, a Scandinavian model could cure the cycle of unrestrained and uncontrolled capital being bailed out with our tax money as we feed unregulated corporations the money they need to savage the environment, our bodies and our minds.

Christmas

December 23, 1997

At a recent meeting of the Santa Monica City Council an item regarding the right of dogs to run free in the park took precedence over the national emergency of homelessness. It could have happened in any American city. It seems, however, to represent the moral bankruptcy in which we are living.

It is not an accident that dogs are given priority over people in Santa Monica. It is part of an attempt to erase the homeless from our agenda. Time and again I have seen homeless people wait patiently for up to six hours to have their urgent issue once again delayed or ignored by the Santa Monica City Council. Some of those waiting so patiently are sick, some are mentally ill, many are undernourished. This time they were exited to the streets and told to come back next month. Many of the people present had just been forcibly expelled from an abandoned hotel. As a result of the occupation, their leadership is being vigorously prosecuted. Representatives of the homeless community have every reason to expect that their concerns will be once again ignored or delayed at the next council meeting as they have been in the past.

We appreciate the affection people have for their dogs. We think, however, that human tragedy deserves priority. The dogs in question were well housed and well fed. The most brutal Latin American dictatorships tolerate the occupation of unused areas for encampments of the homeless. They know that people must live somewhere. But the richest city in the richest country in the world refuses to treat the ongoing brutalization, not of dogs, but of people.

Until such time as our city, state and nation can deal as humanely with the homeless as the Humane Society deals with dogs, we must allow people to camp in parks and beaches. Once functional alternatives are established, we can rightfully enforce anti-camping legislation.

Mayor Holbrook commented, "One thing is clear to me is that the members of the public believe they control our agenda." Mayor

Holbrook, if the members of the public do not control your agenda, exactly how are you serving the people who selected you as their servant?

Councilman Genser commented, "Look, if people are going to keep talking about homelessness, it's keeping us from doing our business." Councilman Genser, homelessness is your business!

As we prepare to celebrate the birth of a homeless child why do not we do a little soul searching about our values. Do we really believe there is no room for "them?" We know this is a national issue. The demand for food and housing has never been as great as in 1997. It is incumbent, therefore, on the City Council of Santa Monica and all city councils, to demand help from their state governments and from the Federal Government to meet this urgent state of emergency.

Mexico

December 30, 1997

The strategy and style of the massacre in Chiapas bears the marks of training exported from the United States.

Last year the U.S. Army 7th Special Forces Group began a massive training program for Mexican Special Forces. 3,200 Mexican soldiers received this training in terror at Fort Bragg, North Carolina. The trainers were the same who committed endless human rights abuses in Honduras and El Salvador in the 1980s. They trained the Contras. The mastermind behind Mexico's counterinsurgency strategy in Chiapas, Gen. Mario Renan Castillo Fernandez, received his instruction at Fort Bragg. He also served as an honorary witness at a ceremony where the state government of Chiapas handed over 1/2 million dollars to the paramilitary group *Paz y Justicia*.

The two biggest recipients of U.S. military aid in the Americas are Colombia and Mexico. These are also the two Latin American countries with the greatest number of paramilitary massacres. Now the paramilitary do nothing in Colombia or Mexico without the approval of the military. Just as in El Salvador and Guatemala, the paramilitary are assigned the acts of terrorism which would embarrass the public relations office of the official military.

The following seems clear:

1. The financing and training of paramilitary is being taught and has been taught at the School of the Americas in Fort Benning and by Special Forces at Ft. Bragg. We have the instruction manuals to prove this.

2. Our military has now openly announced that its recent gifts of Huey Helicopters in the name of the war on drugs can be used for counterinsurgency.

President Zedillo is slavishly obedient to economic policies dictated by the International Monetary Fund and the World Bank and Wall Street which kill thousands of indigenous and poor Mexican citizens every year through hunger and curable diseases. He only becomes defensive when the killing is done not by banks but by bullets. How can President Clinton complain? He is responsible for the endless supply of weapons to Mexico. Did he think the weapons would not be used?

Similar and worse atrocities taking place in Colombia have led to even more U.S. aid to that country. Mexico has every reason to believe that more massacres will result in more military aid from the United States.

After years of using the drug war as a facade, both Mexican and United States military officials now say there is nothing to stop the transfer of American trained army officers to special forces units that might be deployed against insurgents in states like Guerrero and Chiapas. The war of the rich against the poor continues in Mexico and the United States.

Acteal

January 13, 1998

This week I stood at a mound of dirt over some forty-five massacred bodies buried at Acteal in the municipality of Chenalho in Chiapas, Mexico. I lit some candles in their memory and shuffled through children's homework papers scored with bullet holes. Today we have news from San Cristóbal de las Casas that police commander Felipe Vazquez Espinoza has provided a direct link between government officials and the massacre. Vazquez reported to Nuevo Amanecer Press that he had been ordered to check if civilians carrying illegal weapons were members of the Institutional Revolutionary Party (PRI, the party of President Zedillo). If they were PRI members the police commander was instructed not to detain them. Mexico's Office of the Attorney General has yet to name any state officials as suspects.

We interviewed Bishop Samuel Ruiz Garcia at length and were struck by how much he reminded us of the late Archbishop Oscar Arnulfo Romero of El Salvador. He said that the attack at Acteal was the twenty-fifth such atrocity since April of 1997.

We and much of Mexico were astounded by the hysterical effort of Gen. Jose Gomez Salazar, Commander of the Mexican Military in Chiapas to "prove" a link between Bishop Ruiz and the Zapatista rebels. His proof was to find a secret supply of weapons topped with religious texts in the Tojolabal language which were translated by the bishop. The texts included the gospel according to St. Mark, a hymnal, and a catechism. The diocese of San Cristóbal accepted the charge that the books were theirs and asked just how such a find was to be considered as proof of the bishop's alleged involvement in an armed movement.

While the vast majority of the Mexican media, government and people considered the General's claims to be stupid, the charge remains a clear threat to the life of Bishop Samuel Ruiz. Fanatical members of the PRI paramilitary death squads can take such a charge as a mandate to kill the bishop.

After hearing these charges we proceeded to the general's command post in Tuxtla Gutiérrez, asking for an interview. We were told he was in the field and could not see us. But what we did see at the command post were large posters of approval for the very death squads that killed the citizens of Acteal.

We were reminded of the exact same relationships between death squads and military which we had witnessed in El Salvador, Guatemala and Colombia. This methodology was developed by the United States in 1961 and has continued to the present. We refer to *Field Manual 100-20*, Chapter Six, "Foreign Internal Conflicts," (United States Army College, Fort Leavenworth, Kansas, 1997.)

Any U.S. citizen who is aware of the role of our government in the killing of innocent people in Mexico would surely say, "We are better than that." The strongest response to the bloody militarization of Mexico and the example of militant moral authority of the highest level was shown by the women of X'oyep and other villages of Chiapas. With their bare hands they physically pushed heavily armed Mexican troops out of their villages and they will continue to do so, even at the cost of their lives.

Driven from Their Land
in Choco, Colombia

January 20, 1998

This week a tape aired, which was edited from material recorded by Blase Bonpane in Uraba, Colombia. Refugee Voices did the edit and aired the tape on forty-seven radio stations. A transcript of that tape follows.

Abstract:

Driven from their Land in Choco, Colombia (3:54)

At the end of February 1997, paramilitary troops ordered families of Choco to leave their farms. After walking a few weeks in the jungle, the people found refuge in the sports stadium of Turbo. Two children and a mother tell what this upheaval has done to them.[†]

Transcript: (Volume 51, Module No. 3)

Featuring testimony from displaced persons from Choco, Colombia, located temporarily in the city of Turbo.

MUSIC AND INTRO: This is Refugee Voices. Bringing you the stories of refugees regardless of race, religion or politics. (20 seconds)

NARRATOR: The children of Choco, Colombia, live temporarily in the sports stadium of the city of Turbo. They are witness to the trauma of having had to leave their homes abruptly, because of paramilitary operations on their land.

CHILD NO. 1: *Nos dijeron que a tres días nos salieramos. . . . Seco.* They told us that we had three days in which to leave. What made me most afraid was that we got all of our things together at the River

---

[†] (The original taped interviews were recorded by Dr. Blase Bonpane of the Office of the Americas, Los Angeles, California)

Seco. Then they sent a man to ask us if we were leaving, . . . Almost everyone was on the road when they began to bomb our homes.

NARRATOR: Many households of Choco lost family members during this forced expulsion. One family of seven children lost their father.

CHILD NO. 2: *Mi papa un día se fue a trabajar . . . no aparecio más.* That day my father went to work and they took him from there and he hasn't appeared since. They killed him and here we are. We don't have anything. Every day my mother feels very sad. We, too, because we are left without our father.

NARRATOR: This displacement of over 200 people from the country-side of Choco occurred at the end of February in 1997. Now, in the makeshift shelter at the sports stadium in Turbo, they are housed side by side, with little food and inadequate medicine. One of the mothers explains clearly and graphically their current situation.

WOMAN: *Nos da mucho pesar porqué sufrimos mucho . . .* Here, we are very depressed; we suffer a lot. Where we were, we always didn't have everything we needed, but we lived with the little we had. It is painful for us when one of the children asks: "Mommy, give me this thing," or "mommy, I want that." You touch your pocket and you don't have what you need to buy that little thing that the child needs. It makes you feel bad. It is a shame because the ones who are paying are the children. We are not accustomed to suffering pain like this. Therefore it hits us like a glass of cold water.

NARRATOR: The people of Choco have been living in this upheaval for over nine months. They long to return to their farms but the lack of peaceful conditions prevent them from doing so. In the meantime they seek international assistance to alleviate their physical needs and to support them in their efforts to regain their former lives. The following song will help us to remember their hope of returning.

Music begins softly so that translation can be heard—
The Choco has many children. Many children has the Choco. I am one, you [are] too. As brothers and sisters we will return.

Music turns up—
El Choco tiene muchos hijos. Muchos hijos tiene El Choco Yo soy uno, tu también. Como hermanos retornaremos.

NARRATOR: For more information, call Refugee Voices at 1-800-688-REFUGEE.

End of Transcript

Ethics

January 27, 1998

Let us be sure that our children understand the ethical compass of government so they will never be tempted to imitate it. Certain criminal elements are now plotting, planning and conspiring to commit murder in Iraq. They wish to extend the Iraq massacre of 1991 into 1998. They are not at all repentant of the death dealing embargo they have imposed on Iraqi children. They are preparing to expand it from denial of food to snuffing out lives by terrorist bombings. This government amorality is reported as if it were a noble act. It is, in fact an act of infamy.

Iraq was asking for fewer U.S. inspectors. Now we will fight a war to deny them their request, and we will in the midst of it destroy any hope of finding what we were looking for in the first place. This will only further alienate our former allies and make the United States more isolated internationally.

There is some similarity between the adversaries of Saddam Hussein and the case of Bill Clinton. In both cases the adversaries want proof of a presumption. Mr. Saddam Hussein, prove to us that you do not have nuclear weapons. Prove that you do not have biological weapons. Of course we have them and Israel has them, but we want you to prove to us that you do not have them. (Personally I think Iraq would cooperate if we supported the abolition of nuclear weapons and complete international inspection). Mr. Clinton, prove to me that you are not sleeping with your secretary.

This style of adversarial and accusatory questioning is becoming institutionalized and has the potential for the formation of a police state. This is an inquisition. Logical sequences from the Iraq and Clinton accusations would be the following: Prove to me you do not have dope in your house or I will blow up your house. Prove to me you are not a terrorist. We are losing it. Our outrageous and dictatorial behavior overseas is coming home to roost. Our paranoia can be fatal, "Prove to me you are not trying to kill me."

Certainly more brash accusations can be made in a few moments than can be answered in a lifetime. But let us attempt to look at the scales of ethics. Which is worse? Killing a million Iraqis or engaging in consensual sex? One does not have to justify promiscuity or the customary lying that goes with promiscuity. But it takes an extremely naive and easily manipulated public who will fail to see that the paramount evil is killing 3 million people in Indochina. The evil is killing a million people in the Americas. The evil is killing a million people in Iraq and imposing an embargo that continues to kill Iraqi children. Can we attempt to grow out of our ethical immaturity and weigh alleged traditional presidential indiscretion, dalliance and womanizing against cold blooded, calculated, hateful and racist murder? Indeed, patriotism is the last refuge of scoundrels.

A Lose / Lose Situation

February 3, 1998

Let us take a look at the logic of the current U.S. diplomacy.

Current Diplomacy:

- Secretary of Defense Cohen says that air strikes will not topple Saddam Hussein.

- Kuwait, which was the excuse for the 1991 massacre in Iraq, does not support any U.S. military action.

- The Secretary General of the Arab League states any such military action is rejected and unacceptable.

- The foreign minister of Egypt Amr Moussa states such military action will create more problems than it will solve.

The *Los Angeles Times* correctly stated on January 31 that Saddam Hussein would welcome a major military assault. In the wake of such uncalled for slaughter, international public opinion would insist on an end to the sanctions which are destroying Iraq. We might add, his people would continue to see him as a crucified messiah. France and Russia are opposed to military action. International sympathy would all be on the side of the Iraqi people.

Our street gangs would be happy with the assault, it would instruct them that if there is one bad guy in an opposing gang. It is best to kill the whole gang.

Our role in the Middle East will be destroyed forever. James Placke, former diplomat in Iraq and now with the Cambridge Energy Research Associates says, "Afterward, Saddam can crawl out of his fox hole and say: 'You didn't get me. With all those ships and all that firepower, you couldn't accomplish your purpose.' Then who will be perceived as the winner?"

After such a strike, Hussein could also kick out all the UN inspectors and blame it on Washington. The French envoy put it well when he said, "Demonstrating Iraqis could then take down the monitoring equipment, so the danger is that a military strike could end up jeopardizing all the efforts we've made for seven years, we'd be far worse off than before."

Aside from the international opposition to our air strikes, there is absolute international opposition to any consideration of U.S. ground attacks in Iraq. Then why is it that the polls claim the U.S. citizens support an attack on Iraq? William Randolph Hearst gave us the answer to that question at the time of the Spanish American War. Media tailors the news to suit corporations which pay for media. The largest corporations make money on war. It is good for profit. Therefore the news is fit to print just the way they want it to be. But wait, the media says that many countries are privately supporting the coming war, while they publicly oppose it. That particular approach, which was sold to us prior to the 1991 massacre, was created by intelligence agencies. Unfortunately such agencies as the CIA are well represented on the foreign desks of our major papers.

Give peace, logic and morality a chance!

Unabomber

February 10, 1998

The Unabomber has been found and it is us. We unabombed Vietnam. We unabombed Panama, Grenada and Libya. We unabombed Iraq once before, and now the forces of empire have become a cheering section for another unabombing massacre.

What logic. Our Ambassador to the United Nations, William Richardson is saying that the silent majority of foreign nations support our actions. This is twice-dead Nixonian propaganda right out of Vietnam. And here is Mrs. Albright crossing land and sea to find one convert and when she does, to paraphrase the *New Testament*, she makes that nation a two-fold child of hell. International war mongering has replaced international diplomacy.

If you were outside of the United States, as I was last week, you would have seen headlines stating Mr. Yeltsin's opinion that a U.S. strike at Iraq could trigger a Third World War. Of course it could. World War I began in the wake of the assassination of a single Archduke.

As the Russians make serious efforts to seek peace, just as they did before the massacre of 1991, our highly censored press decides that Russian efforts are ludicrous. See Carol Williams' piece in the *Los Angeles Times* for February 9, 1998. The Russian peace delegation is declared "a group of grandstanding nationalist lawmakers." The fifty deputies from Russia are said to be angry because of their "stalled publicity stunt." Their hunger-strike is disparaged and even their aircraft is belittled. Whatever the Russian motives, they are in search of a peaceful solution. Can we say the same of Mrs. Albright?

What we are about to do in Iraq not only has the potential to trigger a Third World War, it can also lead to an unintentional nuclear exchange between Russia and the United States. Former Senator Nunn considers the potential for an accidental nuclear exchange more perilous now than at any time during the Cold War. Add to that existing peril a unilateral bombing frenzy by the United States and the possibility of losing Chicago or New York increases dramatically.

Then we have the comments of Senator McCain. He is telling us that we must have fortitude knowing that innocent people are going to be killed. I do not think it requires fortitude to take the responsibility for killing innocent people, I think it requires a policy of state terrorism.

Our blindness is a sign of profound moral decay. Theodore Kazinski has killed some, Timothy McVey has killed more and now our government wishes to establish terrorism as a national policy. Should such treachery begin, I recommend that all activity cease in our country until the mass murder stops. That is right, a general strike. The good people who live in this country are not murderers. Corrupt officials are.

Mr. President

February 17, 1998

Here are some thoughts taken from a letter signed by International Physicians for the Prevention of Nuclear War, the Office of the Americas and many other organizations:

Dear Mr. President,

Please consider what you are threatening to do.

You are threatening the lives of hundreds of thousands of innocent people, including women and children, to punish one man, a dictator. You are threatening to destroy Iraq's chemical and biological arsenals by bombing them; therefore, releasing their poisonous contents into the atmosphere to be breathed in by the Iraqi people and the people of other countries. You have not even excluded the ultimate threat: the use of nuclear weapons on civilians.

You admitted this morning that you will undermine inspection by your attack, just as such inspections were undermined by the 1991 massacre. United Nations inspectors have done an excellent job, in fact they are still present in Iraq. History will say that simply lessening the number of U.S. inspectors could have averted a second Iraq Massacre. United Nations inspectors have destroyed more weapons of mass destruction than our dropping 88,500 tons of bombs in 1991. Are you going to use even more bombs this time?

UNICEF verifies that 1,211,285 Iraqi children died of embargo related causes between August of 1990 and August of 1991, which together with the bombing represents one of the great holocausts of the twentieth century.

The depravation of food and medicine by a foreign power (The United States) has only served to draw the Iraqi people closer to their leader. 4,500 children are dying every month from starvation and treatable diseases because of the embargo. Your barbaric final solution mirrors the cruelty, contradiction, brutality, ignorance, and racism of the Third Reich.

What depravity! Mordechai Vanunu is held for twelve years in solitary confinement for telling the world that Israel has secretly developed nuclear weapons, and now the Iraqi people must be annihilated because their leader has allegedly tried to build similar weapons. This is the moment for international disarmament. Weapons of mass destruction can be eliminated from the entire world. The United States can lead in this effort. It has been proven that inspections can work, let them be used internationally. We will not assist international disarmament by initiating another war of aggression against Iraq. History tells us clearly that any power hungry demagogue can start a war. It also tells us that years and decades of terrorist activity could follow. U.S. citizens are already in danger by virtue of their status in many countries of the world. A war started for the frivolous reason of refusing to limit our inspectors rather than empowering competent technicians from anywhere else in the world, will place all citizens in grave danger of retaliatory attacks wherever we may be.

Mr. President, we beg you to see reason. Do not bomb Iraq.

Kofi Annan

February 25, 1998

It is time to dust off a Nobel Peace Prize for Kofi Annan. I think he has saved the world from a Third World War. We have some questions to ask President Clinton as he arrives in Beverly Hills this week:

1. *Why was no diplomat sent to Iraq from the United States?* Any first year student in Foreign Service would have suggested this as step number one.

2. Iraq is an ash of a nation almost obliterated from the face of the earth by 88,500 tons of bombs. What masterpiece of military intelligence determined that it was a threat to the rest of the world? Was it not obvious that none of Iraq's immediate neighbors shared the hysteria of Tom Brocaw and Dan Rather (Dan was so eager to please his sponsors that he accidentally started the war by satellite).

3. Mr. President, were you unaware that the chemical and biological arsenal used by Iraq was sent directly from the United States to our ally, Saddam Hussein, for use in the Iran-Iraq War of the 80s?

4. Why was there no objection when Iraq used these weapons during the war with Iran? Saddam was not even taken off of the CIA payroll when he used these illegal weapons. Now, you are searching for the same material that we sent to Iraq in the first place.

5. Are you are aware that Iraq did not use these weapons during the 1991 massacre? You certainly knew that if Iraq were to use any of these weapons as a death rattle, that Israel would have responded with a nuclear attack. Such an attack would have probably been the beginning of World War III.

6. Do you have any understanding of the history of war? It is clear that any third rate demagogue can start a conflict. Unfortunately, such opportunists have no idea how to stop what they have started. Do you know that many wars are started by a contrivance?

A hundred years ago people were shouting, "Remember the Maine." But no one knew how or why the Maine was sunk. It was a contrivance. Lyndon Johnson lied about a Tonkin Gulf Crisis that never existed. It was a contrivance. As citizens we must be on our guard that we are not victimized again by some contrivance allowing your generals to send our youth and a purported enemy to their deaths.

Careful analysis will prove that the entire "weapons of mass destruction" scam was a contrivance. The true weapons of mass destruction are on your aircraft carriers ready to use against Iraqi civilians. The most toxic weapon of mass destruction is your embargo on Iraq.

The founding parents of the United Nations had an even more sacred mission than the founding fathers of the United States.

Bring your troops home now, Mr. President and do not let any warmonger talk you into a Tonkin Gulf style of contrivance.

World Capitalism
or World Federalism?

March 3, 1998

As the century wanes we have a choice. We can choose world capitalism or world federalism. World capitalism will corrupt and destroy the globe if measures like the Multilateral Agreement on Investments become international law. This approach identifies money as an end in itself. How it is amassed, mal-distributed, or legally stolen becomes irrelevant. There is no democracy in world capitalism, only corporate power. The savagery of this power is evident in a century of war. Now our military establishment has become the primary enforcer.

World capitalism is comfortable giving $40 billion of welfare to Dictator Suharto as it prepares to bomb Dictator Saddam. World capital expresses its love for Nazi Agosto Pinochet Ugarte, and spends four decades trying to assassinate Fidel Castro. The selectivity of world capitalism has less morality than organized crime. It does not hit one traitor to its mob, on the contrary, it is willing to annihilate civilians under the control of a dissident system. Such selectivity is based on expansion of profit and bereft of all morality.

Do not despair, there is another model. It is called "world federalism." This model is not a fantasy, it is actually contained in what the best of our founders had in mind. The Bill of Rights and the Constitution are not capitalist documents. They are Federalist documents. Capitalism does not imply democracy. The most vicious dictatorships in the western hemisphere have been capitalist.

The essence of federalism is to give governmental autonomy within overlapping spheres. The family and the tribe have their autonomy and make decisions democratically and locally.

Systems are developed for pubic education, public utilities, public health, public parks, public hospitals, public libraries, public transit. A public welfare for those who are in need. There are public prisons for people who are a danger to public safety. At their best, none of

176

these entities are based on the profit motive, they are based on the expressed needs of the public and are designed to fill those needs for the common good. This is not capitalism. It is the federalism of the common good. But currently the fanaticism of international capital is attacking each and every one of the above mentioned public systems. Such attacks require our noncooperation.

Our noncooperation must include the promotion of world federalism which is in the process of development through the United Nations Charter and International Declaration of Human Rights. The United States alone must not attempt to solve international problems any more than the state of Utah should attempt to resolve a national problem. International conflict resolution is beyond the reach of any nation state. President Wilson attempted to foster a League of Nations after World War I and his goals were dashed by the U.S. Congress. A Second and even more violent conflict followed. The United Nations was established in the wake of World War II with the goals and objectives of world federalism. Our Congress remains as its chief adversary. We must not allow the anti-democratic forces of world corporate capital to destroy the common good which is the objective of world federalism.

School of the Americas

March 10, 1998

Twenty-two people including veterans, nuns, clergy and a college professor have been sentenced to six months in a federal prison and fined $3,000 for criminal trespass onto Fort Benning, Georgia. The twenty-two were among 601 people arrested on November 16, 1997 as they entered Fort Benning, carrying white crosses and coffins filled with petitions containing some 1 million signatures calling for the closing of the School of the Americas. Their attorneys entered a necessity defense based on years of documentation of human rights violations by School of the Americas graduates and multiple efforts by the defendants to persuade Congress to cut School of the Americas funding.

Judge Robert Elliot presided over the trial in front of a packed courtroom and gave the School of the Americas protesters the maximum prison sentence for this offense. Elliot had previously exonerated Lieutenant Calley for the My Lai massacre.

Defendant Sister Rita Steinhagen, sixty-nine, a nun from Minneapolis said, "There's something wrong when we who participate in a solemn funeral procession are sent to prison, while School of the Americas graduates who did the killing get amnesty and will not spend one day behind bars." Ann Tiffany, sixty-two, a nurse from Syracuse, New York said, "It's a crime to spend millions of dollars to teach combat skills to Latin American soldiers, while school budgets for our children and social programs are cut." Rev. Kenneth Kennon, sixty-two, a Disciples of Christ minister from Tucson, Arizona stated, "I believe our going to prison will inspire others to join in calling on Congress to close this 'School of Shame'." Congressman Joseph Kennedy writes to his colleagues that the December 22 massacre in Chiapas links the School of the Americas with the Mexican government's failed Chiapas policy.

At least twelve School of the Americas graduates have played a key role in the conflict in southern Mexico.

Those officers include:

- **General Jose Ruben Rivas Pena**, who helped design the counterinsurgency strategy in Chiapas which included psychological operations against civilians.

- **General Juan López Ortiz**, who was the commander in Ocosingo where suspected Zapatista sympathizers were rounded up and shot in the town's marketplace.

- **Colonel Julian Guerrero Barrios**, who has been charged with the crime of torture and massacre.

How can our country engage in a solution to the aggression of Serbia in Kosovo when it is complicit in fostering and training for even greater crimes in Mexico and Colombia? Ask your member of Congress to support House Resolution 611 to close the School of the Americas and to release the nonviolent demonstrators who have called our attention to our criminal policy.

Nuclearism

March 17, 1998

Today's discussion is about a psychosis that can be fatal for the planet. It is called "nuclearism." The United States has just developed a new nuclear weapon called the "B-61-11." This weapon is a serious threat to the United States and the rest of the world. In the recent Iraq crisis, the Clinton administration once again refused to rule out the use of nuclear weapons thereby inflaming relations with Moscow.

In violation of the Antiballistic Missile Treaty of 1997, the administration plans to spend $4.5 billion a year for a so-called "modernization" of our nuclear arsenal. At any given time the United States has some 2,300 warheads on alert. This represents a combined explosive power of 550 megatons (550 million tons of TNT or the equivalent of 44,000 Hiroshimas.)

Popular mythology stating that nuclear weapons exist only to insure that they will never be used is not part of our military strategy.

In a conflict with Russia, our current plans include hitting Chekhov, the Russian general staff main command post just forty miles south of Moscow. It would be hit by 69 nuclear weapons. Moscow would be uninhabitable for generations.

Our current policy betrays the treaties we have signed. We declared in 1978 that we would not use or threaten to use nuclear weapons against a non-nuclear state that was a member in good standing of the nuclear non-proliferation treaty.

In 1980, a computer chip failure at NORAD, the U.S. command post in Colorado, generated a false alarm of an all out Soviet missile attack.

As recently as 1995, a harmless American research rocket, sent up off the coast of Norway, so alarmed the Russians that they were ready to retaliate with a nuclear barrage. You may ask why the Start II Treaty ratified by the U.S. Senate in January of 1996 has not been ratified by the Russian Duma. Boris Yeltsin proposed a ceiling of 2,000 missiles on each side. The United States insisted on 3,500 missiles. Russia said no and refused to sign. But the matter of Start II is minor compared to the serious agitation caused by NATO expansion. Approval of such expansion by the Senate Foreign Relations Committee is a most hostile message to Moscow. A nuclear capable enlarged NATO moves the nuclear threat even closer to Moscow. We can think of the parallel of Germany after World War I. The failure of Versailles was in the fatal miscalculation of how to deal with a demoralized former adversary.

Russia does not need to be excluded from the world community by NATO expansion. Hundreds of billions of our tax dollars would go into this wasteful and hostile action making the possibility of nuclear disaster even more acute. We must say "no" to NATO and to our reckless expansion of nuclear terrorism.

Korea

March 24, 1998

Nearly drowned in the meaningless hype, sex and con of non-journalism, a tiny notification appeared in the press this week. Four-way talks aimed at a permanent peace settlement on the Korean peninsula collapsed with the refusal of the United States to discuss the withdrawal of 37,000 troops from South Korea.

It has been forty-five years since the armistice was signed on July 27, 1953. North Korea is simply asking for a peace treaty between Washington and Pyongyang prior to further talks. The whole world knows that North Korea is in a condition of extreme famine. Exactly what harm could be done by signing a treaty that should have been signed a half century ago?

Let us do some history. At Potsdam, in July of 1945, the United States military urged the Soviet Union to enter the war against Japan. General order number one, drafted on August 11, 1945, provided that Japanese forces north of the 38th parallel in Korea surrender to Soviet commanders while those south of that line were to surrender to the United States command. United States troops arrived in South Korea on September 8, 1945 and received the Japanese surrender at Seoul. The Soviet Union then asked the United States to form a trusteeship leading to the unification of Korea. The United States refused. That refusal, in 1947, was followed by the Soviet Union recognizing the People's Republic of Korea as the only lawful government in Korea. By 1949 President Harry Truman declared that Korea had become a testing ground in the ideological conflict between communism and democracy, Military aid began to flow massively from the United States to South Korea.

On June 25, 1950, North Korean troops launched a full-scale invasion of South Korea. There were 4 million casualties in the war that followed. The United States lost 33,629 killed in action. In short, we refused to accept unification of Korea in 1947. Our refusal was followed by Soviet aggression in 1950. We refused to sign a peace treaty in 1953, and we have this week refused to remove our 37,000 remaining troops causing the peace process to collapse once again.

I remember when people said that Germany would never reunite. But it did so quite successfully. If we could liberate our press from its sexual slavery, we might see clearly that most Koreans want reunification of their country now. Tell your servants in Washington that you want the troops to come home from Korea and to end our obstruction of a permanent peace pact with a very hungry country.

A Letter
from Bishop Samuel Ruiz

March 31, 1998

I received an email message today from Bishop Samuel Ruiz
Garcia in San Cristóbal de las Casas. I would like to share a
summary translation of that message with you.

To all men and women of good will:

Today, as another storm of persecution calls at our door, we must
share with you reflections from our faith. The mystery of the people of
God, in the midst of persecutions, continues to give birth to a new
humanity free from the slavery of demonic oppression. We cannot
feel ourselves as victims today, since the option for the poor takes for
granted experiencing the same suffering as the oppressed. Today we
feel ourselves moved by the action of grace. Humanly it is difficult
and overburdening for us to suffer such defamation and injury. But we
recognize the splendid gift of grace. "Rejoice, and be glad . . ." the
Lord tells us (Matt. 5:12).

Only the truth will make you free. The truth is our standard of
action in this ministry of reconciliation. For this we have been sent, to
give testimony to the truth. We know that the truth is inconvenient and
gives rise to violent responses. We have been warned about this. That
which we have seen and heard, that which we have contemplated and
touched with our hands, that which we proclaim, is the visage of the
suffering Christ in the indigenous people who are undergoing a sys-
tematic aggression against their fundamental rights. That which we
have seen and heard is the virus of war artificially injected from the
outside. That which we have seen and heard with profound sadness is
death in Acteal and so many other communities.

Now the world is coming to see us. Solidarity with suffering knows
no boundaries and goes far beyond the concept of sovereignty based
on the interests of privileged groups.

For our part, we cannot conceive of refusing to proclaim this enduring gospel. If we keep silent, the stones will cry out and would reveal us as imposters. We are not ceasing in hoping against all hope (Rom. 4:18) that one day in our beloved Chiapas and in our beloved Mexico, "no more will there be children who live only a few days, and old ones who are not able to live out their years" (Isa. 65:21-22). From the metal smelted into AK-47s, they will forge themselves tractors (Isa. 2:4) and in place of sending taxes, the fruit of our labor, to pay tuition for the military at the School of the Americas, we will see classrooms, operating rooms, storerooms, laboratories as well as dignity in the ravines and jungles of Chiapas, in the valleys and in the mountains of our homeland.

The Godless Left

April 7, 1998

Fundamentalist atheists of the left are at least as much an annoyance as fundamentalist right wing Christians, Jews or Islamics. Actually they are the same. They have the truth. The institutionalized left in its flawed political correctness has a religious phobia. Religion can be the opiate of the people. It can also be the hot fudge sundae of the people.

Congratulations to *Nation Magazine* for finally dealing with their problem by publishing Michael Kazin's article on the "Politics of Devotion" in their April 6, 1997 issue. Kazin, an atheist, identifies the arrogance, snobbery and effete Fifth Avenue elitism of the *Nation*. He quotes Katha Pollitt from an interview in the *New York Times* saying: "Religion is a farrago of authoritarian nonsense, misogyny and humble pie, the eternal enemy of human happiness and freedom."

Such arrogance is enough to explain why there is no substantive left in the United States. Actually, there is no effective movement without a mystique. This includes symbols, music, poetry, religion and mythology.

One would have to be trapped in a Fifth Avenue Jewelry Shop for life not to know the history of the religious left. Did you hear about the abolitionists? Has anyone told you about the civil rights movement? Did you ever march with the farm workers and their image of Our Lady of Guadalupe? The only effective socialist campaigns in the history of the United States were conducted by Eugene Debs and Norman Thomas, who both found biblical grounds for a cooperative commonwealth.

Where has this ivory tower left been hiding? Do they think Bishop Belo of East Timor won the Nobel prize for kissing up to Suharto? Do they think Archbishop Tutu was in the pocket of apartheid?

They fail to understand that the religious left is nonsectarian. Dr. Martin Luther King never asked his followers to become Baptists. The religious left does not see faith as a formula. On the contrary, faith is the willingness to do what has to be done in spite of all the odds.

The eleventh chapter of St. Paul's epistle to the Hebrews has an excellent definition:

> It was faith that made the parents of Moses hide him for three months after he was born. They saw he was a beautiful child, and they were not afraid to disobey the king's order. (Heb. 11:23)

That is right, faith includes civil disobedience.

The snotty religion bashing of the arrogant left will continue to do nothing but turn off people of conscience. Is *Nation* phobic about the international leadership of Father Roy Bourgeois, the religious women killed in El Salvador, Father Philip Berrigan and his plowshares movement and Bishop Samuel Ruiz Garcia who represents the only hope for peace in Mexico? It is time to ask "what is your problem?"

Christopher Hitchens may revel in his glib attacks on such people as Mother Theresa. Does he have any idea of what it is to "get down" with the poor?

Abolishing the war system will not be accomplished by sass, "I'm smarter than you snobs." It will be accomplished by people of faith who want to turn swords into plowshares and who want to study war no more.

For a free copy of this [or any other] commentary,
call the Office of the Americas at 323/852-9808
or visit the OOA web site at http://www.officeoftheamericas.org.

This is Blase Bonpane.

The

Peace Reports

and other works

December 10, 1985 to August 15, 2000

The International March for Peace in Central America

December 10, 1985 to January 24, 1986

Columbus sailed the coast of Panama and called it "Veragua." Here Balboa "discovered" the Pacific Ocean in 1513 and here Pizarro used the isthmus to transport his Peruvian plunder to Spain.

By 1572 Francis Drake was attacking the mule trains of treasure as they crossed the narrow link from Pacific to Atlantic. William Parker and Henry Morgan followed the example of Drake and burned Panama City to the ground in 1671.

Everyone wanted the isthmus. What the Spanish lost and what the British plundered was formed into a tiny nation by the sculptor Theodore Roosevelt. Since its creation in 1903, Panama has survived the presence of fourteen U.S. military bases and a Canal Zone. The country does not claim to be part of Central America. Nor is it thought of as part of South America although it was formerly part of Colombia.

Now it was our turn. We hoped that our presence would not be as negative as those who came before us. While the Panamanians did not seem afraid of us, carefully contrived press of dubious origin made our people appear to be a combination of the conquistadores and the barbarians.

The International March for Peace in Central America had begun. Early in December internationalists began to assemble in Panama City at a humble suburban retreat, Centro Gomez y Gomez. The Danes came, the Swedes, the Norwegians, the Germans, the Finns, the Australians, the Dutch, the Japanese. There was Iceland, and Canada, France, Mexico, Argentina, Guatemala, England, New Zealand, Scotland, Ecuador, Belgium, Costa Rica, El Salvador, Nicaragua, Honduras, Panama, and the largest delegation of all: The United States of America.

There was something pentecostal about the spirit, the languages, the singing and the sports as these nations gathered, communicated and celebrated the beginning of this historic march.

As a member of the directorate, I was preoccupied about how we were going to keep ourselves together for the six weeks ahead. Our logistical problems were endless. For months we had planned on how to maintain over three-hundred people in a tropical setting. We had not answered all the questions. But we were determined to begin. While the marchers had little knowledge of Central America, they did have a great desire for world peace.

These were not passive people. There was pronounced individualism, almost adventurism; an eagerness to try anything in the name of peace. The only quality in absence was fear.

We gathered at the National Lottery Building in Panama City for the official opening of the March in the late afternoon of December 10th, 1985. After an opening statement by novelist Graham Greene, Panama's senior spokesman, Jorge Illueca, gave the opening address. Illueca reminded the audience that today was the 37th anniversary of the Universal Declaration of Human Rights and that, as a nation involved in the Contadora Process, Panama sought a solution to the Central American conflict without war. Illueca spoke of the heroic sacrifices of the marchers saying that this was a struggle not of soldiers with arms but of messengers of peace, as the dove which brought good news to Noah in the biblical account, we marchers were bringing the olive branch to the convulsed isthmus of Central America to promote worldwide peace.

We were welcome in Panama in spite of the red-baiting of the Panamanian press and paid ads placing slogans foreign to our march under our logo, in other words, sabotage. Aggressive, rhetorical, dogmatic, psuedo-revolutionary phrases were listed below our peace dove. It seems that some entity, most probably the CIA, had been hard at work to discredit the March. I asked a reporter from *Newsweek* to remind the CIA of the peril such propaganda could cause for us.

Panamanians, however, did not seem afraid of us. But only a few joined our ranks. Our first action was in commemoration of the raising of the Panamanian flag over the Canal Zone in 1964 when twenty-four Panamanian high school students were killed. This act led to the breaking of relations between Panama and the United States by President Chiari. We retraced the steps of the students. But we were an undisciplined unit. Hence we decided to dedicate a good bit of the next day to discipline and preparation for our next action, the march to Fort Howard.

We gathered at the tomb of General Omar Torrijos which is located in Balboa within the Canal Zone. It was a time for speeches by us and by the Panamanians. Torrijos' father and sister were present. Our homage was genuine but some of our marchers had to take cover from the tropical sun and sit under trees. The critical need for hats and canteens was demonstrated at this event. Monitors were trained, and we became a more serious marching group.

We stood at the Miraflores Locks of the Panama Canal and sang peace songs to the passengers of various ships including the famous Love Boat as these vessels sank low enough to pass on into the waters of the Pacific.

Jesse Jackson called me on that same day saying,

> The Rainbow Coalition supports the International March for Peace in Central America. It is as Ghandi's March to the Sea and King's March to Washington, to Montgomery and to Selma. People who are willing to put their lives on the line are bringing light to Central America by this March.
>
> This is a time of genocide in Central America This is a time of military oppression. The U.S. government should meet with President Ortega. It would be mutually beneficial. This is not the same as Somoza's period of tyranny. We must respect the sovereignty of Nicaragua and end our sanctions. We must create relations which will make us all proud. We must support the Contadora process not by ignoring the Contra Invasion of Nicaragua but by acknowledging it, and stopping it.
>
> Many are dying on bloody battlefields, others are choked off by the International Monetary Fund and bear the burden of years of economic domination.
>
> I am happy that Reagan and Gorbachev met in Geneva, but they made no accord on human rights. This is not a matter of peace between East and West This is a matter of peace with justice in Central America.
>
> I want to express my support for the gallant men and women marching in Central America. Political colonizers have been conquered. Economic colonizers have not been conquered. We must remove the debt. People want peace as opposed to quietness.
>
> My prayers are with you and know that peace is the presence of justice, health care, housing and job training. The golden rule is the measure of foreign policy and there is no way we can have peace without justice. We must light candles in the night and in the day. We must look for honest people.
>
> This march will have an impact on the United States. We cannot turn the lights out on Central America.

I will be with you soon, brother, and remember,

The Lord is our Shepherd, we shall lack nothing.

Though we walk through the valley of the shadow of death, we shall fear no evil.

The words of the 23rd Psalm had never been more meaningful to me than on that torrid day in Panama when Jesse called.

Our march at the Southern Command was disciplined and effective. Torrill Eide and I went ahead to make sure we were at the proper entrance of Fort Howard, and we made a few wrong turns before we were ready to give the signal to the marchers waiting on the highway. Our tactic was to tell the military exactly what was about to happen so they would not panic or overreact.

This demonstration had no historical precedent. People from twenty-five countries marched up the hill to the entrance of Fort Howard to be met by the commanding officer, a Panamanian. While the officer would not permit passage of the March through the base, he did cooperate fully with our alternate plan. Each and every one of the three hundred marchers would request permission to enter the base, and he would subsequently deny permission individually. This was done in the spirit of the Posadas: the Christmas custom in Latin America to reenact the search of Joseph and Mary for a place to stay. Had the officer not been a Latin American, this cultural act would have been impossible. It was a Central American custom which he knew and accepted. Group after national group arrived at the main gate singing and waving the flag of their country.

This base was selected because it is the center for the forces of state terror in Central America. From here bombs are delivered to El Salvador for the indiscriminate bombing of the Salvadoran people. From here the training of Contra mercenaries takes place. Standing behind the Panamanian commanding officer were two U.S. Air Force officers who were not anxious to talk until someone brought up the subject of retirement in Panama. They were for it. The entire demonstration took about three hours. We left Fort Howard knowing our position in history had been established. Our efforts would have been a success if we had gone no further.

Even now we are aware of trouble at the next nation up the Pan American Highway. We have received word that it may not be possible to enter Costa Rica. Our visas have been cut back to twelve hours. The March may reach a dead-end at the northern border of Panama in the state of Chiriqui.

I called Ambassador Lewis Tambs in Costa Rica, and he assured me he would seek cooperation from the Costa Rican government for an extension of our visas. He said, however, as it stood now we would be undocumented aliens in Costa Rica after twelve hours. We certainly have many friends in the United States who share the same status.

Later the same day Ambassador Tambs assured Senator Cranston's office that a political officer of the U.S. Embassy would be at the border to observe the International Peace March. We were leaving Panama with warm feelings for and from the Panamanian people. The critically important help of the Panamanian support committees led us to understand the need for local assistance in each country.

To deal with the impasse at the Costa Rican border, Torrill Eide, Daniel Moore and I flew from Panama City to San Jose. Costa Rica, to seek full governmental permission and to remove any fears the government might have of our presence. As we departed by air, the March continued by land toward the Costa Rican border. Neither we nor the rest of the marchers knew that they would be detained for some 48 hours at the Costa Rican border.

When our delegation of three arrived in San Jose, President Monge had already denounced the march as an action of the extreme left. Terror was in the faces of our Costa Rican preparation committee when we arrived at 3:00 AM. They knew we had arrived at the airport at 9:00 PM. They could not understand why it took us six hours to get from the airport to the city. Well, it took us two hours to get through customs. When we finally realized some people were looking for us, we avoided them because they looked suspicious; we did not recognize anyone we knew. We did not acknowledge our reception group until we had studied them for some time. After successfully communicating with our hosts, we started toward the city and had car trouble half way there. Hence the preparation committee thought we had been arrested or kidnapped.

Word from the border informed us that the March was being threatened by Costa Rica Libre. Until this time I did not know there was such an organization. I called the Minister of Security and ran into a flood of negativity. The march could not go to the university because his Ministry does not have jurisdiction over the university; we could not have any public meetings; we must be out of the country in twelve hours: we may not visit anything or anyone. We are in transit and we must keep going. Those who are now at the border must not come to San Jose. If there is a confrontation of any kind, he said, the March would be expelled by police escort directly to the Nicaraguan border. I was speaking to Benjamin Pisa, and he insisted that groups of rightists were waiting to attack us. He said that sixty to eighty taxis representing the extreme right were preparing to blockade the Pan American Highway.

This was the first of various phone calls to Pisa. I wanted to maintain contact at all cost. For some reason I found the man accessible. Finally on a Sunday morning I called to say, "May I come by your home and talk to you personally?" He agreed. Here was the godfather. Research from nationals enlightened me; Benjamin Pisa is not only the Minister of Security, but he is also the founder of Costa Rica Libre. Sitting in his palatial home, I was told that he did not think he could protect us. I had heard the same words almost twenty years before in Guatemala. But at that time it was from the U.S. Ambassador. The phrase is, of course, a diplomatic threat.

I asked Pisa if he could please allow our marchers to come to San Jose for humanitarian reasons. By now they had been held up at the border for almost 48 hours with little food and less water. They had no shelter and Costa Rica Libre was there to taunt them. It was ironic; on the horns of their cabs they were playing the Nicaraguan song, "No pasaran," but in this case the words applied to the March. At last Pisa agreed to let the group come into San Jose if they remained in effect under house arrest at the youth hostel where the three of us were staying. We agreed that this would be better than nothing and word was sent to the border to let the March pass. Pisa kept repeating that if there is a confrontation of any kind the entire group would be expelled to the border of Nicaragua under police escort.

After a long tense wait, the marchers arrived in San Jose. A substantial number of Costa Rican security forces stood guard in front of the youth hostel. Literally hundreds of Costa Ricans had come onto the property to welcome the March. This angered Benjamin Pisa.

As the marchers arrived in full force, the security officers began to fade away. But as uniformed security officers disappeared, plainclothed individuals of Costa Rica Libre multiplied. Hand grenades of CS gas [†] were thrown at us. We picked up the empty canisters to read "Made in U.S.A." This is not old fashioned tear gas. It is much more powerful and much more dangerous. Marchers were sickened by it as

---

[†] O-chlorobenzylidene malononitrile

they attempted to enter the youth hostel. A deadly barrage of bricks and stones followed. We were under attack for about two hours, and we were wall-to-wall people. Every missile was hitting someone. Tables were placed in front of windows. The youth hostel was in shambles. The Red Cross arrived to take away some of the injured. Marchers called the embassies of their homelands asking for protection. I awakened a sleepy Marine at the U.S. Embassy at about 2:00 AM. He said he would, "Do what he could."

At approximately 2:30 AM, just as we were expecting the attackers to invade, Benjamin Pisa himself arrived and waved off his organization, the Costa Rica Libre. Then he entered the hostel and ordered us to be out of San Jose by seven in the morning. We were being expelled from Costa Rica.

Our marchers were very tired. Some were emotionally upset and others were injured. The directorate of the March determined not to awaken the group for a 7:00 AM departure. It was now close to 3:00 AM. We determined to simply let them sleep, which they did.

The following morning, we were not ready at seven. We were not ready at eight. By nine, Benjamin Pisa appeared and said, "If you are not out of here by noon, I will remove all of my security people." This was a clear threat to give us back to Costa Rica Libre. Our group was so combative, especially the young, that they did not care. They were ready to confront Costa Rica Libre once again. It would have been a one-sided bloody confrontation between armed violent fanatics and unarmed pacifists. I could not help but think of the early Christians being fed to the lions. Initially the Costa Rican preparation committee had stated they would cooperate with anything we wanted to do. But finally and prudently they said: "Look, we think it is best for you and for us if you are out of here by noon." In spite of this counsel, some marchers still wanted to vote on whether or not we should leave. Fortunately, in their respect for the Costa Ricans, they agreed to leave at noon as they were ordered to do. Some wanted to be dragged on to the buses. I had to explain to them that there is no Central American custom of U.S. civil disobedience and that it is hard for soldiers to drag anyone while trying to balance an M-16 at the ready. We were expelled from San Jose under heavy security.

During this entire March, we had press contacts from CNN, McNeill-Lehrer, CBS, UPI, AP, all local media, radio, etc., and in spite of these constant contacts with national and international press, we heard from the United States that the press coverage was quite light. This seems to indicate a heavy-handed editing at the U.S. end. It is not that they did not have the material, it is quite obvious that they did not want to promulgate this material.

We were still finding it hard to believe that the March was a reality, that we were actually walking in the jungles of Panama and the mountains of Costa Rica. We made many friends and received some resistance, but we were becoming a unit. We were thinking together, making decisions together, and making mistakes together. We looked forward to becoming even more united, but perhaps this was unrealistic. It seems to me that if five people were walking together planning to have a picnic, that they should have disagreements and different ideas as to how to have that picnic. It would be very unrealistic to presume that over three hundred people could make decisions about traversing seven countries without severe disagreements. We were not in a posture of military discipline, and it probably would have been easier if we were, but the kind of discipline represented by the military is exactly what we were trying to avoid. So we practiced the democracy of listening to people, hearing them out, and attempting to come to collective decisions, in most cases with consensus. This was time consuming, and our meetings could be lengthy.

There was little complaining about the hardships of the journey. Within a few days people became accustomed to sleeping wherever they could, be it in the open, or in some cases, inside of schools or union facilities. Most of the time, sleeping was on the ground. Insects, of course, were a great problem and there were many bites. Water is an eternal problem in Central America, not only because of the shortage of quantity in some places, but also the dubious quality. There were the usual gastro-intestinal diseases. Food at best was simple, and sometimes sparse. But most of the decisions, discussions and differences were on matters of tactics and strategy rather than on the living conditions.

Prior to this summary expulsion from Costa Rica, a few of us had two significant meetings unobserved by the Costa Rican authorities. The first was with Jose Figueres, former president and senior statesman of Costa Rica. As president in 1948, he had discontinued the Costa Rican military. He, as other Costa Rican citizens, was ashamed of the growth of the neo-fascist Costa Rica Libre organization. He told us to have all of the marchers come to his hilltop home and assured us that such a meeting could not be considered public because his home was private. Don Pepe Figueres is up in years now, but he is still willing to confront corruption in his beloved Costa Rica.

Our second unobserved meeting was with Archbishop Arieta of San Jose, Costa Rica. After attending Mass at the Cathedral, I approached the Archbishop in the sacristy. He recognized me immediately and said in English, "Father Bonpane, we understand your program." I asked him if he would support the Peace March,

and he began a ten minute ethereal commentary on how he could not support the Peace March and how the Church was for peace. To our surprise, the prelate concluded his discourse by saying, "Yes, you can celebrate Mass in this Archdiocese for your Peace March . . . but not in my Cathedral." We had planned to go ahead with such a Mass in the open air, but the Ministry of Security had other plans.

Speculating on the impact of the International Peace March in Costa Rica, the revulsion of Costa Ricans at the brutal attacks on us may have led voters away from the hawkish Angel Miguel Calderon and contributed to the election of the more centrist Oscar Arias.

We were asking ourselves, however, "If things are so difficult in peaceful Costa Rica, how will it be in El Salvador, Honduras and Guatemala?" But this apprehension did not last long. The spirit of the March was one of achievement and optimism. Some weeks after the attack in San Jose, we were pleased to read that the Costa Rican Association of Jurists had demanded of President Monge that Costa Rica Libre be dissolved precisely because of its attack on the International March for Peace in Central America. Government officials were living in terror of the organization. Costa Rica Libre was directly linked to the Contra mercenaries and as such opened up employment opportunities for rapists murderers and thieves.

One sudden current of concern jolted the March as we were nearing the northern border of Costa Rica under heavily-armed escort; we were prisoners. The Costa Ricans could turn us over to the ARDE Contras because there is no direct contact with Nicaraguan authorities at the Costa Rican border station. The Nicaraguan station is inland some five kilometers after a no-person's land of devastation. It was not bizarre to speculate that the Contras would be waiting in that sinister location.

But the Nicaraguans were not about to let this happen. They personally came through the no-person's land to meet us at the Costa Rican customs gate. This was a risk for the Nicaraguans, but they are accustomed to taking risks for their friends. We were extremely pleased with this heroic reception. We had left word with our Costa Rican committee to please inform Managua that we would be arriving in Nicaragua early and against our will. Father Ernesto Cardenal had been waiting all day until he became ill and had to return to Managua. We passed through this devastated, dismal, destroyed region without incident.

When we arrived at the Nicaraguan customs gate, we were admitted as a group with no complications or paper shuffling. A few kilometers up the road an entire community was waiting for us. We were recipients of gifts including a well preserved deer head and neckerchiefs. We exchanged greetings with town elders, children and Mothers of Heroes and Martyrs. The latter group is everywhere as living witness to the terrorism inflicted on Nicaragua by Contras.

Much of our time in Nicaragua was in areas with a Contra presence. There was a strategic value to such a presence. The Contras were aware of our international mix and were less apt to attack. Marching from town to town, we were spontaneously received by people who refuse to be terrorized. In Palacaguina we began singing "Cristo ya Nacio in Palacaquina" and the townspeople continued as a choir.

Nicaraguan students welcomed us at the coffee co-op known as *El Chaguiton*. The danger here was such that we could go no more than one kilometer from the camp during the day and no more than 50 meters at night (that was the distance of the outhouses). Devastation of the Contra war was everywhere. Our limitations were taken seriously by all but the Spaniards who wandered off into the mountains and who were not expected to return. By some good fortune they came back unharmed.

Throughout Nicaragua we received nothing but good will and welcome. It was a country at peace. Its peaceful and nonviolent people were being attacked from the outside, and they were responding as peaceful and nonviolent people by defending their families and their country.

But there was a pall hanging over us within this island of good will in Central America. Word was coming from all sides; we were unwelcome in Honduras. Honduras is the only country to the north with a Nicaraguan border. El Salvador has no border to Nicaragua (Washington does not seem to know this). In short, we began to fear that Nicaragua could be the northern terminus of our odyssey.

We made our way up the Pan American Highway to the border town of El Espino in the province of Madriz in Nicaragua. The town had been completely destroyed; there was no living soul in El Espino. This was to be our stand for seven days in an attempt to enter by land into Honduras. We were greeted by the Cobras, an elite group of Honduran troops who were adorned with gas masks and rifles at the ready.

Behind the Cobras was a contradictory emblem, *"Bienvenido a Honduras"* (Welcome to Honduras). We stood at the very line of the border; we sang, we chanted, we talked to them, but no one would respond to us. We tried every way of getting some kind of communicative response, and after some four hours I personally received a gesture from a man dressed in white. At his insistence I crossed into Honduras and asked him if our group could enter. He said, "No, you will never enter Honduras." He asked me if I was a priest, and I said that I was. He said that priests should be in their churches, and should not be involved in political activities. He asked me if I had seen the arms in Nicaragua. I told him that I was not a military man, and was not able to tell him the kinds of arms. He told me that Nicaragua had shown us only what they wanted us to see. He further said that Nicaragua had to disappear. He then asked to see my passport, and read it through page by page. He said, "You have been in Nicaragua too many times. You must know more than what you are saying. I do not believe that you do not know more about Nicaragua. You say you have seen schools. You say you have seen churches. I want to know what else you have seen." His tone was threatening. He repeated, "You will not pass." I asked if we could pass simply in transit to El Salvador or to Guatemala. He said, "No," he said, "Honduras is a country of peace. We do not need a peace march in Honduras. We are a peaceful people."

I told this man, who would not identify himself but who was obviously in charge of the customs house in Honduras, that I had visited recently with Edgardo Paz Barnica, the Foreign Minister of Honduras. This was the result of another quick trip made by me and two other members of the March to Tegucigalpa. We had flown from Managua to Tegucigalpa in order to visit with the Honduran Peace March preparation committee. We found them receptive, helpful; members of the University community, members of the unions, women demonstrating in the Plaza of the Cathedral demanding that we be admitted; and in spite of the fact that we were there on Christmas Eve, we were able to visit the home of the Foreign Minister, who indicated that we would be allowed to enter the country legally. We spoke, however, with the Minister of the Interior, who gave us another message. In Honduras the lines of governmental authority are not clear, but certainly the ultimate authority is the military.

While we could not enter some areas by road, we were having success by air. That is, by arriving in small groups, and without much fanfare.

Getting back to the man in white: When I told him that Paz Barnica had been enthusiastic about our visit to Honduras, he was not impressed. He seemed to view the government officials and ministers with nothing but contempt. He obviously represented the military, the actual political, visible power in Honduras.

The International March for Peace in Central America was the major item in the Central American press from December 10th through January 22nd. We were very pleased to receive positive press in Honduras, revealing that the nation was making a grave mistake by not allowing us into that country. After seven days on that Honduran border with little food or water, it was time for the march to plan on entering Honduras, El Salvador and Guatemala by air. We retreated to Managua to reconnoiter.

We rented one room at the Intercontinental Hotel to serve as a communication center. From there, we distributed marchers throughout the three countries. The plan was simple: Send a few by air to Tegucigalpa, have them report back by phone and with their approval, send another group, and another. They assembled as a unit. The plan was successful. Our Honduran team spoke to Miskito Indians forced to serve as Contras. The Honduran people expressed bitter opposition to occupation by the United States military. People on the street are quick to express their antipathy for the denationalization of their country. Honduran misery has not been limited one bit by hundreds of millions of U.S. dollars expended for military purposes. Literacy has not improved, infant mortality has not decreased and unemployment is the rule. Honduras remains a conquered, occupied country with a high level of resentment.

While sending people into Honduras, we simultaneously began to send small groups into El Salvador, once again awaiting their response upon arrival, and then sending more after them. We were inspired by the response of the Salvadoran preparation committees. Our arrival in El Salvador in early 1986 was greeted by a march of over a thousand Salvadorans who declared their march to be our march, the International Peace March in Central America. They used our slogans and symbols. This was undoubtedly the boldest gesture of any of the nationals on the March to this point. The Salvadorans together with the international marchers began a trek towards San Francisco Gotera from San Salvador. They were physically stopped, forced to turn around and return to the capital. There were interrogations by the military. Brigido Sanchez, a Salvadoran, was arrested and imprisoned. The Salvadoran commander put his arms around Brigido and stated cynically, "We will take care of you, Brigido." The Salvadoran marchers occupied the basement of the Cathedral of San Salvador, and stayed in that location for three days together with our marchers. The next attempt for the combined group was to march west to Santa Ana. The Salvadoran military intervened and the group was once again ushered back to San Salvador.

We had asked the Salvadorans if we would be jeopardizing their safety by marching with them. They insisted that whether we were there or not they were always in danger and that our presence would not hinder their safety. They were determined to continue marching with or without us. They urged us to continue doing what we were doing. In each country the greatest wisdom came from the citizens who were indigenous to the country, and in each case the safety of our marchers was assured only by listening to the wisdom of the local people. There are no experts on such matters. Many of the people we had consulted prior to the march had rejected our proposal. Nobel Prize laureate Perez Esquivel of Argentina was convinced a march of this type was much too dangerous and could not succeed. Many told us we would never get out of Panama. Others said we could in no way get beyond Nicaragua. Here we were, already crossing Panama, Costa Rica, Nicaragua, Honduras and El Salvador and now waiting for the greatest challenge of all, that of Guatemala.

The time was right for Guatemala. The country was preparing for the inauguration of Vinicio Cerezo Arevalo, the new president, and was attempting to give an image of democracy to the world. We considered chartering a plane from Managua to Guatemala City to get the entire march into Guatemala, but if we chartered a plane we would come under the jurisdiction of the Guatemalan military, and the Guatemalan military would never authorize such a charter. By arranging regularly scheduled flights, we were able to fly group after group into Guatemala, in the form of tourists, and to prepare for the unveiling of our march on the day of Cerezo's inauguration, January 14th. It worked. Our people unveiled their posters and banners as part of the inaugural celebration. There was no opposition from the Guatemalan military.

The March was joined by members of the GAM (*Grupo Apoyo Mutuo*), the families of the disappeared, in Guatemala City. Local citizens joined us in the streets. The Peace March in Guatemala City will be remembered as the first international peace demonstration since the CIA destroyed democracy in Guatemala in 1954.

The March went on to Quetzaltenango, and again took to the streets. The March was welcomed by the Mayor, a gesture no one expected. On into the high country of Huehuetenango. A jubilant international throng marched through the devastation to be joined by Indians as if long expected and long awaited. Almost two hundred marchers were now together in Guatemala. None of us had thought this possible in this nation with one of the world's worst human rights records.

A delegation from the March was permitted to visit a "Model Village." These camps are modeled on the strategic hamlets of Vietnam. People are thrown together from various linguistic backgrounds living in utter misery. The schools are non-functional, and terror is in their faces. Hundreds of thousands of men are now part of the civil counterinsurgency patrols. Movement from place to place is by permission only. Even the flow of refugees to Mexico has stopped.

We were aware that all of Central America was talking about the March. Personally I was concerned that after the jubilation of the Guatemala experience, marchers might think they were home free in Mexico. As the marchers were still in Guatemala waiting to cross to the Mexican side, the Mexican committee began to chant some revolutionary slogans. I had to ask them to stop and at least give our people a chance to get on the Mexican side before they started that type of chanting because the Guatemalans could have clamped down at any time.

As we poured across the border at Cuauhtemoc in Chiapas, we were in a distinctly new political situation. All of the Mexican political parties endorsed our March including the all-powerful PRI. Minority parties took advantage of us by surrounding us with their banners and their symbols. We had a meeting with representatives of most of the minority parties and asked them to respect the fact that we were an autonomous march representing no partisan interest. We were here to support: nonintervention, self-determination, human rights, and the Contadora process. Two representatives of one of the more rigid parties objected saying, "Don't we have a right to use our banners as we wish?" Our response: "This is not a matter of rights; it is a matter of tactics among compañeros." Our meeting led to full agreement and for us demonstrated the maturity of the Mexican parties. Beyond this agreement was the accord that we would not focus on Mexican domestic problems which are many. Our attention was on Washington, D.C. (Mexico is not aiding the Contras). We believe that Mexico is the key to a successful Contadora process.

The Mexican preparation committees were in accord with us. We proceeded to San Cristóbal de las Casas to be received by hundreds of people including the great Bishop Samuel Ruiz Garcia. He is responsible for the welfare of over one-hundred thousand Guatemalan refugees in Chiapas. The Mexican government refused to give us permission to visit the refugee camps, but all we had to do was visit the hillsides around us. They were everywhere.

A march around this frigid high-altitude city was followed by a festive ecumenical celebration at the Cathedral. Some of the anti-religious Europeans were reborn at this celebration expressing their comprehension of a liberation theology experience. They had not previously seen Buddhist monks receive holy communion. They had not heard the marimbas in the sanctuary, They had not heard the commentary of people applying scriptures to the here and now. They had not heard a bishop break into tears on the first sentence of his sermon saying: "The people of Latin America are oppressed and I'm sorry to say many of the oppressors call themselves Christians."

The March proceeded to Tuxtla Gutierrez and was again received by large crowds of people as it proceeded on its way to Juchitan and Tehuantepec to be received by another model Bishop. Bishop Arturo Lona Reyes. He is generally dressed in Levis and a T-shirt with a tiny wooden cross around his neck. Because of his opposition to the Mexican land-owning class, it is often necessary for him to sleep in different locations night after night.

As we approached Puebla, a town I had last seen when the Pope was present in 1979, the crowds became massive. Thousands of people were there to march with us. We began to feel a culminating spirit of the March. We felt the impact of six weeks of nonstop Central American press, both pro and con. We began to realize the historic impact of this March and were able to prepare ourselves, at least in part, for what was to greet us in Mexico City.

It was overwhelming to arrive at the Juarez Monument in Mexico City and understand that the crowds were there for us. Fifty thousand people marched with us to Chapultepec Park to the Monument of Niños Heroes to culminate the March with a stirring speech by Archbishop Mendez Arceo. Members of the Mexican Congress marched with us. The Mexican press was extremely positive; Mexico City probably has more daily newspapers than any other city in the world. It was hard for us to realize we had reached our goal; we had completed the March.

The energy and enthusiasm of everyone was certainly at a high point in that frigid Mexican cold, zero degrees Centigrade, where we celebrated the final hours with a huge fiesta, and where all the participant nations gave their cultural best for the Mexican people. We stayed at the Sports Palace that night. I could not believe the energy of the participants. After a day of marching, singing and celebrating, they began a soccer game at 1:00 AM.

The United States delegation went directly to Washington early the next morning, January 24, 1986, and demonstrated at the Vietnam Memorial. Local and national press arrived. From that point, we went to the State Department for an hour-long demonstration and vigil, and spent the rest of the day lobbying in Congressional offices.

The March will now continue in nations around the world as an international secretariat for peace. Our objective in such a march is to change the means of change; to ask the whole world to think about the fact that military methods are not the only methods to bring about change. Once people understand these new methods of change, they will surpass the old methods of change. Fidelity to the past requires the ability to change. Those who repeat the ignorance, the racism, the brutality of the past, are unfaithful to the past. Those who are willing to change, to understand change, are the faithful to the past because they have learned from the past. Our intention is to take the methods which Reverend James Lawson, Dr. Martin Luther King, Cesar Chavez and Ghandi applied on a national level and extend them internationally. We are very grateful that the March was completed without the loss of life. We had anticipated that lives might be lost on a march of this type and we had talked about that eventuality with all of the marchers.

We were moved by the absence of fear and the willingness of the marchers to do almost anything in order to make their plea for peace. Speaking personally, it was necessary for me time and again to restrain people who had adventurist or bizarre ideas they would have carried out spontaneously. Some of the marchers were inclined to do things that would have brought harm not only to themselves but to all of the other marchers as well. I think that the greatest safety valve for the March was the national preparation committees. We listened to them. Even if people were not concerned about their own lives, we were able to convince them to be concerned about the lives of those who remained behind after we left.

Some Reflections on the March:

I kept thinking about the Book of Exodus. After fleeing the oppression of Egypt, Moses was confronted by people who missed the Egyptian food. There were complaints. They had set out not knowing where they were going. In similar fashion, our day to day insecurity led to anxiety. We made no attempt to claim this as the best possible march in Central America. It happened to be the only March in Central America and, as such, one of the hopes for nonviolent change in Central America.

Success does not depend on how far we walk but rather on the fruits of our labor. Our unity is in our agreement on the objectives of the March, not on when, how or where we march. There were differences on such matters. Some of the young people wanted to log in more kilometers per day. Often it was not possible to walk even five kilometers in a day. Many times it was necessary for me to repeat the axiom of Jesus, "Sufficient for the day is the trouble thereof." Calm and confidence were essential to combat anxiety and disaster. The luxury of losing control even for a moment was not acceptable. It was often necessary to debate other members of the directorate publicly. What people want to do is simply what they want to do, not necessarily the best thing to do. We had to ask people not to be so in love with their idea of what the March should be that they could not accept anything else. Many great actions in history were matters of waiting. Gandhi was frequently waiting out the British. Desmond Tutu waited out some situations in South Africa. It is harder to endure than to attack.

The Buddhist monks were the contemplative heart of the March. Their constant prayers, their constant chanting, their drums, served as a great unifying element. Several days in Managua they chanted from sunup to sundown. They prayed through the day at the destroyed Cathedral in Managua and did not eat or drink until evening.

One of the very bizarre ideas during the March was to attempt to take launches from the town of Potosi, Nicaragua across the Gulf of Fonseca to the Salvadoran town of La Union. These launches were actually dug-out canoes with motors on them. This launch proposal was made in a demagogic, can-you-top-this fashion. I opposed it.

In spite of the fact that the action was admittedly being done for media purposes (another reason I opposed it), a substantial number of our people, especially the Danes (the Vikings), proceeded north toward Potosi, Nicaragua. They were interrupted on the way with word that the Salvadorans would not permit the launches to land at La Union and that any such action would be considered a provocation by the Sandinista government of Nicaragua. Without a doubt, adventurism was one of the occupational hazards of this march.

At worst, I thought of some individuals as suicidal. But that was generally not the case. I was quite worried during the seven-day vigil at the Honduran border that some people were simply going to walk across in defiance of the Cobras. I heard discussion of this tactic and even support for it from sources that I thought would know better.

While our March was in El Salvador, Archbishop Rivera y Damas was with a group of priests and sisters in Chalatenango and came under heavy bombardment from the Salvadoran Air Force. They were in the community of Guarjila when A-37 aircraft of U.S. manufacture indiscriminately attacked the city with bombs and rockets.

One of my happiest recollections of the March was a personal visit with Rigoberta Menchú (please read her book: *I, Rigoberta Menchú: An Indian Woman of Guatemala*, Verso Press, London, 1984).

It is important to mention a criticism of Rigoberta's book which was written by David Stoll, *Rigoberta Menchú and the Story of All Poor Guatemalans*. (Westview, 1999). But even more important is the scholarly response to Stoll's criticism written by Julie Bolt, "Towards an Active Utopia: Truth-making in Menchú, Stoll, and the Classroom" an article in *The Review of Education / Pedagogy / Cultural Studies*, Vol. 21, No. 3. pp. 265-279. A linguistic expert told me that Rigoberta, now a Nobel Laureate, actually speaks in verse. Here are some of her words to me translated into English:

The new president will make demands
But his demands will not be permitted.
The Military is going to select the Minister of Defense
Not the President.
Power has been militarized.
Our men are mobilized into Civil Patrols.

A special cedula (internal passport) awaits
Those who are accepted by the Fundamentalist
Churches.
People of Nahuala have become fundamentalists.
People who used to be Catholics.
Why have they changed religions?
Because they are allowed to go further from the village
To look for firewood if they have a Fundamentalist Cedula.

People are forcibly acculturated.
They build highways.
They grow wheat instead of corn.
We are now living in total misery.
The new government will change names
But not reality.

We lack salt.
Salt is sold by pinches.
It would be three or four quetzales per pound.
No one buys a pound
So it is sold in pinches rather than pounds.

We are losing our culture.
There is no other way to preserve our lives
But to lose our culture.

Our people are prisoners in Chiapas.
We lack water.
Those in Campeche have it better.

Do you know that two thousand people died in Alta Verapaz
Rather than to give in to the army.

The army was going to put them into open prisons.
They refused.
This was not the only massacre.

They use certain churches to oppress us
The Mormons.
A woman told me recently that she could no longer
Make huipiles (blouses woven of many colors).
But now that we cannot make huipiles
We must make history instead. After we make our own history
We will make huipiles again.

Perhaps we were guilty of triumphalism.
We thought victory was right around the corner
But this is not the case.

We must remember the slogans of
Grupo Apoyo Mutuo
To Die Honoring the Name of our Beloved.
They took them away living. We demand to see them living.

The risk is very great
But Grupo Apoyo Mutuo is an obstacle to the new government
And the new government might strike out at Grupo Apoyo Mutuo.

I know my parents are dead and I am very proud of them
But in my dreams I see my brothers and sisters.
I do not think they are dead.
Many times I dream they are alive.
They were captured by the army
Taken away by night.
I don't know if they are dead or alive.

And now I live in airports
An international diplomat for the Indian people of Guatemala.
I do not have a house, a family, a roof.
I do not have a country
But hundreds of families are supporting me.

I have hope
We can arrive.
We can have greater joy.
Drugs take people away from the realities of life
But I have a vision of great change in the world.
People must make history.
I am disturbed at the level of ignorance in the U.S.
I am disturbed at the degree of illiteracy in the U.S.
Your culture wants people to say, "Oh, I didn't know that."

While the March was in El Salvador, we heard about an attack from a U.S. warship. It appears the FMLN forces were attacking the Salvadoran battalion Cuscatlan in the area of Usulatan, that is a hundred and thirty kilometers from the capital of San Salvador. This represents another violation of United States law which forbids U.S. forces in El Salvador from any acts of war without an executive order. The ship described was said to be similar to the destroyer 963 Spruance, the same type that contains missiles capable of carrying nuclear warheads. The U.S. Defense Department of course denied the presence of this ship and also denied the attack.

A few of the marchers returned to El Salvador to find out exactly what happened to Brigido Sanchez. They insist on pursuing the case until he is released. He symbolizes the many Salvadorans held without charge.

After delays, opposition, attacks, injury, insects, hunger and thirst, anxiety, disagreements and some sleepless nights, we were in Mexico exactly on the day planned. We were on schedule in good spirits, and we believe we have had an impact on Central America as Central America has had an impact on us.

At times I found it difficult to be in a position of authority while living together with all of the marchers. Military tradition separates officers from enlisted people to retain authority. But we were the antithesis of military tradition.

As a white male, over fifty, and a U.S. citizen, I think I symbolized everything that is wrong in contemporary society. Some people had difficulty with that, but most did not.

Group Three was the directorate; it consisted of some seven leaders who deliberated on issues and projects. *Group Two* were representatives from each of the national groups. *Group One* was the assembly of national groups. The Spaniards observed that Group One and Group Two did not function well and that the entire body vote on all things submitted by Group Three. We gradually accepted the Spanish demands, and put many things to a popular vote. This was, of course, enormously time consuming, and I think *too* many issues were dealt with in this deliberative fashion.

The Danes and the Spaniards were quite similar—they were aggressive, defiant, fearless, adventuresome and ready at the proper moment to give a united front. These people were initially anti-religious. At the beginning of the march they had no understanding of the concept of theology of liberation. The militant example of the Buddhist Monks, however, gave them a new outlook on religion. The most memorable musical event was the incredible Danes marching defiantly up to the Honduran Cobras, who were ready to kill them. The music was Beethoven's Ninth, *The Hymn to Joy*. The image of these tough, hard-drinking people will remain forever in my memory.

Some of the pious, selfless, obedient, thoughtful and generous members simply could not take the strain, and left the March. The Danes and the Spaniards could sing all night, joke at the world, pay no attention to the fact that some people wanted to sleep. They could be categorized as thoughtless and selfish, but these thoughtless, selfish people were making history and they seemed to know it. This ability to complain and to be one's self, as they were, seemed to keep them going. I do not know what we would have done if they had stopped complaining.

A few the British women had served at the Greenham Common anti-nuclear demonstrations. How great people can look with no make-up, no laundry, no water, no fancy clothes. Their femininity seemed enhanced as did their courage. They complained less than the men. Occasionally one of them would get understandably hysterical. I recalled the hymn, "How beautiful the feet of those who preach the gospel of peace," and thought, not only the feet, but the whole person. At times I would look at them and they seemed to glow with a spirituality that was not pietistic, that was not self-righteous and was not sectarian. It was *whole*.

Occasionally, in my view, some of the marchers looked like children, angry at their father, and apparently I was the father figure. "We're going to live our own life, this is our project and we're going to do it our way," they said. It was necessary to point out time and again that the most dangerous project was not necessarily the most effective and that sometimes the most selfish project was the most dangerous.

One lad was so desperately ill he could not hear; he remained behind in Esteli to rest and to get some medicine at the local hospital. Coming down from the Honduran border I went to his sickbed, moved him into a cab and took him to Managua. "We are going to the Military Hospital," I said. He responded, "I don't want to go to the Military Hospital. I'm a pacifist," he said in obvious pain. I insisted, "You *are* going to the Military Hospital." The efficient Nicaraguan doctor carefully diagnosed a mastoid infection, gave shots, medicine and a series of future appointments. The young man improved rapidly. Of course, there was no charge. Medical care was free in Nicaragua, for all, including foreign visitors.

This March is a beginning; it is a beginning of the family of nations observing areas of dispute and arriving as family to attempt peaceful settlement. We are extremely grateful to all of the people of the globe who contributed their time, their effort and their money to support the International March for Peace in Central America.

The Impact of the March on Central America

Personnel for Service in Central America:

Many marchers returned to do long term volunteer work in Central America.

Revitalization of the Contadora Peace Process:

On the day our march began we were addressed by the former president of Panama, Jorge Illueca, a pillar of the Contadora nations. At that moment, December 10, 1985, Contadora was at its lowest ebb. Illueca made the following prophecy:

> The March of these messengers of peace will light a flame of hope in the region and will contribute to creating a climate to stimulate and revitalize the Contadora negotiations.

We marched for a full month before the Contadora Group met again. Our daily reports and press conferences were major news in the region during each day of that month. We believe that our constant support for Contadora as the avenue to a peaceful settlement prepared the way for the bold proposals of the meeting at Caraballeda in Venezuela on January 11th and 12th. We believe the prophesy stated by Jorge Illueca on December 10th was fulfilled on February 10th when all eight Foreign Ministers present at Caraballeda presented themselves to Secretary of State George Schultz in Washington, D.C. (the countries represented were Mexico, Panama, Venezuela, Colombia, Peru, Brazil, Uruguay and Argentina)with the following demands:

- A permanent solution to the Central American conflict must be Latin American. It must not be considered part of the east-west conflict.

- Self-determination, nonintervention and respect for territorial integrity.

- Observance of human rights.

- Suspension of international military maneuvers.

- Formation of a Central American Parliament.

- Reestablishment of conversations between the United States and Nicaragua.

- No political, logistic or military support for any group intending to subvert or destabilize the constitutional order.

Censorship:

While the Caribbean Basin was saturated with news of the March, the U.S. media was not. But why call it censorship? Journalists from major U.S. television, radio and print media traveled with us filed reports from each of the seven countries on our route. Press conferences were held in all seven countries; attendance was excellent. The largest delegation on the march was from the United States. Editors in the U.S. received this material and for the most part it was shelved. Why was its shelved? Because of a general support for U.S. foreign policy by major media. Certainly an opinion piece here or there is accepted as an example of press freedom. But hard news is generally reported with the implication that our side is right. Certainly no major media outlet is about to say that the United States is practicing state terrorism. And that is why our march was declared to be non-news. We are proud to say, however, that the media crew of the march produced fifty hours of professional quality video tape. This material was used to make the award winning documentary *Viva La Paz* (The International March for Peace in Central America).

Relationship of U.S. Foreign and Domestic Policy:

We can only hope that by sharing briefly with the Central American people the brutalization they have suffered, we can be motivated to stop the billions of dollars in military aid which have contributed nothing but misery to Latin America. The relationship between such malicious military adventures and the dismal domestic conditions in the United States should be obvious.

Judiciary Action:

The Costa Rican Association of Jurists demanded of President Monge that the pro Contra organization Costa Rica Libre be dissolved because of its violent attack on the International Peace March in Central America.

Election Results:

Revulsion of the local citizens at the attack on the march by Costa Rica Libre was so intense that it may have tipped the scales away from the favored pro-war candidate leading to the presidential election of the underdog Oscar Arias who was later awarded the Nobel Prize for his peacemaking efforts.

Mass Mobilizations:

The March represented the first demonstration of U.S. internationalists at the Southern Command in Panama. The huge reception in Mexico City was the largest that country had seen for any event in five years.

Exposure of Lies:

Witness to the devastation caused by Contra Mercenaries in Nicaragua will bring to the international community an authentic definition of these so-called "freedom fighters."

Accompaniment:

The presence of marchers and other foreign visitors in Contra zones of Nicaragua and with the Indian people of Guatemala had strategic value in protecting these people from attack.

Investigative Action:

An Australian attorney on the march identified the forced recruitment of Miskito Indians for service as Contras. He judged the Honduran judiciary to be non-functional and declared Honduras to be a de facto military dictatorship.

Timing:

Inauguration Day in Guatemala was possibly the only time for such a march to "invade" that country. Citizens in every part of the country joined us and spoke of the repression in which they live.

Assurance of Future Assistance:

The people of El Salvador and the rest of Central America know that they can call on the international peace community to join them in their times of struggle.

Strategy for the Future:

Such Guerrillas of Peace are apt to strike anywhere they might be needed; Seattle, Washington, D.C., Los Angeles, Philadelphia.

LA MARCHA CONTINUARÁ! (The March will continue).

Circles of Hope

May 12, 1995

With very short notice, the Director of Pastors for Peace, Tom Hansen, asked me to lead a delegation to the peace talks at San Andres Larrainzar in the state of Chiapas, Mexico. Picture an indigenous village in the highlands of Chiapas where clouds float in at any moment and obscure the verdant landscape. Here live the Tzotzil (Bat People).

With weeks of planning, and following up on the meetings of the month of April, 1995, the latest session began on May 12th. What we saw was a model for international conflict resolution. Through the unrelenting efforts of the Mexican non-governmental network of human rights and the persistent effort of Bishop Samuel Ruiz Garcia, a complex and effective system for the dialogue of adversaries was developed.

Circle one:

These are the Mexican Military Police. Actually members of the Mexican Army, these troops have arrived according to the agreement armed only with riot sticks. Everyone is aware that the back-up forces of the Mexican Army are not far from this village in the surrounding mountains. These troops are ready at a moments notice to storm the peace talks "if necessary." Approximately 50 thousand troops of the Mexican Army are now in Chiapas.

Circle two:

Representatives approved by the National Commission of Mediation (*Comision Nacional de Intermediacion*) known as CONAI. The president of this commission is Bishop Samuel Ruiz Garcia of San Cristóbal de las Casas. This inner circle is made up of Mexican human rights networks, and international visitors seeking a peaceful resolution to the conflict. Inside of this circle, and in sync with it is a belt of indigenous people from the surrounding villages. These groups are also under the umbrella of CONAI. Together they represent *El Cinturon de Paz; Sociedad Civil* (The Peace Circle of Civil Society).

Circle three:

This is the Mexican Red Cross and it borders the building where the talks are to take place. Participants in the three circles are on duty for approximately four hours at a time followed by a rest period.

In between the Military Police circle and circle two is a huge stage which is available to 250 journalists eager for a story. Intermingled with the journalists are the "journalists" of the Mexican Secret Police who are eagerly taking moving and still pictures of everyone present. With everyone in place and hours of waiting, the International Red Cross four wheel drive vehicles spattered with mud arrive with the players in this dangerous dialogue for peace. Circle two had been instructed to avoid cheering and slogans . . . but there was some cheering even from the journalists when the Zapatista Commanders descended from the vehicles in their indigenous garb, multi-ribboned hats and black ski masks. There were no cheers for Marco Antonio Bernal Gutierrez who led the delegation representing the government of Mexico.

With the smiles and handshakes and an effort to project informality there remained in San Andres Larrainzar an obvious fear of treachery. Why? It is a matter of history. Mexican Emperor Iturbide took the state of Chiapas from Guatemala by force in 1823. By 1867 the indigenous people of Chiapas revolted under the direction of Pedro Diaz Cuscat who heard the stones talking and giving counsel to disobey the *Ladinos* (Mestizos) and to take back all of the lands stolen by the hacienda owners. Just as the indigenous warriors were in a position to capture San Cristóbal de las Casas they entered into a dialogue with the government of Mexico.

The peace talks of 1869 were followed by the capture an execution of the leaders and everything went back to "normal." Then there is the ghost of Emiliano Zapata. The new Mexican ten peso bill is emblazoned with Zapata's piercing stare. It was Zapata who developed the Plan de Ayala which evolved into Article 27 of the Mexican Constitution of 1917. But Zapata's plans for the peasants of Morelos were a threat to the urban based Mexican Federales and the hacienda owners who wanted certain political changes (one term, no re-election) without an economic restructuring of Mexico. Zapata was asked to come to dinner for peace talks with Colonel Jesus Guajardo. Guajardo's troops sounded the honor call on the arrival of General Zapata, they presented arms and shot him to death on April 10, 1919. The opportunist President Venustiano Carranza promoted Jesus Guajardo to the rank of brigadier general and paid him 50 thousand pesos for the assassination.

In the spirit of Carranza, President Salinas abrogated section 27 of the Mexican Constitution in 1992. Sub-Commandante Marcos and his advisers are very conscious of this history of treachery. With this in mind, Marcos explained that he would not arrive at San Andres Larrainzar. He knew that the Mexican power structure still thought they could eliminate the leader and end the movement.

All of the commanders who arrived at the dialogue were indigenous. Marcos also wanted the world to know that the indigenous commanders could negotiate for themselves. They did not need him. The model designed by the Zapatistas of 1995 is not the model of Latin America revolutions of the twentieth century. They do not seek state power. "We did not come here to ask for the National Palace," said one indigenous commander, "we came to seek, justice, democracy and liberty." Even as the dialogues of 1995 took place there were reports of the Mexican Army advancing in the areas of Guadalupe Tepeyac and Ocosingo. The night of Sunday, May 14th was one of ominous signs. Thunder, lightening, wind, rain, fog and clouds struck San Andres Larrainzar. The Zapatistas were tired of being lectured to by the Mexican government representatives. The eldest rebel, a woman, Commander Trinidad, accused the government of lies. Rhetorically the Zapatistas said, "Why are we here? Why should we continue if you have no substantive offers?" Actually the Zapatistas had begun the meeting with an audacious statement that they were stronger than the Mexican government. "The rhythm of the Mexican government is not our rhythm," said the Zapatista leadership.

A singular lightning bolt was created by the General in charge of the Military Police at about midnight. In an instant the metal detectors were removed and the Military Police were ordered away from their circle. Everyone knew this was a signal for the armed troops in the mountains to descend on San Andres Larrainzar. The indigenous men of circle two sent their wives and children to a safe area and actually expanded their numbers as some of the other circles began to be depleted. The indigenous were clearly putting their bodies on the line in defense of the Zapatistas in the conference hall. The engines of the vehicles of transport for the government were started and the vehicles were pointed toward San Cristóbal de las Casas. An imminent departure of government representatives was expected.

Bishop Samuel Ruiz Garcia moved from delegation to delegation seeking a continuation of the faltering dialogue. The Zapatistas took the initiative by saying that they would respond to the government's statements at 10:00 AM on Monday morning, May 15th. Reporters asked Marco Antonio Bernal Gutierrez, head of the government delegation, just who gave the order to the Military Police to take such precipitous action. Bernal shrugged his shoulders. When the General was questioned he explained that he had evidence of arms on the compound. None of the journalists present were able to verify the presence of any arms.

Monday, May 15th was a day of substantive communication. The government has proposed a plan for routes to open space for the EZLN (Ejercito Zapatista de Liberacion Nacional) to group its contingents reciprocally and proportionally in defined communities. The areas identified are principally near Guadalupe Tepeyac and Ocosingo. The government gave assurance that the Mexican Military would stay a large distance from these proposed routes. It further stated that the Zapatistas were neither required to surrender nor put down their arms. The Mexican Government even conceded to the Zapatistas the maintenance of public order and security in rebel areas. On their part the Zapatistas responded that they would consider the offer and return with their reply on June 7th. In a unique model of substantive democracy, the EZLN will bring this proposal to all of their communities for consultation.

Commander David offered a formal invitation:

> The government is invited to our indigenous communities to see how we carry on consultation with the people on a local level. The government is invited to walk in our villages, to talk to our people, to talk to the women and the children. The government is invited to observe the life of the poor ... see how we eat, see how we sleep. Even if it is only a brief moment to share the experience. You can accompany us for a time.

The final observation by Mr. Bernal of the Mexican government was his desire to succeed in finding a mechanism to convert the armed Zapatistas into a legal entity. Our delegation left San Andres Larrainzar understanding why the audacious Zapatistas said they were more powerful than the Mexican government. Any effort to eliminate them militarily will trigger a national response from the Mexican people. A million Mexican died in the Mexican revolution of 1910-1929. It is urgent that the United States not foster any effort for a military solution to this conflict. The peace process will continue in Mexico if the treachery of the past is rejected and the root causes of the conflict are addressed.

Pastors for Peace and the Office of the Americas urge the nomination of Bishop Samuel Ruiz Garcia for the Nobel Peace Prize. This will enable the Bishop to have a larger forum to give a voice to the voiceless. Reinstatement of Article 27 of the Mexican Constitution of 1917; recognize the absolute failure of neo-liberal economics, and end of murderous structural adjustment policies of the International Monetary Fund and the World Bank are part of the solution.

Back in January of 1994, when we originally visited this war in Mexico, we heard the clear objections to NAFTA. The missing elements in the agreement are accords on social justice, human rights, the rights of labor and environmental protection. We do not support war in any form. In our opinion the greatest achievement of this historic meeting in San Andres Larrainzar is the fact that it happened. We urge continuation of these dialogues for months, years or decades if necessary.

Let this be the end of nineteenth century laissez-faire economics and the beginning of a century of cooperativism. The Tzotzil, Tojolabal and Tzeltal people of Chiapas in Mexico can show us how to do it.

The Death of the Dinosaur
and the Saber Tooth Tiger

A Foreboding of the Death of Militarism

March 10, 1997

Take a look at the La Brea Tar Pits numerous millennia ago. The saber tooth tiger attempts to attack a wild horse. The tiger gets stuck in the tar. The most ferocious animals are generally on the endangered species list, the lions, the tigers, the bald eagle. Animals of prey are endangered. Many of their frequent victims are not. The rabbit may appear defenseless but has a much greater future than the saber tooth tiger or any tiger for that matter.

In human history we see the same analogy. The last stage of every major civilization is to be ferocious. The twentieth century has been a century of war. As we examine world history the "rabbits" may seem defeated, but the rabbit species is undoubtedly the victor. The irony of defeat must be examined.

Did the Christian Crusaders defeat the infidels? On the contrary, the Moslems considered the Christians infidels and the Crusaders were neutralized by the Sunni Moslem Saladin on July 4, 1187. The concept of *Jihad* (Holy War) did not begin with the Moslems, it was a Moslem imitation of the "Holy War" of the Christian Crusaders.

Was Japan defeated in World War II? Ask one of the world's major economic powers. Were the Mexicans defeated in the war with the United States in 1846? Look at the very areas of their so-called defeat. The very region "conquered" by the United States will soon have a Latino majority. The history of militarism is a history of apparent victories, of Pyrrhic victories. Did the Conquistadores conquer Latin America or were they simply absorbed into it? Indigenous people were devastated but they are now resurrected and remain as environmental messengers to a dangerously "developed" world.

Without getting into absolutes we wish to say that most of the world's wars were unnecessary and counterproductive. The goals of the strong against the weak have rarely been achieved. The defense of the weak (David vs Goliath) against the strong has a rationale of legitimacy.

Let us look at some examples. The Cold War began at Hiroshima and was confirmed at Nagasaki. The two atomic bombs were meant to announce a new world order. They were a message to the Soviet Union that the United States would have international military hegemony.

The Soviet Union was in ashes after World War II but it took up the challenge from its former ally. Every child in the USSR knew, "The United States uses atomic bombs against civilians." The Soviet Union began a frantic effort to imitate the bomb used against the Japanese. The USSR never led in the arms race. But it successfully bankrupted itself mimicking the runaway military spending of the United States. Some scholars speak of value free social science. If there are no values, what could be a more perfect investment than the arms business? It appears to be heaven sent! The source of capital is a bottomless pit of gold; the treasury of the United States. Created from the tax money of the hard working people of the United States, this source is limitless and is counted in billion dollar increments.

The Characteristics of this military industrial system:

- **Greed:**
  Militarism is collective theft. Its only "ethic" is that might makes right.

- **The manipulation of fear:**
  "The enemy is coming and it is going to destroy us. But give us your money and we will protect you." If there were no Soviet Union after World War II, military industrialists would have had to create one. Foreign competition with our economic system was viewed as a threat to the people of the United States. "National interests" became a slogan to define corporate interests.

- **Instant obsolescence:**
  Whatever weapons currently operational must have immediate improvement. It can have a higher kill ratio. It can be faster, fly higher, carry more bombs.

- **Patriotism:**

    We are programmed to accept and even to love war. Years of prayerful recitation of The Pledge of Allegiance and a romanticized study of "history" prepare the way for the arrival of military recruiters on our high school campuses. High unemployment makes the "poverty draft" a certainty. (Centuries ago this kind of patriotism was identified as, "the last refuge of scoundrels."

- **The military budget becomes a sacred cow:**

    An uncritical posture is taken by legislators, as half of the national budget is designated for military purposes. Certainly there must be no cheap competitive bidding on military contracts. Such patriotic service will be done by the best and the brightest. Actually bids are determined by political power. Former generals serve as lobbyists to speak as "experts" for the benefit of corporations. Campaign coffers of cooperative candidates are filled by corporate Political Action Committees (PACS).

- **The search for enemies:**

    As the Defense Department became the largest entrepreneur in the United States, the CIA was avidly seeking new enemies. And there they were: Korea, Indochina, Dominican Republic, Chile, Grenada, Nicaragua, El Salvador, Guatemala, Panama, Iraq I and Iraq II, and Serbia to mention a few. Most of these conflicts were linked to that "evil empire," the Soviet Union, under the doctrine of anti-communism.

But the doctrine of anti-communism was never a doctrine of democracy and the United States supported dictator after dictator in the name of this vapid ideology. The world's dictators flooded to the United States to ask for financial and military aid to stop communism when they should have been trying to stop hunger.

The greatest crisis for U.S. corporate, military, prison, police and gun government actually did come from the Soviet Union. Rather than a first strike nuclear war which we were prepared to conduct, it came in the form of Mikhail Gorbachev. He realized there would never be any winners in the Cold War and he took the initiative to end it. The CIA was unknowledgeable and unprepared for this "revolution."

What a tragedy for the arms business! Gone were the endless preparations for nuclear war. The financial heaven they had discovered in the arms business was so great that they began to believe in the inevitablity of nuclear war. They did not negotiate. They did not speak values. But they did have values. Making money was the most important thing in the world. Nothing made money like arms. In the spirit of Dr. Strangelove, they were prepared to go to hell and to bring everyone else with them rather than to lose their "principles."

For over four decades our country used nuclear weapons in the same way a gunman robs a bank, brandishing the weapon, demanding the money and thankfully not killing the teller. This nuclear threat mentality took the place of diplomacy. Cold warriors were prepared to eliminate hundreds of millions of non-combatants in a nuclear holocaust. Possible massacre of entire uninvolved nations was seen as simply "collateral damage." Historians will surely identify this conduct as a form of homicidal mania.

To understand all of this, we must look to the military socialization of the world's people. "Fight like a man," was a formula designed by kings to create armies out of peasants. "Do what you are told," whether it be the monastic vow of obedience or the military, "mine is not to reason why, mine is but to do or die!" There is little difference.

There is no better example of the religiosity of militarism than the Christian Crusades (1095-1291). Pope Gregory VII viewed his calling to be the unity of Christendom under the papacy. The Christian Knights would attack the infidels (Moslems) who occupied the Holy Land. Emperor Michael VII of Constantinople had asked the Roman Pontiff for help and protection from the Turks and the Moslems. Here was a chance to bring back the schismatic Eastern Church to Rome and turn the Christian Kings and Princes into Papal servants and repossess the Holy Land.

It was the second successor of Gregory VII, however, Pope Urban II, who actually sounded the alarm and called all Christian Knights to attack the infidel and reconquer the Holy Land.

The beginning of the twelfth century the Crusaders reached Jerusalem. Their chronicler reports:

> One of our knights, Letold, clambered up the wall (of Jerusalem). As soon as he was there, the defenders fled along the walls and down into the city, and we followed them, slaying them and cutting them down as far as the

Temple of Solomon, where there was such slaughter that our men waded in blood up to their ankles . . . The Crusaders ran about the city, seizing gold, silver, horses mules, and pillaging the houses filled with riches. Then happy and weeping with joy, our men went to adore at the sepulcher of Our Lord, and rendering up the offering they owed. The following morning we climbed to the roof of the Temple and fell upon the Saracens who were there, men and women, beheading them with the sword.

Even in the first Crusade we see something akin to the 1992 massacre of Bosnia. Almost a millenium later, Orthodox (Serb) and Roman (Croatian) Christians walked ankle deep in the blood of their Moslem enemies in the name of ethnic cleansing.

Pope Eugenius III and King Louis VII of France asked St. Bernard of Clairvaux to foster a Second Crusade 1147-1149 to stop the great Muslim growth which was alleged to be swallowing up both Roman and Greek Orthodox Christianity. By hindsight we can see the fallacy of his vision. St. Bernard was instrumental in founding the order of Templars which he described in 1125:

They are not lacking in proper bearing at home or in the field, and obedience is not lacking in esteem. They go and come according to the order of the Master; they put on the clothes he gives to them and demand from no one else either clothing or food. They avoid opulence in both; only essentials are cared for. They live with one another happily and with modesty without wenches or children in order that they do not lack evangelical perfection, without property in one house, of one spirit, endeavoring to maintain the bond of peace and tranquility so that in all of them one heart and one soul appears to live. At no time are they idle or wander about with curiosity. When they rest from their struggles against the infidels, in order not to eat their bread for nothing, they improve and mend their clothes and arms. Chess and board-games they despise, they do not cherish the chase nor the bird-hunt. They hate the vagabonds, the minstrels, all excessive singing and acting as vanity and stupidity of the world.

They do not go into battle stormily and without thought, but with due consideration and caution, peaceful like true children of Israel. But once the battle has begun they press into the enemy without fear, considering the enemy mere sheep. And if there are only a few of them they trust in the help of Jehovah. Therefore one of them has managed to drive a thousand before him, and two ten thousand. Also in a curious combination they are gentler than lambs and more ferocious than lions so that one has doubts whether to call them monks or knights. Yet they deserve both names, because they partake in the gentleness of monks and the bravery of knights.

St. Bernard has thus given us a perfect romantic fantasy of militarism. Indeed. God is on our side! Recruiters for military service continue in the spirit of St. Bernard.

Saladin was sixteen years of age at the time of St. Bernard. As a devout Moslem he was determined to expel the Crusaders from Palestine. God was on his side as well and he defeated the Second Crusade on July 4, 1187. (Both Saddam Hussein and George Bush insisted that God was on their side during the U.S. bombing of Iraq on January 13, 1991). The Third Crusade was marked by opportunism of the Crusaders and was also a failure for Christendom.

The greed motive became ever more clear in the Fourth Crusade which became a battle of Christian vs Christian as Roman Catholics attacked the schismatics of Constantinople where there were far more riches to be sacked than in the Holy Land. It went on for two centuries. Long before the conquistadores from Spain and Portugal or the Puritans from Europe, the essential religiosity of warfare, had been firmly established. The "humanitarian bombing" conducted by the United States in Serbia is part of this same same drill.

The bonding of the "crusaders" is essential, whether they be the LAPD or the Marine Corps. After months of training and suffering together, if one of their own is killed or wounded, they only fight more viciously against the "enemy."

"I could have killed every Somali I saw," said an African-American Marine after his buddy was shot by a sniper in Somalia (1993).

Can militarism be cured? Of course, but the antidote demands a consciousness of our social and political programming.

The dinosaur of militarism must become extinct. This will happen when we acknowledge militarism as the most vile form of slavery.

Yes, friends, we are called to abolish the war system.

Office of the Americas Report on the Delegation to Colombia

August, 1997

What does Medellin mean to a U.S. citizen? Narco-terrorists, *sicarios* (hired assassins) and drug lords. It is actually a beautiful and mountainous city located at many altitudes, all of them comfortable.

Colombians may joke about sacred things. Local humor might identify the Holy Trinity as *the army*, *the oligarchy* and *the church*. Such shady humor does not apply in Medellin. Church base communities made up of lively clergy and laity reach out to the urban delinquents and former addicts. We sat in a church rectory full of young delinquents in a process of rehabilitation. There was no moralizing. There was only a spirited discussion about the establishment of their new bakery.

Monsignor Hector Fabio Henao Gaviria witnessed a march for peace in Nicaragua some years ago and decided to attempt a similar peace march and vigil in Medellin. Powers of the city were doubtful of the success of such a venture and even feared the program would deteriorate into the violence which has marred Colombia for a half century. Hundreds of thousands of citizens came out to vigil, to march and to pray.

In the wake of this sustained event, Medellin has begun to change. But change is difficult in the midst of an invasion. The invaders are people from the countryside who are pouring into Medellin, Bogotá and all major urban centers. Why? There is a war on and they are being ordered off their lands by paramilitary death-squads. Who are the paramilitary? Some two hundred entities are identifiable. Some are under the direction of large land-owners, some are the "protectors" of oil companies, but most of them are shadow killers who do the dirty work for the Colombia military. It is similar to Guatemala and El Salvador; where death squads operated almost exclusively under military direction. To our chagrin we discovered that the paramilitaries are now part of a legal entity known as *Convivir* (to live together). We left Medellin with data from the Andean Commission of Jurists identifying two percent of Colombia's violence as drug related.

We proceeded to Uraba. Uraba is not a state or a province, it is a jungle region just south of the border of Panama which includes coastal lands of the Pacific Ocean and the Caribbean Sea. We were greeted by the Mayor of Apartado, Gloria Cuartas. It was here we determined that no good deed in Colombia will go unpunished. Some months ago Gloria prepared a school program on peace. While her class was in process the paramilitaries slid by the school, grabbed a young child, cut his head off and threw it into the classroom where she was speaking.

We were invited to visit a community under paramilitary control. Our guides recommended that we travel in a church vehicle over the dank, dirt, jungle path to San Jose. In the torrid humidity, a paramilitary death squad was guarding access to the community. Our diocesan vehicle was allowed to pass. I saw a hungry looking couple approach the food storage center with an empty sack. A brief word was spoken to them and they departed sadly with their sack still empty.

Weeks before our arrival a human rights group including a representative of the United Nations and a bishop was investigating a massacre in the nearby community of Vigia Fuerte. The group received a message to be out of the area within twelve hours or to die. The bishop inquired about the whereabouts of the missing pilot of a small boat they used for travel. The paramilitary leader said, "We have just killed him." The human rights group was told they were interfering with the paramilitary's right to kill.

There is a social center in San Jose. It is staffed by Doctors of the World and other most welcome "internationals" who come to share their lives with the oppressed. One of the women volunteers witnessed the brutalization of a peasant by the paramilitary and said, "Why don't you kill me instead?" The peasant was released.

But where are the guerrillas? They are virtually everywhere. There are over a thousand municipalities in Colombia, over half of them are under rebel control. The rebels are of the *FARC* (Revolutionary Armed Forces of Colombia) and the *ELN* (Army of National Liberation). These forces were created because of the institutionalized violence of Colombia. The voice of presidential candidate and revolutionary priest Camilo Torres demanded social justice and human rights for Colombia's masses. He was killed in combat in 1966. It would be futile to romanticize about the moral perfection of the rebel forces. Actually there seems to be a deterioration of the rebel ethic. While the rebels are not in the drug business, they do tax growers of food crops and coca.

One of the most extreme rebel organizations, the *EPL* (Army of Popular Liberation) has completely dissolved. Some of its members have been recruited into the paramilitary death squads. Paramilitary salaries are said to be $300 per month. Rebel salaries are placed at about $100 per month. The net result of these decades of conflict is one million displaced Colombians, a fate second only to death.

African-Colombians from the Choco were bombed and told by paramilitary forces to leave their homes immediately. They walked for days and finally were settled in the sports stadium of Turbo. We spent an afternoon with these sick, tired and hungry people. A second refugee center in Turbo, under the direction of the Church, was better organized and better fed. But everyone wants to return to their beloved Choco.

After these experiences with refugees, it was time to visit the General in charge of the Colombian Army in Uraba; Rito Alejo del Rio Rojas. General del Rio welcomed us at a large staff table. His intelligence officer was present as well as his human rights officer. The General called in a Special Forces officer and said, "Look at the uniform worn by the Special Forces, it's beautifully made of soft cotton. Look at the coarse material of my uniform. The Special Forces uniform is made in the United States and mine is made here in Colombia."

We introduced ourselves and the general began a long and defensive argument about the role of the Colombia Army. He identified the paramilitary forces as criminals and delinquents operating on the margin of the law. We said that we had just driven to the community of San Jose and that the paramilitary were running the check-point at the entrance of the town. If we could see the paramilitary, why could the army not see them? He shrugged his shoulders.

Why had the army never confronted the paramilitary squads? No answer. The workers in the banana plantations had a major problem, according to the General, they drank. He made no reference to the fact that they worked from 6:00 AM to 6:00 PM in a heat and humidity of international fame. The massive banana plantations pay no taxes to the municipality of Apartado. The people, however, gather some of the rejected produce and boil it into a banana stew.

Here begins the monologue of General Rito Alejo del Rio Rojas:

Eighty percent of Uraba is jungle. There are few roads. We lack resources, educational and health facilities. Most of the homes are minimal, lacking the basic needs for human life. There is an absence of recreational facilities. The principal means of recreation is drinking liquor. There are many isolated communities where the civilization has not arrived. They are isolated in the jungle. This is a complex problem. Groups on the margin of the law have controlled these areas. They have been very radical and have maintained power through force. This included the EPL, the People's Liberation Army. Five months ago, they laid down their arms. Some went into the FARC (Revolutionary Armed Forces of Colombia). Some went into the ELN (Army of National Liberation). When EPL members began to reintegrate into Colombian society, the FARC considered them to be traitors and determined to eliminate them.

Massacres began in URABA. The phenomenon of organized delinquency began. Organized delinquency or what are called paramilitaries began. These are narco-terrorists who imply they are working with the army. But the government and the armed forces consider the paramilitary as narco-terrorists just as the FARC and ELN. They are dedicated to terror. Narco-terrorists of the drug cartels as Pablo Escobar who are dedicated to commerce in drugs.

These groups use terrorism under the control of the drug lords so they can receive income to purchase arms and equipment. This region is especially convenient for the narco-subversives because it is surrounded by two seas, The Gulf of Uraba on the Caribbean and the coast of Choco on the Pacific. The narco-subversives also take advantage of the border with Panama and send narcotics out of Colombia. Arms are sent in by guerrillas of other countries. This area is also the scene of many kidnappings. Such activity facilitated by the jungle. It is almost impossible for the public forces to rescue everyone who is kidnapped.

In spite of these difficulties, this area is very attractive because whoever wishes to develop a business here has a high possibility of getting ahead. The climate is appropriate for every kind of commerce. The zone has 32 thousand hectares of bananas. The area is suitable for cattle, and any other product. We also have the problem of unions. Growers tried to cultivate African palm oil but the guerrillas burned down the trees.

The present cultivation of bananas includes 11,000 heads of families working in the banana fields. Each worker has five or six people under their care who depend on them. But because of the lack of culture they do not use their money well, they spend it on alcohol and therefore they have a low level of life. They have invaded land by invasion. You can see areas of Apartado where there these invasions have taken place. I consider these invasions the greatest social problem of this region.

This book (*Ejercito Nacional de Colombia, Informe Publico de la Decimoseptima Brigada sobre la Situacion de Derechos Humanos en Uraba.* Carepa, Antioquia, Colombia, July 31, 1997) will give you the necessary statistics. The FARC is the bloodiest group. The table of contents indicates that everything is proven. These are the violations of human rights in Uraba. How many died in each massacre and who killed them is clear in this book. You will also see that organized delinquents which are unfortunately called paramilitary are involved as well. There are kidnappings. My soldiers are wounded by land mines. There has been a campaign of extermination against the political movement known as Peace and Liberty.

We conduct Civic Military Action which includes health and social services. But the information which generally leaves this country is not accurate. Non-governmental organizations are partial and try to link the bloodshed to the military. But this book will show you exactly who has been assassinated and by whom. Here we have proof regarding the real culprits. You can see the quantity of land mines which these outlaws have distributed in our communities. Our soldiers have been wounded. Fortunately we were informed of the presence of land mines and we told people not to go near the area until the Army could defuse the mines. If it had not been for our informers some humble workers would have been killed. Their terrorist actions increased. They placed a car bomb in Apartado. Thirteen were killed and fifty-two were wounded. That was the FARC. There was a material loss of three billion pesos.

Then there was the massacre of Currulao in the municipality of Turbo. This was the FARC. They have resources from drug trafficking. They get camouflaged uniforms. We do not have these camouflaged uniforms from the U.S.. Our Special Forces have them, however. But these bandits have camouflaged contraband uniforms. The FARC guerrillas were wearing this kind of uniform in Currulao and they penetrated the area on a holiday. The community was celebrating that night. They were dancing and drinking and the population was confused. They thought it was the army. The FARC rebels went into a bar and according to our testimony, "Fatso" who is the second or third head of the FARC was recognized by a young man. Fatso went into the street and began to assassinate indiscriminately claiming that he was killing paramilitaries. If you go to the Attorney General's office and see the photos, you will see that the victims were humble people and were not involved in any social conflict.

There was a massacre at the finca Osaka in the municipality of Carepa. The FARC killed ten people. These were the same people that committed the assassinations in Apartado. Many of those reponsible for the massacres have been captured. We searched for them. When we placed them in custody, elements of the FARC denied that these subjects committed the massacres and even blamed the Army for committing these crimes. But we can show you clearly the kind of individuals which were captured. We have the background on them and we know the lies they are telling.

There are investigations and reports on all of these aspects. The Army has received calumnies and denunciations. In some parts of the world, people who are linked to the FARC and the ELN are interested in creating a bad name for the Colombian Army. Such reports have no validity when they are placed before competent authority. These people are paid and they are violating international humanitarian law when they ask that actions be taken against relatives of persons linked to the public forces including minors of age who have nothing to do with the conflict.

I am happy that you are here today and I hope you will return to this region. We guarantee you helicopter visits throughout the region so you can talk more openly with the various communities. We would like you to go to Choco. For us it is a marvelous visit. Welcome, and if you come again we will be very attentive to your presence.

Here ends the monologue of General Rito Alejo Del Rio Rojas.

(Ham sandwiches are now served with Coca Cola).

Questions and observations from the delegation:

OBSERVATION: We spoke with the displaced people in Turbo and the group in the gymnasium has an empty storage room. There was no food. They are sick. I have this written request for the things they need.

GENERAL: I spoke to Dr. Cesar Garcia regarding the necessary purchases. We have obtained everything they need. But now I would like to say something that should not go out of this room. We have some communications of the guerrillas talking to each other. They don't care if they kill children, paraplegics, the sick or whatever.

QUESTION: Who are the paramilitary? Why does the Army protect them? Why have their violations not been investigated?

GENERAL: The paramilitary are at the margin of the law. They are delinquents just as the FARC is delinquent. And by the way, I forgot to mention three other massacres. The paramilitary arrived near the border of Panama. They were threatening families. These threats spread throughout the region. We talked to the Minister of the Interior and the mayors.

QUESTION: But who are the paramilitary? Who runs them? If you know so much about the FARC why don't you know so much about the paramilitary?

GENERAL: I believe that here in the book it is very clear. We are speaking about delinquents financed by the people of the region. They are drug-traffickers.

QUESTION: Are you spending as much energy protecting people from the paramilitary as you are spending protecting people from the FARC?

GENERAL: You can see we have pursued them, we have captured them.

QUESTION: Have you visited the people in San Jose and Turbo? Have you received their testimony?

GENERAL: Yes. I visited Rio Sucio. I have spoken to them individually. They are welcome to come here. Because of the reduction in homicides and massacres, the people are coming back to Uraba. This includes businessmen.

QUESTION: But the people in Turbo said they want to go back to Choco and they want guarantees.

GENERAL: It is physically impossible to guarantee them complete safety. Choco includes hundreds of square miles.

QUESTION: We listened to the people of Choco. Planes and helicopters came in and bombed them. Where did the helicopters come from? Do the paramilitary have helicopters?

GENERAL: No. But they could have rented them. We have no proof. In those operations, however, some of the helicopters were damaged, pilots were injured, soldiers were killed and injured. Remember the FARC killed some people they had kidnapped.

Our delegation departed after viewing photos of elderly couples dancing which were presented to us by the human rights officer.

A video camera panned all of the delegates as we approached our vehicle. Back to the airport at Apartado on our way to Bogotá. The military guards at the airport were into an endless stare as we awaited our Otter aircraft. It is hard to be pleasant with people who can take your life with impunity.

From the jungles of Uraba we flew to the cool Andean heights of Bogotá. Our first meeting was at the Colombian equivalent of the Pentagon. The guards subjected us to search after search prior to our admission to this sacred sentinel. Our passports were taken and we were told to proceed to the office of Mery Lucia Garcia Parra, the advisor on human rights in the National Defense Ministry.

Mery Lucia made it clear that her office is not an investigative agency. They simply receive reports and channel them to the appropriate offices. She repeated General Rito's position regarding the paramilitary as extra legal criminals and the enemy of the Colombian Army. The presentation of a military "line" became so clear. It is hard to find a Colombian intellectual or private agency that accepts the line. But what else is new? As U.S. citizens we had been victims of equally irrational military propaganda for ten years in Indo-China, to say nothing about the gibberish slobbered on us during the rape of Central America, the psychotic war in Grenada, the bombing of Panama and the holocaust in Iraq.

The military clique is a closed cult. They create their mythology, share it internationally and then apparently begin to believe it. Just as Jim Jones or David Koresh, the military cult leader's word is sacred. Disbelief is treason. Critical thinking is the enemy. The cult leader is generally an opportunist.

The drill of the Colombian military is clear:

- The civil war in Colombia is a drug war.

- The United States will give us billions of dollars if we claim to be fighting drugs, just as they gave billions to dictatorships which claimed they were fighting communism. Therefore the political rebels are actually narco-guerrillas.

- To maintain our international reputation as a legitimate military we will support a paramilitary apparatus for all dirty war activities. We will identify our paramilitary death squads as the enemy and disclaim any relationship to them.

The relationship between the military and the death squads of Guatemala and El Salvador was absolute and so is the relationship between the military and the paramilitary of Colombia.

Now we can understand how the Generals, the Ministry of Defense and Governmental Human Rights Offices unanimously claim that international and national Non-governmental organizations are "guerrilla sympathizers." Such claims are both insulting and threatening. Similar charges are made against any Colombian officials who attempt to identify the charade of the Official Story.

In the midst of the bloodshed which is Colombia, there is a domestic and functional answer. It is the program of the *Unidad Popular* (Popular Unity), an alternative political party. People of all classes are impressed with the goals and objectives of this party. There is just one difficulty. Anyone who stands up to organize or lead the Unidad Polular is killed. Thousands of party leaders have been brutally assassinated. This is the perplexity of the hermit kingdom which is Colombia. It is a nation which has never encouraged immigration. It has isolated itself in a liberal-conservative pendulum swing between co-existing oligarchs and feudal land barons. The drug lords are at home with and fully integrated with this crowd.

Does this mean that the FARC and the ELN have the answer for Colombia? I do not think so. We cannot ignore the fact that their ideology has focused on the needs of the poor and the oppressed. But together with the military they have helped to create a population of one-million displaced Colombians.

Personally I think the answer to the conflict lies in the proven potential of the United Nations. This international body can be proud of its achievements in Nicaragua, El Salvador and Guatemala. In Bogotá we had a lengthy meeting with Almudena Mazarrasa Alvear, the director of the Office of the High Commission of the United Nations for Human rights in Colombia and her assistant, Javier Hernandez Valencia. It is her opinion and ours that the President of the United States has the ability to promote a United Nations Negotiating Team for peace accords in Colombia.

The current policy of the United States is to promote victory for the status quo in Colombia. This means that a war which is now fifty years old will be one hundred years old in 2047. Such a war will undoubtedly lead to the purchase of a great deal of military hardware. It seems to me, however, that a political economy of peace and distributive justice would be better for everyone.

For Colombian documentation of the absolute relationship between pararmilitary death squads and the Colombian Military, I recommend: *Colombia, the Genocidal Democracy* by Javier Giraldo, S.J., (Common Courage Press, 1996.)

Our current military aid to Colombia, which is well over a billion dollars in recent years, is simply adding fuel to the fires of war and confirming the cult of Colombian militarism.

The Emergency Delegation
to Chiapas

January 13, 1998

This week we stood at a mound of dirt over some forty-five bodies buried at Acteal in the municipality of Chenalho in the state of Chiapas, Mexico. We lit candles in their memory and shuffled through children's homework papers scored with bullet holes.

The weapons used in this massacre came from the United States. 3,200 Mexican soldiers have recently been trained at Fort Bragg by the same Green Berets who trained the Contras for their blood-thirsty attacks on Nicaragua in the 1980s.

Rules of the Game:

Today we have news from San Cristóbal de las Casas that police commander Felipe Vazquez has provided a direct link between government officials and the massacre. Vazquez reported to Nuevo Amanecer Press that he had been ordered to check if civilians carrying illegal weapons were members of the Institutional Revolutionary Party (PRI, the party of President Zedillo). If they were PRI members the police commander was instructed not to detain them. Mexico's Office of the Attorney General has yet to name any state officials as suspects.

Paramilitary Death Squads:

There are a variety of terrorist paramilitary death squads representing the interests of the PRI:

- *Desarrollo Paz y Justicia* (Development, Peace and Justice)

- *Guardias Blancas* (White Guards)

- *Mascara Roja* (Red Masks)

These paramilitary groups and many others spread terror and confusion in their efforts to destroy indigenous movements. A motorcade including Bishop Samuel Ruiz Garcia was fired upon recently. There were three casualties.

The Mexican Military:

Almost half of the entire Mexican military is now in the state of Chiapas. Why don't the people of Chiapas want them there?

1. They are attempting to control communities, not to defend them.

2. Women of the indigenous communities document sexual attacks by the military.

3. Prostitutes are brought in from Mexico City and in some cases local residents have presented their daughters as prostitutes in order to avoid starvation.

4. The military has not restrained its paramilitary terrorists.

5. The military is interfering with the educational system by using local schools as barracks.

6. People cannot get their crops out of the field because of military harassment.

7. Women cannot cook because they cannot gather firewood without being threatened.

8. Constant overflights of helicopters maintain and atmosphere of terror.

In every village there is a demand for the military to depart immediately. Some of the efforts are history making.

Take the case of the village of X'oyep. Thousands of Tzotzil indigenous refugees arrived fleeing the violence directed at them because they do not belong to the official party, the PRI. Their houses had been burned, their belongings stolen, there were indiscriminate murders by the above-mentioned death squads. This month the Army arrived and occupied the lands of the community. At first the people shouted at them to leave immediately and then for five hours physically pushed the Federal Troops out of the village. The troops have not left the area and are currently interfering with the efforts of the people to use the village water supply.

Visiting Zapatista Communities:

Our emergency delegation went to the Zapatista community of Oventic. Here we observed the secondary school building under construction by international volunteers. Oventic is referred to as an Aguascalientes (a major meeting place for Zapatistas). The inhabitants of this large community were forced to flee to higher ground as Mexican troops broke the peace accords and intruded. Citizens were just beginning to return as we visited. The large clinic, however, was still closed.

This Aguacalientes is in the municipality of San Andres Saicamch'en de los Pobres which was previously known as San Andres Larrainzar and was the site of the Peace Accords of 1995-1996. The accords are violated by the Mexican government daily. The Zapatistas were granted freedom of movement through the area, they were allowed to keep their weapons and they were granted a degree of autonomy. That autonomy has not been respected. What about the word "Saicamch'en?" It means "white rocks." These local rocks have cried out to the community on many occasions. Once it was the intrusion of the Aztecs into the Mayan area, another time it was because of Spanish occupation and enslavement and now they cry out again "for the poor." We spoke at length to the President of San Andres. His resemblance to Emiliano Zapata was striking.

At Polho, as in other Zapatista communities, we had to show our authorization as international observers. This authorization is not from the Mexican government; it is from the Aguascalientes. At military stops delegates had to produce U.S., Canadian and Mexican passports. At Zapatista villages we had to produce Zapatista documents. Polho is a major site for the displaced of the region. Mexican and international humanitarian aid is much in evidence at this mountain community.

The villagers of Polho were celebrating an unusual occurrence. Here is their statement:

On the 15th of October of 1997 a dove flew into our community from the north. It landed in the plaza at noon where it encountered a worker drinking pozol. The worker offered the dove tortillas, beans and crackers. The dove ate the meal and stayed for two hours. As the fog came in, various members of the community attempted to keep the dove with us. The dove did not permit this and flew off to the southwest.

The mayor explained that on the evening of October 15, paramilitary death squads "passed over" the village firing only one shot which imbedded itself into the wall of his home. The village looks to the dove as a symbol of their survival.

The villagers elevated a large banner relating the history of the dove as they built an altar to Our Lady of Guadalupe. I was introduced to the community as a priest and was asked to speak. I explained that for centuries Our Lady of Guadalupe was known as Paloma Blanca, The White Dove and I sang the ancient chant in Latin, Salve Regina.

The Massacre Site:

From the Zapatista village of Polho we drove on to the massacre site of Acteal. Police were aggressively interrogating a town official. Before our departure we were informed that some people had agreed with the local police to dress up as soldiers and to review several suspects in the massacre case. The whole thing sounded so bizarre that we thought it might be a trap to eliminate witnesses. Some community members joined us as we drove to the PRI village of Tzajalucum. I thought of the phrase "valley of death" as we descended down a steep rocky dirt road passing numerous burned down homes of non-PRI citizens. We were clearly unwelcome in this location. As we attempted the ascent toward the main highway, our VW van lost its differential and we were stuck with one functional vehicle and a van that was blocking a single lane dirt road. The driver was afraid that any military vehicle passing by might simply push the vehicle over the side to clear the road. We left a group with the vehicle and proceeded to Polho to get a rope. After numerous adventures we arrived back in San Cristóbal at 1:00 AM. We had been told to be off the highway by 6:00 PM.

Bishop Samuel Ruiz Garcia: A Zapatista?

We interviewed the Bishop, a Nobel Prize Nominee, at length and were struck by how much he reminded us of the late Archbishop Oscar Arnulfo Romero of El Salvador. He said that the attack at Acteal was the twenty-fifth such atrocity since April of 1997.

We, and much of Mexico, were astounded by the hysterical effort of General Jose Gomez Salazar, Commander of the Mexican Military in Chiapas to "prove" a link between Bishop Ruiz and the Zapatista rebels. His proof was to find a secret supply of weapons topped with religious texts in the Tojolabal language which were translated by the bishop. The texts included the gospel according to St. Mark, a hymnal, and a catechism. The diocese of San Cristóbal accepted the charge that the books were theirs and asked just how such a find was to be considered as proof of the bishop's alleged involvement in an armed movement. While the vast majority of the Mexican media, government and people considered the General's claims to be stupid, the charge remains a clear threat to the life of Bishop Ruiz. Fanatical members of these PRI paramilitary death squads can take such a charge as a mandate to kill the bishop.

After hearing these charges we proceeded to the General's Command post in Tuxtla-Gutierrez asking for an interview. We were told he was in the field and could not see us. But what we did see at the command post were large posters of approval for the very death squads that killed the citizens of Acteal.

U.S. Manuals:

We were reminded of the exact same relationships between death squads and military which we had witnessed in El Salvador, Guatemala and Colombia. This methodology was developed by the United States in 1961 and has continued to the present. We refer to *Field Manual 100-20*, "Stability and Support Operations," Chapter six, "Foreign Internal Conflicts," United States Army Command and General Staff College, Fort Leavenworth, Kansas, 1997.

Any U.S. citizen who is aware of the role of our government in the killing of innocent people in Mexico would surely say, "We are better than that."

The strongest response to the bloody militarization of Mexico and the example of militant moral authority of the highest level was shown by the women of X'oyep and other villages of Chiapas who, with their bare hands physically pushed heavily armed Mexican troops out of their villages and they will continue to do so even at the cost of their lives.

International Accompaniment:

The Bishop and people of Chiapas are asking for accompaniment from the people of Mexico and the world. The most promising thing we saw in the village of Acteal was a group of young Spanish "internationals" who simply moved in as an act of solidarity. They have hung up their hammocks in the little chapel and are most welcome by the indigenous community, many of whom cannot speak Spanish.

A young physician greeted me saying, "Do you remember me from Colombia?" He was one of the *Medicos del Mundo* (Doctors of the World) who had been working in a savaged war zone of Uraba. They are much needed now in Mexico.

A Cry from Riobamba

September 2, 1998

In his Fedora hat, Quichua garb and with absolute confidence, the indigenous Master of Ceremonies intervened during the discourse of one of many Latin American Bishops present in Riobamba, Ecuador for a hemispheric meeting of the churches.

"Thank you, Monsenor, your time is up." The bishop stopped talking.

This incident is symbolic of a rapidly expanding "leadership from the base" in Latin America. Equally interesting is the honesty of the Bishops themselves.

"There is starvation, slavery, land theft and ecocide in my diocese," said one Bishop from Brazil. "When the Papal Nuncio came to visit, his singular concern was that I shave off my mustache." The Bishop still has the mustache. Perhaps it would be better to keep all of this a secret. But this is the information age!

The Awakening.

Everyone knows about the Conquistadores, the Crown and the Cross, the Inquisition, the Oligarchies and the Armies of oppression. What is not yet known is the awakening of hemispheric consciousness.

It began in 1810 with the Grito de Dolores of Father Hidalgo, the Father of the Mexican Independence. It continued with ongoing revolutions from Mexico and the Caribbean to Tierra del Fuego. Generally, these armed struggles were put down with beastly oppression.

After Vatican Council II (1962-1965), the churches gathered at Medellin, Colombia in 1968 to insist on a "preferential option for the poor" and the pursuit of a nonviolent struggle.

In August of 1976 in the wake of the Medellin Conference, the hemispheric churches met in Riobamba, Ecuador. The material of the conference was considered "subversive" by the Ecuadoran government. Seventeen Latin America Bishops were arrested together with other clergy and laity. They were held prisoner and finally expelled from Ecuador. The church was beginning to accept its call as a servant of liberation. The word liberation replaced the word development. Latin American governments then replaced the objective of liberation with the concept national security state (read dictatorship).

In 1980, Bishop Oscar Arnulfo Romero personified the preferential option for the poor. He was shot through the heart by Salvadoran "authorities" while celebrating Mass on March 24th of that year.

Riobamba, Ecuador, August / September, 1998

Hoping that the Ecuadoran government would not intervene as in 1976, the churches of Latin America convened in the Andes with a new component; macro-ecumenism. With the help of the Ecclesial Base Communities, Protestants, Indiginous religions and the surrounding community, a synthesis of consensus was expressed in *The Cry of Riobamba*.

The document was read in the Colosseum of Riobamba, Ecuador by Bishop Pedro Casaldaliga of Brazil. Triumphal ads for Coca Cola, Sprite, Fanta and again Coca Cola surrounded the stadium. Some ten thousands people chanted their approval to the statement.

Here is a summary:

From the heights of Chimborazo we join in a "Cry of the Excluded" and the hopes of the people of our continent. In an ecumenical spirit we call upon the God of Exodus and of the Passover who always hears the cry of the people in the process of liberation and of life. We are celebrating the 30th anniversary of the Medellin Conference and the second millenium, the Jubilee of the coming of Jesus.

During these days, we have visited the communities and participated in dialogues with the Indigenous people, African-Americans, the pastoral workers and the base communities. We have seen the vitality of a people cultivated prophetically by their pastors and becoming protagonists for the poor.

We direct our attention to:

- The option for the poor. Never has this been more important. More than seventy percent of the people of Latin America are excluded by the new economic order (neo-liberalismo).

- The struggles and the contribution of an alternative by the Indigenous people and the African-American people, especially in the defense of the land while living in accord with their cultural identity and social autonomy.

- The community as an expression of "communion and participation."

- Solidarity among the people and the churches of our country with the churches and people of other continents, especially those of the third world.

1. Regarding the option for the poor:

- We denounce absolutely the iniquity of the new economic order in its totality. It is a system of exclusion, idolatry of profit, and out of control ecocide. Related to this onslaught is the expansion of arms sales together with repressive militarism and paramilitarism.

- As one voice with people from all over the world, we denounce the new and perverse assault known as The Multilateral Agreement on Investment.

- We remain in permanent struggle for the abolition of the external debt and even more, we demand the payment of the social debt which is owed to our people at the cost of their lives and their dignity.

- We intend to pursue the reform of international institutions such as the United Nations, The International Monetary Fund and The World Bank which currently give privileged status to affluent and exploitative countries. We also intend to participate in the reform of the political, judicial and social institutions of our own countries.

- We will support, with effective solidarity, the process of peace and liberation while we simultaneously oppose the impunity and institutionalized violence which has marked our continent, particularly in Guatemala, Mexico, Colombia and Haiti.

- We will promote the participation of the general public in politics and in the promotion of civil society.

2.   We will evolve . . .

... from an ecumenism of intention, discourse and isolated gestures to a mutual recognition of the churches while understanding the complementary nature of the truths we hold and the sanctity of the unique mystery of Christ.

- Overcoming ancient historical conflicts and arguments which are often unrelated to the gospel message.

- Serving prophetically in the community of justice and peace and for the integrity of creation.

- Maintaining a macroecumenical dialogue with all religions, most specifically the Indigenous and African-American religions, to share of the faith in one God and one human family within one welcoming Spirit in self-critical and critical conversion

- Overcoming the attitudes of centralization and authoritarianism of the Catholic Church as well as the atomization of the Evangelical Churches.

- Recognizing all women and men in equality through baptism and for the service of the kingdom. We foster the adult participation of the laity, especially of women, in the churches to exercise various ministries and to hold decision making posts.

- Inculturating with the light of the gospel and the liberty of the Spirit, the liturgy, theology and all pastoral actions.

- Constructing, day by day, the church which we envision as the people of God, with the Bible a living reality in the ecclesial base communities and through the social pastoral ministry with a creativity faithful to the gospel, our times and our America.

We hope that this might be the life style and support system for life in our respective churches and countries; the true and permanent Jubilee established by Jesus of Nazareth. Going beyond occasional triumphalist commemorations, we hope to concretize a Biblical Jubilee in society and in the churches. Therefore we are calling for a personal and structural conversion in our churches and societies which will be manifest by living in faith with coherence and inculturation.

A fraternal community of peace with justice and dignity will lead to great renewal of land tenure, housing, education, communication and work.

We want to recover the historic memory of our churches and our people as we take the responsibility for centuries of struggle and martyrdom. We march with many brothers and sisters from our America, from all of the Third World and from solidarity in the First World, to fight with hope against the fatalism of a system imposed on us. We are confident in the loving presence of the God of Jesus, liberator of the poor, Father-Mother of the human family.

For the Catholic Church
Samuel Ruiz

For pastoral workers
Jose Oscar Beozzo

For the theologians
Jose Comblin

For laypeople
Adolfo Perez Esquivel

For religious life
Magdalena Vandenheen

For the Protestant
and Evangelical churches
Federico Pagura

Riobamba, Ecuador, 30 de agosto de 1998

Translated by: Blase Bonpane, Ph.D.[†]

[†] Blase Bonpane was a participant in the Riobamba Conference and the Southern California Representative of *Secretariado Internacional Cristiano de Solidaridad con los Pueblos de America Latina: Oscar A. Romero* (SICSAL). (The International Christian Secretariat in Solidarity with the People of Latin America: Oscar A. Romero).

A Testimony Concerning
Lori Berenson

June 30, 1999

Testimony of Blase Bonpane, Ph.D., Director of the Office of the Americas, at the Congressional Human Rights Caucus, co-chaired by Representatives Tom Lantos (D-CA) and John Edward Porter (R-IL). Rayburn House Office building (Room 2200) 4:00 PM, June 30th, 1999

Sincere thanks to Congresswoman Maloney, Congresswoman Waters and Congressman McGovern for your presence today, and thanks as well to Mrs.Annette Lantos.

In March of this year the Office of the Americas led the first human rights delegation to visit Lori Berenson.

The members of the delegation:

- Blase Bonpane, Delegation Leader.

- Rev. Lucius Walker, Director of IFCO / Pastors for Peace.

- Amy Goodman, Pacifica Radio, host of "Democracy Now."

- Kristen Gardner, M.I.T. classmate and friend of Lori Berenson.

- Annie Bird, Guatemala Director of Guatemala Partners

- Patricia Todd, Librarian.

As we made plans to visit Lori Berenson at Socabaya prison in Arequipa, Peru, all advice was negative. The Peruvian Embassy here in Washington requested the names of everyone on the proposed delegation and advised us to speak to the Peruvian Ministry of Justice in Lima.

The United States Embassy in Lima suggested that we not come at all on the dates we proposed and expressed an opinion that we would not be admitted under any circumstances.

We decided to proceed as planned. Upon arrival in Peru we presented ourselves to the United States Embassy and conferred with Mary Grandfield, U.S. Consul. Delegation member Annie Bird hand delivered a written request to Colonel Justo Jara Ugarte, Director of the National Penitentiary Institute of Peru asking permission for the delegation to visit Lori. After hours of waiting and a follow up phone request, Annie was told that a decision had not been made.

Our delegation proceeded to Arequipa early the following morning. We hired a vehicle and drove to Socabaya Prison. At each of four military check-points we presented the only authorization we had, a letter requesting our admission to the prison which was written by Peruvian Congressman Gustavo Mohme Llona. Upon arrival at the prison we were instantly admitted and presented to the Director of the women's section, Juana Begasso. Within moments we were admitted to the prison yard and were greeted by Lori Berenson. We sat in a circle and spoke for two hours.

Lori's complexion was red and her hands were purple. Her eyesight is failing and she suffers from poor digestion. We think a crime has been committed against Lori Berenson. At the time of her arrest she had two articles in process about women in Peru, she had also interviewed four members of the Peruvian Congress. She is a freelance journalist. She told us how she was arrested while riding a bus. She was taken to the Secret Police, handcuffed, slammed into the back of a police car and driven to the site of an active shoot-out with the MRTA rebels. She was then taken to the Secret Police headquarters and interrogated at length. She was told that if she made the proper accusations she would be rewarded. If she failed to cooperate that she would be handed over to the military where she would be tortured and raped.

As a result of her non-cooperation she was slapped into a filthy cell on December 28, 1995. She shared that space with Lucinda Rojas who was in extreme pain. Lucinda had five bullet wounds (from the above mentioned shoot-out) and she was using a colostomy bag. A doctor looked at Lucinda and simply walked away saying, "I don't want to deal with that colostomy bag." Rats were ever present while Lori and Lucinda endured this ordeal for eleven days. Lori was dragged from the cell in complete disarray to be presented to the media of Peru. She was righteously angry and had reason to be frightened. She was told she had one minute to speak and that she had to scream because there was no microphone. With great strength Lori spoke of the institutionalized violence in Peru and her love of the Peruvian people. Her statement was viciously misinterpreted by the Peruvian media as proof that she was a subversive.

Further criminal action against Lori was taken by a hooded thug (purportedly a military judge) a loaded gun was held to her head and she was "convicted" of treason. This was a classic example of accusatory law. No evidence was given against her and she had no defense.

After this brutal excuse for a trial, Lori was thrown into Yanamayo Prison near Puno, Peru at 12,750 feet above sea-level. It should be noted that these Peruvian prisons are not sixteenth century dungeons. They are modern instruments of torture built in the 1990s. With barred window open to the frigid Andean air sick prisoners can quickly die of hypothermia.

The very day that the Organization of American States held a hearing on Lori Berenson, she was removed from Yanamayo Prison in a public relations effort to demonstrate "concern for her health." She was delivered to Socabaya Prison at 7,500 feet above sea-level.

When we returned to Lima on the following day and met with U.S. Ambassador to Peru, Dennis Jett, we found him both disturbed and angry that we were admitted to the prison. His references to Lori were blatantly adversarial as has been every piece of correspondence which we have seen from the U.S. Department of State. He implied guilt by association, he referred to Lori's parents as, "Spitting in the face of President Fujimori" because they held signs asking for the release of their daughter when Fujimori visited his daughter in Boston. If Ambassador Jett had shown as much respect for Lori Berenson as he showed for President Fujimori, she would have her rightful freedom.

We are observing the globalization of the world economy. Lori Berenson is in the vanguard of the globalization of the necessary humanity which must join this new world order.

We are well past the era of nineteenth century isolationism where everyone is expected to confine their interests to their own nation. We live on a small planet which is in grave danger. This is the era when U.S. citizens should identify human rights abuses in Peru and Peruvian citizens should identify unnecessary homelessness in the United States. Only in this way will we be able to implement the Universal Declaration of Human Rights.

The time is long past to ask for a "fair trial" for Lori Berenson. In Peru a "fair trial" would mean that Lori would wait in prison for six more years and then be presented to a judicial system which the United States Department of State has identified as corrupt.

A crime has been committed against Lori Berenson by the Peruvian government. The State Department of the United States has failed in its duty to defend the human rights of this exemplary citizen.

The United Nations High Commission for Human Rights considers Lori's imprisonment to be Arbitrary Detention. The Inter-American Commission for Human Rights of the Organization of American States has agreed to give a formal hearing to Lori Berenson's petition against the government of Peru. Amnesty International has issued repeated Urgent Action Bulletins regarding Lori's unjust imprisonment.

It is incumbent on the Congress of the United States to demand that the President of the United States carry out his obligation as stated in Act of Congress (22 U.S.C., section 1732) to come to the aid of an American Citizen wrongfully held in a foreign country. Lori Berenson's health is rapidly failing. She must be released from that hell hole now.

Non-European Holocausts

A Personal Odyssey

University of Colorado, March 1, 2000

I will try to explain U.S. Foreign Policy in Central America as a witness and as a personal odyssey of some years. In today's *U.S. News and World Report*, there is a story of a prisoner in Peru. The prisoner, of course, is Lori Berenson. She has been incarcerated now for more than four years and her incarceration is a reflection of U.S. Foreign Policy. This policy has generally included the support of dictatorial regimes because we prefer to deal with *one* person and insist on conformity to our wishes. The name might be Somoza, he could do no wrong as far as our presidents were concerned. It was true of Manuel Noriega, our man in Panama. Manuel was on the payroll of the CIA until he became a bad boy. Our military destroyed the neighborhoods of San Miguelito and El Chorillo simply to kidnap Manuel Noriega, who was not in sync with our policy in the Contra War. Of course, such a foreign policy was not confined to this hemisphere; Saddam Hussein, our ally in the Iran/Iraq War, used poison gas on the Kurds. No questions asked until there was a question of nationalization of oil. That was serious! And then he is became "Adolf Hitler."

In today's issue of *U.S. News and World Report*, there is a case of another dictator. I went down to visit Lori Berenson recently. We were the first delegation allowed in aside from her parents. Prior to going, of course, we stopped at the U.S. Embassy and we heard from our Ambassador to Peru a long explanation of just what a great guy President Fuijimori is.

I said, "Well, why do you feel that way?"

"Well, he pays his debts. He's letting us have a military base on the Peru/Colombian border. He's a great guy, we don't want to disturb him, and beside that, the Berenson family is spitting in his face."

I said, "Please explain."

He said, "Well, Mr. Fuijimori went to Boston where his daughter goes to school [as Lori went to MIT] and the Berenson family was demonstrating for the release of their daughter."

Of course, is it not spitting in *her* face to have her in a dungeon for four years. What we have to do is get her out. She has been victimized by accusatory law. There is no evidence against her. There was no defense for her. The hearing was by military officers and she was given a life sentence. This is part of policy because it would only take *one* phone call from President Clinton for Lori Berenson to be free.

Is she a member of the MRTA? No. Is she a leader in the MRTA? No. Her parents have been to the National Security Council and talked to Sandy Berger as well as the people in Congress. The majority of people in the House of Representatives have asked that she be released. She is still in that dungeon.

Fujimori is still flaunting a little TV tape made after Lori was incarcerated for eleven days with a woman who was dying of five bullet wounds. She was very angry and she expressed her love for the Peruvian people. She expressed the main problem we have with the Holocaust—the non-European Holocaust—which is the institutional violence killing people throughout the world; the Americas included. That is; the violence of curable diseases; the violence of hunger; the violence of the World Trade Organization. That violence is institutional, because it deals with pornographic realities like cheap labor as a commodity. There is no need for cheap labor. There is only a need for people to raise their children. Cheap labor is an evil sin and has to be abolished internationally. We do not care what the WTO wants; we care about what the people of the world want.

The demonstrations that took place in Seattle were at least as important as the Boston Tea Party. They were *at least* as important because they made it very clear that people are conscious of our policy, which is a corporate policy, showing a regard for corporations far and above a regard for people. This policy is imposed on small nations by way of *privatization*. They do not want to be privatized. The public sector is what has made life liveable in places like the United States. Public schools. Public libraries. Public parks. Public welfare. To privatize this—why? Because of a rigid ideology—far more rigid than *Maoism*, which is the ideology of the World Trade Organization. It is rigid and it is meaningless! It is monetarist. I cannot believe that the world monetary system functions for another day. Seven or eight countries have real money. Everybody else has "Monopoly Money." Are there seven countries in the world? This is policy and the WTO is part and parcel of that Monopoly game. It is a war-like policy. "You will export your Brussels sprouts to the United States from Guatemala. The fact that your children are hungry is not relevant. You will export beef from Chiapas in Mexico and we are going to give you U.S. corn."

I was in Chiapas when the revolution broke out in 1994 and I heard people who did not speak Spanish talking to me with a translator (they were speaking Tojolabal, Tzolzil, Tzeltal, God knows, all the beautiful languages of the area), they knew much more about economics than many of our people, forgive me, perhaps on this very campus—or any campus. Why? Because they are speaking economics from the real world.

They said, "Look, we don't want the peso devaluated. We don't want our ejido system destroyed by President Salinas eliminating Article 27 of the Mexican constitution. We don't want to grow cattle. (Speaking personally, it would be progress to have genocide for the cattle. It would be better for everyone's heart. We don't need cattle.) We need to grow our sacred corn. We need to have our sacred areas and that's what we are fighting about. We want to be self-sufficient."

Well, the WTO is not designed for self-sufficiency. It is designed for dependency. So, these are issues, policy issues, that are extremely important. I am so glad that you mentioned the word "holocausts" because I can never see it in the singular. I have never thought of it in the singular. It is plural. There are holocausts. There is no denying the Holocaust of the Third Reich. But, it is not singular. That is why it is important to identify the reality of such "holocausts."

I am happy that a national debate has begun after Seattle. There is so much activism. I do not know if you realize how much is going on at the present time in our country. I went to the University of Arizona and I thought, this *is going to be a rather rigid place, a rather reactionary place*, and as soon as I got there they said, "You will have to forgive us today, the students are occupying the President's office and they will stay there until he stops allowing the sale of this sweat shop junk in our University stores." This kind of thing is going on everywhere across the country. It is a sign of consciousness not unconsciousness. I think there is more activism in the United States in the year 2000 than there was in 1968. It was sad that a small percentage in Seattle (much less than one percent) decided to be trashers of the area. Naturally, they got much of the publicity. They stole the publicity from more than ninety-nine percent of the people who were absolutely nonviolent. They robbed the press that way. Possibly some of them were provocateurs. I had one report of someone dressed in black as an "anarchist" who was seen handcuffing some of the peaceful demonstrators. That reminds me of things we have seen over the years as part of a policy. We have to think about that provocateur action and realize that when we plan an action, we presume that people should have enough respect for democracy to honor a ninety-nine percent consensus. We can hope that someone else is not going to come in, parasitically and disrupt.

My odyssey began in Guatemala. I was assigned there as a Maryknoll Father in the 60s to work with the students at the national university, San Carlos. At that time, the ecclesiastical leadership was saying, "Look, we have to show that the Church is also interested in social justice not just the Marxists." That was more or less what came with the mandate for me to serve at the university. I realized I was coming there in the wake of the post World War II intervention of 1954.

Our student groups (cursillos de capacitacion social) went throughout the country. The indigenous people dubbed us Guerrillas de Paz (Guerrillas of Peace) because we were unarmed. The movement stressed health care, literacy, and unionization. One day we were up in the *Huehuetenango* area and we realized that one of the ninety students involved in the program had a pistol. We said, "If you want to be part of the rebel forces, go to the rebel forces—we can get you there—we know right where they are—they come and see us frequently—they talk to us. They tell us we're probably going to be eliminated because we are unarmed, but if you want to be part of this movement, get rid of the pistol. Because we are unarmed the indigenous people are not afraid of us."

Well, in a way, the rebels were right, many of us in the clergy were expelled; accused of plotting an armed revolution, which was ridiculous, just as it is ridiculous to say that Lori Berenson is a leader of the MRTA. She is not a leader of the MRTA and neither is she a member of it. What is she being held for? Because she is a leftist. Do you think every leftist should get a life sentence? Is she a leftist? *Yes.* Is she a member of the MRTA? *No.* Was she plotting to blow up the Peruvian Congress? *No.* There is absolutely no evidence of that.

In regard to this period in Guatemala, you might want to read my book, *Guerrillas of Peace.* Being expelled from Guatemala, I was kind of traumatized, realizing I had expected to spend my life there. I came back to the States and found that the leadership of our religious community was also very disturbed.

I was told, "You are involved in rebel activity in Guatemala."

I said, "Who are you listening to?"

"Well, the CIA has come up here, and the FBI, and other groups, and you are involved with rebel activity. So, what we want you to do is to go to Hawaii and shut up. Don't speak, don't organize, don't write. Forget what you saw in Latin America and be quiet."

So, I went to Hawaii, being the obedient person that I am, and I was there overnight. I got up the next morning and said to the various priests there, "This order here, this was just an act of anger, wasn't it? Is it not for real?" They said, "Oh yeah, it's for real. That is the order. You are not to write anything about Latin America. You forget everything about Guatemala." I asked, "When's the next plane out of here?" I went to the airport immediately, flew directly to Washington D.C. and released everything I had to the *Washington Post*, which they released to 400 newspapers. It is called "Guatemala, Our Latin Vietnam."

So, coming back to the States, I figured there might be some anger on the part of the Church at this. I got an apartment in Washington and realized that our policy had upset many people (this in the midst of a war in Indochina—of a Holocaust in Indochina with carpet bombing, agent orange, napalm).

Someone called and said, "Phil Berrigan would you like to met with us at 1620 S Street, Washington, D.C.? We want to talk about something,"

I said, "Sure."

Thirteen of us met in a basement and began to talk about our country burning people alive, about the reality of napalm. Would it not be better to have a symbol of burning paper rather than people? So, the Catonsville action was planned in that basement. Nine people agreed to take part in it (I was not one of them), to go into the Catonsville draft board to take the files into the parking lot and to "napalm" the files! They would then kneel and say the Lord's Prayer until the police came. The action was so superb, so much in the spirit of the Boston Tea Party that it was imitated over 100 times. These were not orders coming from Phil Berrigan or Dan Berrigan. It was imitation as the highest form of praise. It was nonviolent action to denounce a Holocaust.

The Holocaust was part of a policy. We also realized there was provocateur action at that time. There were up to a million people in the streets in Washington D.C. In the midst of this gathering of mostly middle class people, who had given up their work time, possibly gotten fired, there arrives carefully costumed hippies from the security agencies, bringing kerosene soaked flags, which they burned. In the thirty years I have been in the peace movement, I have *never* known anyone to burn a flag. I have known police to burn flags, but I have never known anyone in the movement to burn a flag.

Who is on the front page of the paper the next day? One million people are discredited, a few police dressed as hippies, with their picture being taken, burning a flag. Congratulations, provocateur! Very sad. How many MIAs are there in Vietnam? There are about 300 thousand missing in action who are Vietnamese. I think we have probably accounted for all of ours. In a war with flaming gasoline, some people are going to be incinerated.

At that time we formed, AVILA ("Avoid Vietnam in Latin America"). It was the beginning of a solidarity movement for Latin America. In the midst of this, being an unattached priest, I was to meet someone from the same Order. I was a Maryknoll Priest and I met a former Maryknoll Sister who had left the convent. So, we figured we should get married. We got married, and that too is part of a movement. Good things happen from the base. Nothing grows from the top down. If you want a movement for a married clergy, get married. That is all there is to it. It is that simple. Some people will not like it. Get married. Tens of thousands have done that. Did Jesus say do not get married? I do not think so. We had a married clergy in the Catholic Church for a thousand years. There is a history of it. Actually, we have never had a moment in the Catholic Church without a married clergy. We have seventeen Byzantine rites with a married clergy. What is the problem? There really is no problem. Celibacy is simply a disciplinary law with a very shabby history.

Cesar Chavez became interested in our work. He said to my wife, Theresa, and me, "Would you set up a university for farm workers, so that farm workers can study whatever they want to study?" We said we were involved in the peace movement, but we knew that the domestic policy was equally bad. Children were working in the fields of the San Joaquin Valley. People talking about cheap labor instead of people. We would do whatever we could to end that horror. It was a joy to work with Cesar through those years. He was unforgettable. It was a privilege to be a part of his movement.

Back to academia. I taught at UCLA. At an anti-draft rally on campus I saw the famous Los Angeles Police Department breaking the windows of the draft office with their clubs. Here was another example of police provocateur action with the hope that students would be blamed. Shortly thereafter I was called to a police shoot-out at the Black Panther headquarters in Los Angeles. The press mentioned that a priest/professor was there to ask for a truce. Governor Ronald Reagan had had enough so he came to the Regent's meetings and wanted any professors connected such peace activity eliminated. My tenure at UCLA was quite limited.

We were aware of some organizing going on in Nicaragua. My seminary colleague, Father Miguel d'Escoto, came to my home and said, "Why, I'm really in a situation now. I've got the superiors at Maryknoll in New York. I've got the comandantes. I represent them as their foreign minister and they are, of course, still fighting the war. Would you please do what you can to assist this situation?"

Well, the demonstrations in Los Angeles and San Francisco continued on behalf of the Nicaraguan people against Somoza and on July 19, 1979, an incredible thing happened. There was a massive demonstration in Los Angeles. During the demonstration, we heard that the Sandinista victory had taken place. The head of the demonstration, Manuel Valle, went up to the Nicaraguan Consulate in Los Angeles and said to the Somosistas there, "Get out, we are taking over." They gave him key and walked out. Unbelievable. I mean, truth is stranger than fiction. Manuel evolved from street demonstrator to Consul in one act. On the same day I was asked to celebrate a thanksgiving Mass for the Nicaraguan people at St. Joseph's Church in Los Angeles. I did that as my wife sat in the congregation.

Manuel Valle and I went to Nicaragua after that to begin to work in the wake of the Sandinista victory. Rosario Murillo, wife of Daniel Ortega, asked Theresa and me to please bring people from the United States to witness the revolution. Bring Republicans, bring Democrats, bring people. Bring people of goodwill so they can see what is going on here and they will understand that there is a filthy, mercenary war underway and that your government is paying mercenaries to kill our citizens, to kill our children and to destroy the revolutionary government.

From 1980 to 1990, we were back and forth to Nicaragua with delegations, bringing thousands of people there to see U.S. Foreign Policy in action. As a result of those delegations, the Boulder/Jalapa Sister City Program was developed and many other friendship city arrangements. We became quite aware that there was dope going back to the United States. We became quite aware of what was finally identified as the Iran-Contra Scandal. We were also aware of the Holocaust in Nicaragua. One of many. It reminded me of the history of Indian removal in the United States. President Monroe removed the Indians from everywhere east of the Mississippi. He signed treaties with them so that they would cede their territory, which they did. He did not honor any treaty at all. He, of course, gave us the Doctrine that followed, "Jefferson's

Doctrine." Jefferson actually was the first one to say this is *our* hemisphere. That, I guess, goes along with the Louisiana Purchase. Such "purchases" were a result of, "Will you sell it or do you want us to take it?" That was the message. "If you want us to pay you for it, we will. If not, we will take it."

The Doctrine of Monroe said to Europe, "Stay out of Latin America. All colonization is over." This was U.S. policy coming into 1823. There would be no more colonization in the Americas. This Doctrine was fairly well ignored. In the midst of this, there was the Holocaust of our indigenous people. It was genocide and was joined with a very unpopular war with Mexico. In 1846 President Polk wanted to take a great deal of Mexico, and in that conflict we saw mutiny to our policy just as we saw mutiny in Vietnam. The endless mutinies in that war were a key reason for ending the war. I have had students for thirty years who have reported disobeying orders, who have reported mutiny. I have never asked them to talk about it, they speak about it whether I want them to or not. There was a mutiny of people that came over from the Irish Potato Famine of the 1840s. They had been drafted because they did not have any money. If you had money, you did not have to be drafted. They were drafted and pressed into service, went to the Mexican border, began fighting as a battalion and realized the people they were fighting were Roman Catholics. "This is stupid. Why are we fighting for the Protestants in the United States? We are going to the other side." So, the San Patricio Battalion went to the side of Mexico and fought on behalf of Mexico and every year in Mexico City and in Dublin they celebrate the San Patricio Battalion. Why not in Washington? The men that were caught, were hung. The soldiers that were not caught, stayed in Mexico, are found among many longstanding Mexican citizens with red hair and names like O'Reilly.

So, the policy began with Jefferson and Monroe. But Europe ignored the Monroe Doctrine and continued to colonize the Americas. The United States could not do much about it. After the war in Mexico there was, William Walker who took over Nicaragua in 1855. He declared himself president. He declared the language of Nicaragua to be English and thought the Nicaraguans would serve the Confederacy as slaves. As you recall, this is still pre-civil war. All of this type of behavior was taking place under the name of the quasi-religious theme, "Manifest Destiny." It has not changed much. Religiosity is still the basis of U.S. foreign policy and that is sad.

While the Contra War was going on in Nicaragua we decided to form the Office of the Americas. It is a small organization which is dedicated to building a peace system and dealing with conflicts in the Americas, or anywhere for that matter. We are not going to confine ourselves just to this hemisphere. We call it the Office of the Americas. But, we call it that because our focus is on our country and what our country is doing and how its policies are genocidal. That is our focus. We are not going to go to Nicaragua to tell the Nicaraguans how to run their government. We are going to Nicaragua to tell our citizens that we are responsible for the massacre of Nicaraguan people. Once we opened the doors of the Office of the Americas the response was amazing. Thousands of people went to see the war. Not only in Nicaragua, but El Salvador and Guatemala as well. We never thought this kind of tourism would develop. We were so pleased to see many similar groups develop around the United States. On one such delegation, not from OOA, the Reverend Lucius Walker was shot by the Contras, by a rifle made in the USA. That is what led him to form "Pastors For Peace."

We felt we still were not close enough to the ground, bringing all these people down and having them see the Contra War. Bringing celebrities, bringing high profile people and very low profile people. Any one that was willing to go. We would get closer to the people, however, after a Norwegian physician came to my office and said, "We want to have an international march for peace through Central America. And we think we can bring it off. We want your Office of the Americas to direct the U.S. delegation." That delegation became 100 people. We planned the march in Vienna, Austria. People appeared from thirty countries and on December 10, 1985, we began the march in Panama. Graham Greene was there to kick off the march—to wish us well. Jorge Illueca, the former president of Panama said, "these 'soldiers of peace' will help us to bring about the Contadora Agreements." Many countries in Latin America had agreed to serve as mediators in the war between the United States and Nicaragua. They were called "The Contadora Countries." Panama is one of those countries, and we would begin marching there. We would be able to speak to many people as we went through the war zones of Central America. We had tremendous opposition from the U.S. Embassy. We saw printed materials saying that we represented the PLO and God knows what else. It was all a batch of lies.

Costa Rica had a group of contras living there and a group known as Costa Rica Libre. They were associated with the Contras in Nicaragua. They were waiting for us. They physically attacked us as we came into San Jose. It was there that we realized that these mass mobilizations require discipline. Some people wanted to do near suicidal things. We had to try and keep a balance there through meetings of what we could do and we could not do. We were finally expelled from Costa Rica into the "No Man's Land" between Costa Rica and Nicaragua. The Sandinistas knew that we had been dumped into this open fire war zone and they literally came in and rescued all 400 of us and took us out to the north to Nicaragua.

This was major news everyday throughout the Americas. CNN was with us, CBS, ABC, NBC, UPI, AP, all the press agencies were there on a daily basis walking with us frequently. The amazing level of censorship in this country was beyond description. Hardly a line of press coverage was permitted in the US. People did not even know it that the International March for Peace in Central America took place. Even the warring countries of Central America had far better coverage that our press at home.

We healed our wounds in Nicaragua. It was the only country that received us well. We proceeded to Honduras were the Honduran Cobras were waiting for us on the borders with their gas masks on; their M-16s at the ready. They held us there for seven days. One of them called me over into Honduras, across the line, and asked, "Are you a priest?"

I said, "Yeah. You are a priest forever."

He said, "Priests belong in their churches. What did you see in Nicaragua? What kind of guns? What kind of education?" So, this interrogation begins and finally he said, "You will never come into Honduras," and sent me back to the Nicaraguan side.

We decided to fly into Honduras in small groups. We realized the only way we could get into the countries of El Salvador and Guatemala was by air. We went into those countries and we met with the people there and we marched with the people there. We felt that it was possible to stir up a great deal of activity in this fashion demanding peace in the Americas. We finally all reassembled in Chiapas at the southern border of Mexico.

We were received there by Bishop Samuel Ruiz Garcia and went through Mexico quite peacefully because they were also members of the Contadora group. They said, "You can come through Mexico. You can march through Mexico. In fact, you can have a massive demonstration in Mexico City, but don't say one negative word about Mexico."

That was fine. Mexico was not our objective then. Our objective was to support Mexico as they supported the Contadora process. When we got to Mexico City, fifty thousand people were in the streets. We were received by Bishop Mendez Arceo who gave a closing ritual to the March. From Mexico we flew to Washington D.C. to gather at the Vietnam Memorial and then to Congress to ask them to stop this damn war.

Our protests are responses to a policy that has not changed much since the time of Jefferson. It has been intrusive. It has been interventionist. While we could not intervene much in the nineteenth century, the Theodore Roosevelt corollary to the Monroe Doctrine began the age of U.S. imperialism. As President Monroe was looking at Europe, President Theodore Roosevelt was looking at Latin America, saying, if you behave yourself, we will not intervene. But, if through chronic wrongdoing you do not behave yourself, we will intervene.

Endless interventions followed at the beginning of the twentieth century. With the creation of Panama, the occupation of Haiti, occupation of the Dominican Republic, the war to take Cuba away from Spain with the first president of the liberated Cuba, being General Leonard Wood (1902). These interventions simply did not stop. The attacks on Sandino in the 20s. The first use of dive bombing was against Sandino. The Somoza dictatorship was established, which became our Nicaraguanization of the conflict. This has been our policy. All with the same religiosity.

One of the most ruthless acts of treachery in our history took place with the support of a member of the Nazi lodge of Chile, Augusto Pinochet Ugarte. There had been a lot of Nazis in Chile. Some communities speak German. He was one of them and we knew it. He determined to eliminate medical doctor Salvador Allende. Allende won the presidency of Chile at the ballot box. He had never been involved in any kind of armed activity. He brought to Chile exactly what they wanted and was going to get the copper companies out. He said, "We've already paid our debt to you. You've been taking copper out of Chile all these years. Don't tell us that we owe you anything."

For every dollar invested in Latin America in the past century, at least $3.00 has come back to the United States. We have not given them anything. We have taken a great deal. So, what to do? Organizing on all levels. We are happy that we finally saw some sense of international law with the apprehension of Pinochet Ugarte. Now, we have the admission of the United States that it knew about Mr. Harman. That it knew that he was going to be assassinated by the Chilean junta, just as we knew about so many others. We knew of the Sisters in El Salvador; the Jesuits in El Salvador, to say nothing of the endless thousands of people that were tortured and killed with our knowledge. We claimed to have had one hundred fifty-five advisors in El Salvador from the United States. After the war, several thousand troops came to get their battle pay. We lied about that also (by "we" I mean our government).

The wars continued. The Holocaust in Guatemala went on almost to the present, until the peace accords were signed. It is the only case I know of in our history where a president has apologized. President Clinton apologized to the Guatemalans for our behavior. I do not know if he was chided for that, but he did that.

In the midst of this, there was the war in Grenada, which will probably be recalled as the most stupid venture to take place in the entire history of the United States. With the media saying, "We got there just in time." That was very touching. Just in time to blow up a mental hospital.

To understand this Holocaust in a more profound way, I recommend the best book on the subject, which would be *Killing Hope— U.S. Military and CIA Interventions Since World War II* by William Blum (Common Courage Press, 1995).

We were so horrified to hear what was happening in Iraq that we broke ranks with Latin America. We went to Baghdad in 1991, and it was literally unbelievable. Here was our former ally, Saddam Hussein. Everybody was able to negotiate that one. Mr. Gorbachev was eager to negotiate on behalf of peace. Mr. Bush was not interested. He wanted his war because he was not going to have any nationalized oil in Iraq. Why? Because we will make that decision here. The bottom line might be, "Isn't it awful?" But that is not the bottom line. If it were, we would become cynics and do nothing.

We do not feel in our line of work that there is any room for cynicism. What do we want to do? We want to abolish the war system. The war system is a slave system. You will serve or you will go to a Federal penitentiary. You are a slave. You will keep your mouth shut and do what you are told. If you do not want an anthrax inoculation, we will put you in jail. It is slavery all right. Wars are conducted by slaves.

Now, if in 1850, we were in this room (had it been here at that time) there might have been one abolitionist in a crowd of this size. Maybe one or maybe none. The abolitionist made their point to the reluctant Mr. Lincoln and ultimately they were victorious in eliminating slavery. The response about slavery at that time was very similar to our responses about war. They would bring up slavery and say that is really terrible. God it is awful. It is just a shame. But, you know, it is our economic system and we really cannot function without it. It is the same way today with war.

Since 1991 we have been killing 5,000 children every month in Iraq. That country is in absolute ashes and the propaganda you are getting everyday is, "They might have a nuclear weapon." I know someone who has one. We do! This is very dangerous. We are going to lose Chicago because of it or Los Angeles. We are not going to go on without an accident. We have to get ourselves together and realize that we are brainwashed; we are socialized; we literally believe a media that is absolutely controlled and absolutely involved in censorship. We must save the planet. Save it from our military, who at peace are the greatest threat to the environment. The military at war will destroy the planet.

It is time to build a peace system. Anyone who says we cannot do it is locked into the nineteenth century. If you repeat the past, you show no reverence for the past. The only way to deal with the past is to change it. When we study history, we are studying stupidity; we are studying racism; we are studying ignorance; we are studying superstition. That is what history is. Manifest destiny?

Think about it. Now is the time to build a peace system. Would anyone in government be interested? Yes. Congressman, Dennis Kucinich, of Cleveland is drafting a bill. We are working with him for a Department of Peace and we hope to have that department at cabinet level. I think the Department of War (known as the Defense Department) has made every possible mistake. It is not credible. If any student of mine gives the Pentagon or the CIA as a source. I say, sorry, those are not credible institutions.

I was traveling through Nicaragua with one of the men who planned the overthrow of Guatemala, Colonel Philip Roettinger. He is now part of the peace movement as are many such former officers. We were in a helicopter, flying over the tree-tops during the Contra War, and I said, "Phil, you were in the CIA so long and you helped to overthrow Guatemala; then you became a peace person. Could you give me an example of something worthwhile that the CIA has done?" He said, "No, I can't." The CIA must be abolished. It is not related to U.S. Constitutional Government. It is unconstitutional and a lively Supreme Court would eliminate it immediately. We do not need a secret agency, or a secret government. This is un-American.

Kucinich is formulating the bill. We are inviting him to California. We think that such a bill should be related to conflict resolution between countries. It should be related to stopping the violence in this country. Our military policy is coming home. Our foreign policy is coming home.

Twenty-five percent of the prisoners of the world are in this country. Five percent of the people of the people live here. We have a prison state. The vast majority of those being held at this time are in for nonviolent crimes. Anyone who knows anything about criminology should realize that prisons are for people who are a danger to public safety. If one is not a danger to public safety, there are many other forms of punishment. One can be held under house arrest or allowed to go home and go to work. But, no, we would rather have a military, industrial, gun, prison system. We have been so successful with our "necrophilia" (our love of death) that we maintain the death penalty.

The death penalty has been so successful that we have more homicides in Los Angeles County than all of Europe put together in any one year. Ask yourself how many homicides there are in Japan in a year. I think the death penalty has increased the homicides in the United States because it is *class* punishment. Anyone who studies sociology knows that. These are things that have to change with a Peace Department.

This is included in the draft of the text that we have been literally working on. To deal with these hateful, necrophilic, mean spirited, and counter-productive practices that are going on. People of color know very well that they have much greater opportunity to spend the rest of their life in prison. They know that. It is very clear. Statistics show this.

We hope and pray to have this Peace Department in sync completely with the United Nations. Apparently our Senate hates the United Nations. This is a terrible thing. This has created Holocausts. It created perhaps the biggest Holocaust in the world, which was called World War II. After World War I, there was a formation of a League of Nations. The Senate of the United States hated the concept. They wanted to run things from here. As a result of not having a League, there was a World War II. The Great Holocaust of the Century.

After World War II, the United Nations was formed. This was a brilliant piece of work. Together with the UN, what should be our international constitution for the future? The Universal Declaration of Human Rights. We have Eleanor Roosevelt to thank for that and many others.

Our Congress is totally uncooperative with the United Nations. We have just done one of the most destructive acts imaginable by reconstructing the dinosaur known as "NATO" in order to conduct a Holocaust in Serbia and to have people running around and asking, "What else could we do?"

We hope that you will become familiar with the new "Tobin Resolution." It is very important because it would impose a tax on the over trillion dollars a day that is exchanged in doing nothing. That trillion dollar exchange every day is between money lenders. The kind of people Jesus threw out of the temple. There is very little productive action that goes on. Put a quarter of percent tax on that and you have enough money to eliminate poverty and misery in the world. These things can be done.

There is *absolutely* no room for cynicism. You might ask "what to do?" You do not fight every battle. You choose your battles. We chose ours. Our battles do not have to be your battles. You may want to fight an environmental battle. You may want to fight an economic battle. You organize at the base where you are. You organize in Boulder and you work together, coordinate with other people. I have seen very little conflict in the solidarity movement. We certainly do not sit around arguing ideology. We have not argued ideology since 1980. We discuss what we are going to do and where we are going to do it.

We brought delegations to Cuba. I asked the State Department when I went the first time, "May I go to Cuba?" The response was negative. I left the next day because our legal advisers considered it unconstitutional for the State Department to give such a mandate. The State Department may say no, but it does not have a right to say no. So, we went in violation of the blockade, which has been a Holocaust on the Cuban people. An act of war for some forty years.

Now, we are involved in national child abuse with Elian. There is no question about where he belongs. His father took care of him five days a week. National law says he should go home. International law says he should go home. The child molesters of Washington are going to impose, or try to impose, U.S. citizenship on him. Child molestation as policy. He belongs with his father at home. There should be no further legal discussion. Ask Mrs. Reno.

We have these problems. We are called upon to organize and protest the embarrassing things that our country is doing. We have to do that. We have to decide what we are willing to do. If we are willing to be part of C.D. (Civil Disobedience), then we do what the intelligent movement does, we get the people interested in C.D. to segregate themselves completely from the others that want to be in a legal demonstration. This way there is no confusion, no one is arrested who was not planning on it.

Perhaps you will never see a better ordered demonstration than the School of the Americas Watch gathering at Fort Benning, Georgia. Father Roy Bourgeois is another colleague. He is a Vietnam Veteran. He organizes those incredible demonstrations that take place every. He has spent almost five of the last ten years in federal prisons. The demonstrations are a great statement against the School of the Americas, which is also known as the School of the Assassins. It is the school, of course, that trained the murderers of Archbishop Romero. It trained the murderers of the nuns in El Salvador. It trained the people who killed Bishop Gerardi in Guatemala. It is a school of assassins. What did Father Roy do? When the Salvadorans were training there, he came into the base dressed in military fatigues, climbed a tree over their barracks, and put a boom box in the tree with the final sermon of Archbishop Romero. The Archbishop very clearly told the troops to mutiny. He said, "No soldier is obliged to obey an order against the law of God that says, 'You shall not kill.' In the name of God, then, and in the name of this suffering people whose cries reach up to heaven with greater intensity every day, I beg you. I implore you. I command you in the name of God; Stop the repression." The Salvadoran soldiers came out of the barracks terrified. It was midnight. The M.P.s got Roy out of the tree. He served a couple of years for that one. This will be remembered. Happy are you peacemakers. You shall be called "the Children of God."

What is in store for the war makers? You answer that. What I am saying is we can abolish a war system. We can certainly look at the wars and say, well that one was unnecessary. That one was unnecessary. That one was unnecessary.

The problem is war itself. It is not a matter of who is right. Some people get it into their heads that it is all right to kill other people. That is the problem. It is not—was I right—or were you right? The war is the problem. Preparation for war is the problem. Where your treasure is; there your heart will be. Where is our treasure? Fifty percent of it is in war making. Military trash being produced which has no legitimate use. It has no value except destruction. It is not protecting us. It is endangering each and every one of us. We are in greater danger of a nuclear accident at this time than ever before.

War is destroying our universities where about half of the research is military. It has made academia the last place where we hear a new idea. New ideas are not coming from academia. They are coming from whoever writes a book, whoever has an idea. That is tragic. Universities were to be the centers of critical thought, not centers to repeat the past.

Office of the Americas is a very small organization. We are one of many hundreds of such organizations. We believe that solidarity is nothing but another word for love. That solidarity is love. We understand there is one race on the planet. Anything else represents unscientific superstition. There are no separate races. There is one race. It is called "the human race." A difference of color or size is philosophically and scientifically irrelevant. It is known as, in philosophy, as an "accident." It has nothing to do with the essence of the situation. The essence is the human race.

National boundaries have become outdated. National laws are outdated. The laws of the United States are not going to stop the pollution of the ocean. The laws of the United States are not going to stop the pollution of the air? International Law and Order, is required including a world federalist polity. That has to be where we go. The thirteen colonies prior to forming the United States had less in common than the 200 nations of the world at this time.

As serial killers, nations today are saying, "Stop me before I kill again." Some legal entity must stop Orthodox Catholics from killing Roman Catholics in Serbia and Croatia. Christians killing Christians. Islamics killing Islamics. Need we mention Israel and Palestine? We have to stop the manipulation of fear which is the methodology of the cheapest and lowest form of politicians throughout the world where they get one group through demagogy to hate another group for their questionable political objectives.

That manipulation of fear goes on right here. It went on all through the long years of *the Communists are coming, the Communists are coming, the Communists are coming.* God, that was used as the excuse for any new idea, for any progressive idea, and it was dead from the start. It had no relationship to Democracy. There was no relationship between anti-Communism and Democracy. There never had been. Neither is there a relationship between capitalism and Democracy. They are totally unrelated. Pinochet's Chile was classic capitalism in the Milton Friedman sense. It was a Nazi dictatorship.

To presume that capitalism implies democracy is nonsense. The economy has to be based on humanity. It must not be based on a concept of profit. Some say, "Well, there won't be incentive if people can't take in billions each year as Mr. Gates does. I would simply ask, where is the incentive for those who win Nobel Prizes? The vast majority of such world class experts are people on a fixed salary. No, it is not necessary to take in billions each year, actually such greed represents a direct theft from the poor.

Take the case of Disney's Mr. Eisner, is it fair for him to receive $100,000 to $200,000 and hour? He pays his help in Haiti, eleven cents an hour. That is a crime on the face of it. That is what the WTO protests are about in Seattle, in Washington, D.C. and in Prague. It is not fair to allow a clandestine group in Geneva, representing the short term goals of international corporate capital, make rules that are to be carried out by the rest of the globe to the detriment of the human race and its environment. We must not tolerate this.

The movement will continue. It is not going to stop. We would like to make that clear to citizens in this country who think we live in a monarchy. Some ask questions like, "I wonder what the President wants." Since when were we to care about what the President wants? The President must understand that people in government are to act like servants, look like servants, behave like servants, or get out of government? They are supposed to take the lead from us. Right now the corporations have taken over the United States of America. They have taken over with their power. They have taken over with their ability to give us the best government money can buy. It is really a pathetic situation. I believe we can turn it around. And, if I did not, I would not be here. We are firmly convinced we can do that. We see it everyday in places that we travel where people tell us, "This is a very conservative area." But they are so ready to listen, they are truly in pain with our mean spirited corporate/military state.

People all over the world want to end the war system, which is a system of malice and ignorance that should not continue another day. We can end the war system if we want to. We do not want to pay taxes and witness over fifty percent of our budget wasted on the corporate/military system. We heard somewhere that taxation without representation is tyranny. We do not like tyranny. I want to be able to determine where more than $3.00 of my annual tax money goes.

I think we can get something good going here.

Why We can't Refrain from Protest at the Conventions

Democratic National Convention, August 15, 2000

Why don't we respect the desire of the two great parties to celebrate their conventions without protests? It is because the two great circus meetings in Philadelphia and Los Angeles are about nothing; nothing needed by the people of the United States. The two great conventions are about a government of the corporations, by the corporations and for the corporations. Abraham Lincoln, the republican, spoke of this danger when he said in 1864 that the corporations made windfall profits on the civil war:

> I see in the near future a crisis approaching that unnerves me and causes me to tremble for the safety of my country. as a result of the war, corporations have been enthroned, and an era of corruption n high places will follow, and the power of money will endeavor to prolong its reign by working upon the prejudices of the people until all wealth is aggregated in a few hands and the republic is destroyed. I feel at this moment more anxiety for the safety of my country than ever before, even in the midst of war.

Seventy-four years later, we have the comments of President Franklin Delano Roosevelt, the Democrat: "The liberty of a democracy is not safe if the people tolerate the growth of private power stronger than their democratic state itself. That, in essence is fascism." These warnings of Lincoln and Roosevelt have not been heeded, therefore we have to protest. Our protests are mainly directed at what the conventions are not addressing. Their silence indicates their approval of gross injustice.

In our "colony" of Puerto Rico the citizens have demanded an end to the endless bombing of their island of Vieques. As the G-8 countries met in Okinawa, 25,000 people surrounded our air base with a message of "it's time to go home now." The South Koreans are demanding an end to another endless bombing at our range in Maehyang Ri, near Seoul. The Salvadoreans are demanding that we do not establish a new military base in their country.

It seems to me that the world is tired of violence and militarism. The entire matter of hundreds of thousands of working U.S. citizens who have no roof over their heads is a non-issue at these circus gatherings of Republicans and Democrats. Both parties support *Star Wars* in spite of the opposition of 50 Nobel prize winners and millions of people throughout the United States and the world who consider it a war mongering project. The internationally counterproductive war on drugs has no opposition from Republicans or Democrats. The new flawed welfare programs will not be discussed at these great conventions. An attempt to win the Vietnam War in Colombia will not be discussed. Both parties seem unaware and uninterested in the fact that peace talks are currently taking place in Geneva between the Colombian rebels and the Colombian government. How can we sell helicopters and arms if there is no war? NAFTA and the WTO are acceptable, as is, to both parties at these circus conventions. I think it is now clear why intelligent people must state their objections in the spirit of Dr. Martin Luther King, Cesar Chavez, and Mahatma Ghandi. The great conventions are an insult to our intelligence.

Need we mention the infanticide our government is fostering in Iraq? The cradle of civilization is now in ashes while our paranoid corporate Pentagon planners continue the illegal and immoral bombing of that country for ten years. There are more victims of genocide in Iraq than there were as a result of the genocide of Pol Pot in Cambodia. People are still pointing the finger at the lack of response to the Holocaust of the Third Reich over fifty years ago. What is our response to the Holocaust our country continues to conduct in Iraq?

We believe, as the builders of ancient cathedrals did, that we might not see the finished product of our protests. The struggle itself is the victory and we intend to remain in that struggle. now can you understand why we have to protest?

We are building a peace system instead of a war system.

Blase Bonpane, Ph.D., served as a Maryknoll priest and superior. He was assigned to and expelled from Central America. In addition to being a UCLA and California State University Northridge professor, contributor to *Los Angeles Times* and the *New York Times* and former commentator on Pacifica radio station KPFK 90.7FM (Los Angeles, California), Blase is the author of many publications. As a U.S. citizen, he is especially concerned about the role of his own country in fostering conditions of injustice. In 1989 he was named "the most underrated humanist of the past decade" by the *Los Angeles Weekly.* He is currently Director of the Office of the Americas, a non-profit educational corporation dedicated to peace and justice in the western hemisphere. The Blase Bonpane Collection 1950-2000 has been established by the Department of Special Collections of the U.C.L.A. Research Library. This is a compilation of his published and unpublished writings together with tapes of lectures and a complete file of the "Focus on the Americas" programs which were uplinked to the National Public Radio satellite.